RADIO ADVERTISING
The Authoritative Handbook

RADIO ADVERTISING

The Authoritative Handbook

Bob Schulberg

NTC Business Books
a division of *NTC Publishing Group* • Lincolnwood, Illinois USA

Published by NTC Business Books, an imprint of
NTC Publishing Group, 4255 West Touhy Avenue,
Lincolnwood (Chicago) Illinois 60646-1975 U.S.A.
©1989 by Robert S. Schulberg. All rights reserved.
No part of this book may be reproduced, stored in a retrieval
system, or transmitted in any form, or by any means, electronic,
mechanical, photocopying or otherwise, without the prior
written permission of National Textbook Company.
Manufactured in the United States of America.
Library of Congress Catalog Card Number: 88-62126

8 9 0 BC 9 8 7 6 5 4 3 2

To Lorraine, Clare, and Peter

Contents

Foreword

I have long thought, and still think, that radio is magic. Television is OK, but radio is magic. If television had been invented first and *then* radio had come along, people would think, "What a wonderful thing this radio is! It's like television except you don't have to *look* at it!"

When I sign off my television newscasts by saying, "See you on the radio," it's my way of saying that radio is like television, but with better pictures. They haven't come out with a TV screen big enough, bright, clear, and colorful enough to equal the capacity of the mind to create its own vivid images. This is vitally important to me because I spend most of my time telling news stories on the CBS Radio Network. What makes radio such a terrific "telling" medium also makes it a terrific "selling" medium. Nobody understands this better than Bob Schulberg.

Long before I ever met Schulberg, I used to steal from him regularly. He is the author of a fascinating and informative monthly newsletter called *Tuned In*. I would attack every issue with a Magic Marker and shamelessly appropriate material for my own speeches and presentations. I never thought of it as plagiarism. I considered it "research." I reasoned that Schulberg wouldn't mind because all he wanted was to get the word out.

Well, that was what he wanted but it wasn't *all* he wanted, as this book clearly demonstrates. What I later found out about Bob when we became friends is that he is a real student of the radio business. I may do a lot of talking into microphones, but he is the one who understands how the business is structured and how it works.

Many of my news colleagues don't know and don't want to know about the business they are part of. They think of the commercial advertising as that which pays the bills *so that* people like us can do what we do on the air. But it's just as true that broadcasts such as ours exist *so that* there will *be* an audience for advertisers to advertise *to*. Neither of us could exist without the other. In a sense, the advertiser delivers me to the listeners and I deliver the listeners to the advertiser. That seems a fair enough bargain, as long as the listener knows the difference between being told something and being sold something.

But whether we are telling or selling, it is important to grasp the nature of the medium so we can do our jobs more effectively. Radio is magic all right. And Bob Schulberg will now explain how the magic works.

Charles Osgood
CBS News

Preface

This book is neither a textbook nor a manual for running a station. Its intent is to enlighten readers to radio's potential, to spark new thinking by advertisers and their agencies, to suggest specific techniques for effective radio advertising, and perhaps to raise a hackle or two among cohorts and competitors.

I see it as an overview of radio as an advertising medium—affirmative in its point of view, critical but not a critique, analytical but not an academic treatise.

Here is how it came to be written.

In the fall of 1975, a CBS executive named John Lack asked me to become the western manager of a business development department that CBS Radio was starting. Soon after I began working for an organization then called CBS Radio Spot Sales (now CBS Radio Representatives).

My eastern counterpart, who had an extensive radio background, started in New York a few months earlier. He was Don Macfarlane who was the general manager of the *Post-Newsweek* radio station in Washington, D.C., before joining CBS. Unlike Macfarlane, I came from the advertising agency world. I had worked for various agencies since the '50s and in my last post had been a management supervisor at Ogilvy & Mather's Los Angeles office.

Arriving at CBS, I faced two challenges. First, I had to figure out how to function in a vaguely defined and newly created job. The objective of this fledgling market development group was to funnel advertising to the radio stations we owned and represented by focusing on the needs of the advertiser. The idea was to help solve advertising problems, not merely media problems.

Second, I had to learn much more than I already knew about the radio business. In those early years at CBS, I consciously studied radio the way I would have boned up on a new client's business at an advertising agency. As an agency account director, I had looked at the broadcast business from the outside in. As a radio marketer, I had to view it from the inside out. And the picture looked quite different from this changed perspective.

I soon recognized that staying in touch with a lot of people was essential if I was going to succeed in this business. I also noticed that Don Macfarlane had started sending a one-sheet newsletter to his prospect list in the East. I blatantly stole his idea. In November 1978, I wrote, printed, and distributed the first issue of my radio newsletter, *Tuned In*. It is now in its tenth year of continuous monthly publication and has a circulation of about 2,500. Regular recipients are advertising agency account, creative, and media people, and client marketing and advertising executives. A surprisingly large number of *Tuned In*'s readers have spoken kindly of this modest publication.

A while back, I noticed that the notebook in which I file a single copy of each monthly issue had become quite weighty. An old advertising agency colleague, John Miyauchi, noting its sheer bulk, suggested that a book about radio was already substantially written. He assured me all I would have to do was some cutting and pasting. I believed him. That turned out to be one of life's great self-delusions. Books take on lives of their own and this one absolutely did not want to be cut and pasted.

Although some of the material contained in this book appeared previously in different form in *Tuned In,* this volume is a fresh distillation of an advertising man's view of radio—its background, structure, strengths, warts, and wonder.

Acknowledgments

I could never have written this book had I not worked over the years with an outstanding group of radio professionals. I am deeply indebted to past and present associates at CBS Radio in New York, most particularly Tom Dawson, Terry Drucker, Michael Ewing, Don Frier, Don Gorski, Bob Hosking, Ed Kiernan, Gene Lothery, Peter Lund, Don Macfarlane, Tony Miraglia, Nancy Widmann, and Bennett Zier. I am also grateful to all my past and present colleagues in California especially Rich Allen, Tom Cosgrove, and Dean LeGras, and to Raif D'Amico in Philadelphia and Roger Murphy in Chicago.

Mary Jean Flamer, Rosemary Paragham, and Scott Springer, of CBS Radio Representatives, and Erik Disen, of KNX Radio, made specific and valuable contributions to this book, as did Gerry Boehm, of Katz Radio; Maurie Webster, of the Radio Information Center; and Bill Stakelin, Ken Costa, and Bob Galen, of the Radio Advertising Bureau.

Special thanks go to my friend, Charles Osgood, of CBS News, New York, for encouraging me to produce this work, assuring me that it will sell and writing the foreword to help the undertaking along.

Until now having been one of the nonbook producers in a family of writers, I wish to pass familial appreciation to those who have encouraged and helped me—my mother, Emma Zeeman Schulberg; novelist/poet sister, Lucille Warner; grammarian/linguist/marketer daughter, Clare; television newsman son, Peter; sister-in-law, editor/novelist/literary counselor, Ann Reit; and close friend, writer of wonderful stuff for kids and grownups, Sy Reit.

For my loving wife, Lorraine, words are inadequate. A professional advertising writer, she served as consultant, editor, copyreader, and rewrite specialist. When you are writing a book and working at the same time, there are no holiday weekends, no lazy days on the beach and damn few family *tête-a-têtes* on weekday evenings. She abided this abysmal situation with good humor, and her support for the project never wavered. She was the quintessential good scout.

Final warm nods of appreciation to Jim Surmanek, of McCann-Erickson, and Gordon Mason, of the Southern California Broadcasters Association, who both took time from their busy schedules to read the first draft with kind but critical eyes, and to Harry Briggs and Dan Spinella, my supportive and creative editors at NTC Business Books.

I regret I cannot thank anyone for typing the manuscript. I did it all by myself using WordStar on a Kaypro II Computer and a Brother Printer.

Introduction

Paradox, thy name is Radio.

In 1948, when television was emerging as the new media champion, there were 2,612 commercial radio stations in the United States and commentators were less than enthusiastic about radio's prospects for the future.

"Television will eventually make radio as obsolete as the horse," wrote *Time Magazine.*

"Radio's days in the big time seem numbered," suggested *Newsweek.*

"Radio: On the way out? Yes!" commented *The New Republic.*

At the end of 1987, however, there were almost 9,000 commercial radio stations whose signals criss-crossed the country—about 5,000 AM and 4,000 FM stations. Net radio revenues increased from $562 million in 1948 to almost $7 billion in 1987. The medium's share of total advertising expenditures has risen over the past twenty years. While television and magazines were enduring uncertain times during the 1980s, national advertisers were rediscovering the value of radio. Radio was hot again—alive, healthy, ubiquitous, and financially robust.

Yet Bill Stakelin, president of the industry's trade association, the Radio Advertising Bureau, was moved to state, "Radio still gets taken for granted. It's the Rodney Dangerfield of media." And Bill Tragos, chairman of TBWA Advertising, commented, "Radio is a new medium to some companies because it's been ignored for so long."

Ken Roman, president of Ogilvy & Mather, was probably closer to the truth when he observed that while "radio may be the most overdiscussed, underutilized" of all media, he foresaw "more advertisers in the 80s recognizing the enduring value of radio in a personal world."

The Cinderella Medium

David Ogilvy himself put it succinctly. He said, "Radio is the Cinderella medium," and he was absolutely correct. Over more than a dozen years, on behalf of CBS's radio interests, I have met and talked with scores of marketing and advertising executives and with hundreds of advertising agency account and media directors. The truth is that most of them perceive radio as a pale, thin relative of television.

This pervasive attitude works itself downward. Young marketing and advertising people usually are well grounded in the complexities of television but only a very few have either knowledge or feelings about radio. Indeed, radio is much like the poor stepdaughter, wearing hand-me-downs and scrubbing the kitchen floor, while the ugly stepsisters are donning glamorous gowns for the ball.

But by wearing the right pair of glass slippers, radio—like Cinderella—can sparkle in its own right.

Radio

The Ultimate
Personal Medium

Radio is the ultimate personal medium, a communication between a radio station and a single listener. It is an indispensable component of American life.

Walter Cronkite, whose broadcasting career began on radio station KNOW in Austin, Texas, arrived at this conclusion: "Radio has its own special strengths and contributions. While TV pulls the big audience, it's still radio that's there virtually every place, all day, all night. It's radio that's there when disaster strikes. Radio is the medium of the single sense and it frees the imagination."

In an advertising sense, radio is more closely related to magazines than to television because it is *format driven*. Readers select magazines because of their editorial content. Radio stations are chosen by listeners because of their programming. As a result, radio and magazines have *audience franchises*.

Conversely, television is a program-driven medium. People have favorite television programs and tune to the channels on which these programs are broadcast. Television programs have loyal audiences but no television station, not even public television, has a true audience franchise.

This is a crucial difference for advertisers.

People, however, listen to radio because of its programming, not to hear commercials. An understanding of its nature is essential before radio can be successfully employed as an advertising medium.

Radio Is Everywhere

The Radio Advertising Bureau (RAB), an industry trade organization, does an annual analysis of the medium's status. Here are some facts and figures released by the RAB in 1988:

Five-hundred-twenty-seven million radio sets were in use in 1987—342 million in homes, 126 million in cars, and 57 million in other locations.

The average household has 5.6 radios.

Two and two-thirds billion dollars were spent on new radios in 1987.

Ninety-nine percent of all homes in the United States have radios. Radios are in 41 percent of all rooms.

Radio is extremely portable. One may be moved from room to room and taken out of the home. Seventy-eight percent of all households have battery-operated radios and 120 million battery-operated sets are in use.

Ninety-five percent of all automobiles have radios. Three out of every four adults listen to radio in a car sometime during the week.

Ninety-seven percent of all cars used for commuting have radios and 86 percent of all car commuters listen to radio.

Sixty-one percent of all adults have a radio at work.

Seventy-eight percent of those persons beyond the age of twelve listen to a radio every day; 96 percent listen every week. The average time spent listening is more than three hours per day.

Individuals, not family groups, listen to radio. Every member of a household may be tuned to a different station.

Each one of these radio listeners, however, turns to only a few stations. The national average is 2.4 stations per listener. In Los Angeles, where there are more than eighty radio stations, the average jumps only to 2.6 stations per listener.

Listeners are loyal and friendly and, in many cases, harbor true familial feelings toward the stations they listen to. But if a radio station is not satisfying its public, listeners do not turn off the radio. They turn to another station.

Radio Is Big

Radio ranks third among mass advertising media. Although it trails newspapers and television, it is big and vibrant.

Radio advertising was a $7.25 billion business in 1987. Radio advertising expenditures have increased two and three-quarters times since 1977 and more than 1,200 percent since 1949, the first year expenditures for television were measured.

Robert Coen, senior vice president of McCann-Erickson Advertising, is the industry's numbers guru and his estimates of all U.S. advertising expenditures are accepted as authoritative. Here are some of his radio totals:

	1937	1947	1957	1967	1977	1987
Radio expenditures *(in millions)*	$165	506	618	1,048	2,634	7,240
Percent increase	—	306.7	12.2	169.6	251.3	274.9
Percent of total advertising expenditures	7.9	11.9	6.0	6.2	7.0	6.6

The fastest growing, though smallest, segment of radio is network radio. Although accounting for under 6 percent ($405 million) of all radio advertising sales proceeds in 1987, it grew 76 percent from 1981. Local radio is where the money rolls in. In 1987, 76 percent ($5.5 billion) of all advertising expenditures in the medium were local. Spot radio—nationally placed market-by-market business—made up the remaining 18 percent ($1.32 billion) and is the slowest growing category of radio sales.

By comparison, network television is the largest but the slowest growing television category. Overall, more than three times more advertising money ($24,155 billion in 1987) goes to television than to radio. In 1987, radio, however, drew 31 percent more advertising dollars ($7.24 billion) than magazines ($5.53 billion).

The late Senator Everett Dirksen was the man who, in talking about government outlays, said, "A billion here, a billion there—and pretty soon you're talking about real money." No matter how you approach it, $7.24 billion is real money.

Sounds in the Mind

If Confucius actually said that one picture is worth ten thousand words, the old Chinese philosopher was off the mark. Perhaps he should have said a few words are worth ten thousand pictures. Radio listeners who are old enough can sing every word of commercials like "No brush, no lather, no rub-in" for Barbasol, and "Pepsi-Cola hits the spot," both of which last ran more than forty years ago. That's because the mind retains information best when it is received through the ear.

Psychologists have concluded that hearing memory in humans is stronger than sight, touch, or smell memory. The response to sound, which goes directly to the brain, is on the average of 140 milliseconds. The response to light—words and pictures—is 180 milliseconds. The 40-millisecond differential is the time it takes for the visual image to be routed to the aural portion of the brain for identification before it moves to the brain's visual reception system.

Listening and understanding spoken language is more basic and occurs much earlier in life than visual comprehension of language. When children begin to learn reading in school, they are taught to translate aurally received phonetic sound into written language.

Being born deaf is a far more onerous burden in terms of language comprehension than being born blind. Researchers have determined that blind people can comprehend spoken language as well as those who can see. The deaf, on the other hand, usually do not read as quickly as those who can see and hear, and, in fact, on the average, read more slowly than the blind using Braille.

Dr. Tony Schwartz, in *Media: The Second God* (Random House, 1981), has carefully examined hearing and media communication. He observed that someone will often say, "I'm a slow reader," but no one ever says, "I'm a slow hearer."

He also notes that

> whatever environment people may be in, all the sound that is in that environment goes into their ears. We can shut our eyes because we have eyelids. But we cannot shut our ears because we have no "earlids." . . . We know that (in hearing) the brain registers a fleeting momentary sound vibration, but also remembers previous registrations and anticipates future ones. (pp. 19–21)

Radio is not television without pictures. Because no literal image exists, when radio is used creatively by programmers and advertisers alike, it can leave impressions in the mind that are beyond the wildest vision of the most adventurous television producer.

Goodman Ace with his wife, Jane, were radio pioneers whose daily program, "Easy Aces," was one of the broadcast delights of the 1930s. He was a superb writer and a great humorist who artfully, but grudgingly, made the transition from radio to television. Goodman Ace fervently believed that words told the story and you really didn't need pictures. He felt you could visualize scenes on "the little one-inch screen in your brain." Though he was reportedly TV's highest paid writer at the time of his death in 1982, his great love was radio.

Roger Angell, in a *New Yorker* profile of Roy Eisenhardt, president of the Oakland A's, quotes him as saying:

> Baseball is a terrific radio sport, by contrast to television, because radio feeds our imagination. I was a Tiger fan all the time I was growing up, and I have a perfect memory of George Kell and Hoot Evers making certain plays that I heard but never saw. I remember them to this day. I'd be lying out on the grass at home listening to the game, but I was really there in the ballpark.

Radio is the most intimate of all media and the one medium that is larger than life because its screen is the brain. Albert Einstein once stated that the gift of fantasy meant more to him than all his talent for absorbing positive knowledge. Radio is the arena of fantasy, the theater of the mind, with an unlimited potential for visions created by words, for the imagined image.

When People Listen

There are striking misconceptions about radio listening habits. Deep in the psyche, individuals feel that everyone is a bit like themselves and reacts as they do; and such individuals attribute their habits and actions to others. "I only listen to the radio driving to and from work, therefore everyone like me only listens to the radio driving to and from work. I listen to station XYZ—doesn't everyone like me listen to station XYZ, too?"

The answer to that question and others like it is a resounding "No!"

Radio breaks down into fairly standard segments called dayparts. *Morning Drive* is 5:30 or 6:00 A.M. to 10:00 A.M.; *Daytime,* 10:00 A.M. to 3:00 P.M.; *Afternoon Drive,* 3:00 P.M. to 7:00 or 8:00 P.M.; *Nighttime,* 7:00 or 8:00 P.M. to midnight. *Overnight* spans the late evening hours from midnight to the start of Morning Drive.

Enormous numbers of people are listening all the time, but many advertisers overvalue the two drive times and depreciate the other dayparts. They either have not examined or have not accepted the documentation that charts radio listening over twenty-four hours a day and seven days a week. (See Table 1–1.)

People *are* listening to the radio all the time. It is not merely a drive time medium or daytime medium. Two out of three Americans listen to the radio during television's 8:00 P.M.–11:00 P.M. prime-time hours. Almost 40 percent listen to the radio between midnight and 6:00 A.M. More than 80 percent listen every weekend, a percentage consistent with weekday listening. Weekend television viewing drops sharply over weekends.

A major 1986 research study sought answers for the question, "How much time do prospective customers spend with various media during the course of a day?" The study showed that radio and television are close in share of media time during the twenty-four-hour day but that radio dominates between 6:00 A.M. and 6:00 P.M. (See Table 1–2.)

How Radio Time Is Sold

An advertiser can buy time on four different "kinds" of radio: local radio, national spot (i.e., individual market), wired network, and unwired network. To the casual listener, the commercials all sound the same, but the differences between the four radio categories are significant.

Local Radio

Local radio, which accounted for 76 percent of all radio advertising dollars in 1987, is just what it appears to be: a local advertiser buys time on a

Table 1-1. Percentage of Population Reached on Radio by Daypart

Monday–Friday	Persons 12 +	Men 18 +	Women 18 +	Teens 12–17
6:00 A.M.–midnight	95.0	94.8	94.3	98.7
6:00 A.M.–10 A.M.	84.5	84.9	83.2	87.8
10:00 A.M.–3:00 P.M.	74.9	75.1	76.7	66.6
3:00 P.M.–7:00 P.M.	79.0	79.2	77.0	87.0
7:00 P.M.–midnight	60.8	59.1	56.6	86.1
Midnight–6:00 A.M.	37.9	38.9	35.3	45.1
Saturday/Sunday				
6:00 A.M.–midnight	79.1	77.5	78.5	87.7
6:00 A.M.–10:00 A.M.	48.3	49.0	48.6	44.1
10:00 A.M.–3:00 P.M.	58.3	56.3	59.0	63.3
3:00 P.M.–7:00 P.M.	46.5	45.1	45.8	54.9
7:00 P.M.–mid.	36.3	34.1	33.6	57.6
Midnight–6:00 A.M.	19.1	18.7	18.3	24.3

Source: Percentages based on Fall 1987 RADAR® (Radio's All-Dimension Audience Research) Reports. Copyright by Statistical Research, Inc., as analyzed by the Radio Advertising Bureau.

Table 1-2.   Media Use on Average Weekday by Adults 25–54

	Time Spent/ Combined Media (hrs.:mins.)	Percentage of Time Spent/Each Medium			
		Radio	Television	Newspapers	Magazines
6:00 A.M.–12:00 M.	2:05	58	24	14	5
12:00 M.–6:00 P.M.	2:07	49	34	9	8
6:00 P.M.–midnight	2:49	15	72	6	7
6:00 A.M.–6:00 P.M.	4:12	53	29	11	7
6:00 A.M.–midnight	7:01	38	46	9	7
24 hours	7:20	39	46	9	6

Source: *Media Targeting for the 90's,* produced by R.H. Bruskin Associates for the Radio Advertising Bureau. Reprinted by permission.

local station. The transaction may be made directly with the radio station by the advertiser, or through an advertising agency. In either situation, the station will be represented by a member of its "local sales" staff.

Where the order is placed determines whether it is local. A car dealership in St. Louis would be a local account on a St. Louis station, but so would St. Louis-based Anheuser-Busch, one of the country's largest advertisers, as long as a St. Louis advertising agency placed the schedule.

There is a pervasive belief that local advertisers are able to buy time less expensively than national advertisers. There are radio stations who use different rate structures for the two categories, but they are usually in smaller cities. Unlike newspapers, most radio stations in the major markets do not offer price concessions to local accounts.

Spot Radio

National spot radio is radio advertising, other than local, placed on a market-by-market basis. It accounted for 18 percent of radio advertising expenditures in 1987. If Anheuser-Busch's St. Louis agency were also buying advertising time in New York, Chicago, and Los Angeles, it would customarily negotiate and place its spot radio orders through national radio station sales representative companies.

In the last few years, these companies have been consolidating. A decade ago, when each radio station insisted on sales exclusivity in its own market, there were scores of independent representative firms. Today the business is dominated by two giant organizations who often represent four or five stations in the same city, and thousands of stations throughout the country. These multidivisional giants, Katz Radio and Interep, have parallel divisions that compete against each other. Together they account for an estimated 75 to 80 percent of all national spot business.

There are still a small number of independent representative companies. CBS Radio Representatives, with a list of approximately fifty stations of which only eighteen are owned by CBS, is the sole radio representative firm operated by one of the three major broadcast companies.

All representative companies maintain offices in all major cities and a radio time buyer frequently will buy time in a number of cities for one advertiser through one sales "rep."

As with sales representative firms, advertising agencies have been consolidating into larger entities, many of whom regionalize their buying. The proliferation of large advertising agencies that buy regionally for their clients has had a negative effect on national spot radio business. Regionalized buying frequently turns what is ostensibly national business into local business.

Regional buying agencies like J. Walter Thompson or Bozell Jacobs Kenyon & Eckhardt have offices in many cities. When Detroit-based Ford Motor Company, out of Thompson, or Dallas-based American Airlines, out of BJK&E, wants to place radio schedules in Los Angeles, the Ford media plan will be prepared in Detroit and the American Airlines media plan prepared in Dallas. Then the agencies will have buyers in their Los Angeles offices place the orders for Los Angeles schedules. In this example, Ford and American Airlines are local.

The same Los Angeles buyers in the same agencies placing schedules for the same advertisers in the San Diego market, where they do not have offices, would do so through the national sales representatives. In this situation, Ford and American Airlines are national spot radio advertisers.

According to Radio Expenditure Reports Inc., the top twenty-five spot radio advertisers in 1987 (in millions of dollars) were:

1. Anheuser-Busch	43.6	14. Melville Corp. *(retail)*	13.8
2. General Motors	34.8	15. Bell South	13.3
3. Philip Morris Companies	29.5	16. Coca-Cola	13.0
4. Sears Roebuck	21.2	17. Bell Atlantic	11.3
5. PepsiCo	19.8	18. G. Heileman Brewing Co.	10.8
6. Delta Air Lines	19.7	19. Adolph Coors Company	10.1
7. Southland Corporation	18.3	20. United States Govt.	10.0
8. Chrysler	17.1	21. Cap Cities/ABC	9.2
9. Pillsbury	16.4	22. Greyhound Corporation	9.1
10. American Airlines	16.1	23. S & P Holding Co. *(beer)*	9.0
11. Texas Air	15.6	24. R. J. Reynolds Industries	8.8
12. Ford	14.9	25. U. S. West Inc.	8.6
13. Walt Disney Productions	14.8		

Network and Syndicated Radio

Network radio, a national advertising medium, is the fastest growing but smallest radio segment, accounting for 6 percent of total radio advertising revenue. Networks provide programming of various types to independent affiliated radio stations throughout the country. The CBS Radio Network, for example, has approximately 450 affiliated stations to which it supplies a variety of programming. Only a handful of these stations are actually owned by CBS.

Two major broadcast companies, ABC/Cap Cities and CBS, and the largest radio syndicator, Westwood One, owner of NBC and Mutual Radio Networks, control the conventional radio networks. There are also a large number of ad hoc networks created to carry various syndicated programs. Networks generate income by selling spots to national advertisers. They, in turn, compensate their affiliated stations.

The effort, and cost, required to buy network or syndicated radio is well below that required to buy spot radio. One network buyer, dealing with a handful of salespeople, can buy for the entire country, while equivalent spot buys would require a number of buyers who would have to negotiate with scores of sales representatives.

Buying network time is a relatively simple procedure. Each network has its own sales organization with offices in the media centers, such as New

York, Chicago, and Los Angeles. In contrast to buying spot radio where each station is purchased individually, an advertising agency places one order for its network schedule and receives one invoice for the entire purchase. Advertising agencies love to make radio network buys.

Networks are customarily referred to as "wired" networks to set them apart from "unwired" networks, an administrative amalgamation of technically unrelated stations. With present technology, the term *wired* is a misnomer because virtually all network feeds are made from satellites and not through telephone lines.

According to the Radio Advertising Bureau, the top twenty-five network radio advertisers in 1987 (in millions of dollars) were:

1.	Sears Roebuck	52.7	14.	Dow Jones	9.0
2.	Warner-Lambert	24.6	15.	Philip Morris	8.9
3.	Procter & Gamble	23.7	16.	Lever Bros.	8.6
4.	Anheuser-Busch	23.5	17.	Mars	8.6
5.	Bayer AG	22.0	18.	State Farm Insurance	8.3
6.	Ford	19.8	19.	William Wrigley, Jr.	8.2
7.	General Motors	19.0	20.	K Mart	6.8
8.	TeleDisc	15.8	21.	Dow Chemical	6.4
9.	AT&T	15.0	22.	FTD Florists	6.1
10.	Campbell's Soup	14.8	23.	Whirlpool	5.8
11.	U. S. Government	13.5	24.	IBM	5.4
12.	Cotter & Co. (True Value)	12.5	25.	Avis	5.3
13.	Schering-Plough	10.6			

Unwired Networks

Unwired radio networks, the creations of the national sales representative firms, emerged as a significant component in the late 1970s. Sold like wired networks (i.e., one order, one invoice), they are flexibly organized coalitions of large numbers of individual radio stations. In 1986, their business accounted for under 10 percent of total national spot volume and sale increases just equaled the sluggish 3 to 4 percent increase of the total spot market.

Technically, unwired networks are not networks at all because the advertiser's commercials are broadcast independently by each participating station. Accordingly, the market list can be tailor-made for an individual advertiser, schedules may vary in different markets and commercials may be customized for each market.

Several needs are satisfied by the unwired networks. In addition to the advantages of flexibility, network choices have been expanded. Today a national advertiser will frequently run a campaign using both wired and unwired networks.

Unwired networks offer the market-by-market advantages of spot radio coupled with the buying and administrative economies of wired network radio. Most advertising agencies perceive unwired networks as a packaging tool for national spot radio. Whether unwired networks offer rate economies, however, is a question widely debated in the broadcasting and advertising communities.

With the consolidation of sales organizations, there has been a sharp reduction in the number of unwired networks. By 1988, only three unwired networks were competing for this segment of the radio business—Internet (1,000+ stations), Katz Radio Group Network (1200+ stations), and Supernet (600 stations).

The need to have stations available for unwired networks has been a major factor in the consolidation of radio sales representative companies. These companies, with rare exceptions, do not sell wired networks or syndicated radio. They are, however, the major packagers of unwired networks and the more stations they represent, the greater share of this business they can control. For example, parallel sales staffs at Interep, who compete for spot business, work together in structuring unwired network buys.

The unwired category is not broadly used. A handful of individual advertisers plus the moving picture category account for almost half of all unwired business.

2

The Beginnings

Every government in the world considers the electromagnetic frequencies used for radio communication to be public property and their use is universally regulated. This unique public character sets radio, and television, apart from printed media.

Without regulation, stations operating on the same frequencies could interfere with one another and have difficulty identifying themselves. This was the situation before 1912 when the proliferation of radio signals from ships and land stations (whose function was to communicate with vessels at sea) created a tangled mass of competing signals. An international agreement to assign call letters was reached in that year. The United States was given all call letters beginning with W, K, N and AA–AL. That same 1912 agreement assigned C to Canada, X to Mexico, F to France, D to Germany, and so on.

All U.S. commercial broadcasting stations now use call letters beginning with W and K. The call letters of most, but not all, stations in the eastern half of the country begin with W and those in the West begin with K, but this is no longer required by regulation. A and N are used by the armed forces, civilian aircraft, and ham operators.

Until 1921, however, there was no licensing procedure for radio stations, and only in 1923 were the more powerful stations assigned their own frequencies. These stations promised the federal government quality programming in the public interest, and, at the same time, they had to agree *not* to play phonograph records.

A voluntary system to keep all other stations from infringing on one another's wavelengths had been established in 1922, but by 1927, when there were over a thousand stations on the air, the system was breaking down and the federal government took over complete control of frequencies.

Present day broadcast regulation in this country is based on the Radio Act of 1927 and the Communications Act of 1934. The Communications Act replaced an earlier body called the Federal Radio Commission with the current regulatory entity, the five- member Federal Communications Commission. Because airways have no respect for state boundaries, broadcasting was classified as interstate commerce in the earliest regulatory act.

Broadcasting, by definition, means "to cast in all directions." As a method of communication, it is in contrast to point-to-point wireless, which had been in use since Guglielmo Marconi made his first sale to the British War Office in 1898. The concept of broadcasting—reaching an unknown audience indiscriminately—was not readily accepted. Radio was expected to replace existing wired communication systems, the telegraph and telephone, and its lack of privacy was considered to be a serious weakness. By the early 1920s, however, broadcasting's potential was becoming apparent.

Acceptance of Advertising

Virtually from the start, U.S. broadcasting has been run as private enterprise with advertising as its primary source of funding. Our system of broadcasting is not widely copied throughout the rest of the world. Most countries maintain strong governmental rather than commercial control of the airwaves. In the United States, this method was briefly considered and rejected.

Advertising was not without its detractors. In 1922, Secretary of Commerce Herbert Hoover said, "It is inconceivable that we should allow so great a possibility for service, for news, for entertainment, and for vital commercial purposes be drowned in advertising chatter." Despite this feeling, then shared by a majority of the public and most of the radio industry, advertising-supported broadcasting prevailed. As a result, popularity with listeners became the criterion for programming.

Sidney W. Head, in his definitive *Broadcasting in America* (4th ed., Houghton Mifflin, 1982), writes,

> The profit incentive, minimally hampered by government regulation, results in catering to the widest possible audience. Operating within the permissive framework of the free enterprise system, American commercial broadcasting has all the pragmatism, aggressiveness, materialism, improvisation, expansionism and free-swinging competitiveness of American marketing. Whatever the critics may say, the overall result has been a more lively, inventive and varied broadcasting system than can be found elsewhere in the world. (p. 5)

The nonregulatory pattern established in the Reagan years is likely to continue in subsequent administrations. The desires of radio listeners, rather than what a paternal government thinks is good for them, are almost certain to shape the medium through the rest of the twentieth century.

The Oldest Station

What is now KCBS, San Francisco, is the oldest radio station in the United States. It *broadcast* for the first time from San Jose, California, in January 1909, when Dr. Charles David Herrold, principal of the Herrold College of Engineering and Wireless, sent out a signal on a fifteen-watt transmitter that he had built himself.

The 1912 agreement mandating call letters initially affected only ships and land stations, so until Congress enacted the legislation requiring licenses, Dr. Herrold's announcers identified the station by saying, "This is San Jose calling." His station provided a means to publicize Dr. Herrold's wireless school to its best prospects, young radio amateurs. The programming consisted principally of recorded music and news dispatches.

In 1921, the Department of Commerce assigned the pioneer station the call letters KQW. Dr. Herrold sold the station in 1925, and a year later, when it had moved to San Francisco, its first advertiser, the Sperry Flour Company, sponsored a daily fifteen-minute cooking program. This made KQW truly commercial.

The Columbia Broadcasting System (now CBS Inc.) bought KQW in 1949 and changed the call letters to KCBS. Still a trailblazer, in 1968, KCBS became one of the earliest radio stations to employ the All-News format. Later KCBS became the first news station to employ a computerized, completely electronic newsroom—a far cry from Dr. Herrold's day when the station's announcers simply read aloud news stories from the local newspaper.

Another pioneer radio station, WRL, started as a radiophone land station at Union College in Schenectady, New York, around 1916. It was operated by college students under the direction of the renowned electrical engineering professor and inventor, Charles P. Steinmetz, using equipment provided by the General Electric Company. WRL was the first broadcast station to run regularly scheduled radio programs. It also engineered the first remote broadcast, which originated from a remote transmitter in a baby carriage on State Street in Schenectady, a few miles from WRL's location on the Union campus.

When WGY, General Electric's own station, began operations in 1922, WRL folded up. WGY's manager, Kolin Hager, was a programming innovator. He literally invented radio drama. He created the memorable series "One Man's Family," which eventually became a daytime mainstay of the National Broadcasting Company's network. Most broadcast historians also credit him with devising the three-note chime still used to identify NBC. The musical notes "G," "E," and "C" stood for "General Electric Company." It was a fitting symbol. Thirty-three years later, in 1985, GE became NBC's owner when it acquired RCA, NBC's parent company. In 1987, however, although retaining the parent company, GE sold the NBC Radio Network to Westwood One.

KDKA, Pittsburgh, claims to be the nation's first broadcasting station because, in 1920, it was the first station to become federally licensed. KDKA was also the first commercial radio station to be assigned four call letters. This pioneer station began, during World War I, as an amateur radiophone station operated by Frank Conrad, a Westinghouse engineer, whose employer took over ownership in 1920. Its first regularly scheduled program relayed the election results of that year's Harding–Cox presidential race. By 1921, KDKA was broadcasting live symphony orchestra concerts, professional baseball, and college football games. Among its other trailblazing accomplishments, KDKA transmitted the first church service and the first World Series broadcast.

Radio stations as we know them, however, had their genesis with old Dr. Herrold and his San Jose fifteen-watter.

The Start of Networks

In 1923, WEAF, New York, hooked up with WNAC in Boston and this was the start of "chain broadcasting," or networking. A year later, by using its own telephone lines, American Telephone & Telegraph, owner of WEAF, was operating a coast-to-coast network of twenty-three radio stations. A rival network of four stations was owned by the Radio Corporation of America, a consortium of radio set manufacturers. AT&T, fearing the loss of its telephone monopoly, got out of the radio business in 1926. It sold its radio stations to a new subsidiary of RCA, the National Broadcasting Company (now NBC), who thereafter operated two radio networks, the Red and the Blue.

Early networking simply involved sending sound on AT&T's high-efficiency cable from the originating station to other stations with enough fidelity to allow a wireless rebroadcast. David Sarnoff, the head of NBC, created network broadcasting as it is known today on November 14, 1926. That night, those who listened to twenty-four NBC Red Network stations heard a program that included, among others, cowboy commentator Will Rogers broadcasting from Kansas City, opera singer Mary Garden from Chicago, and comedian Eddie Cantor from New York.

In 1946, the NBC Blue Network, consisting of RCA's pre-1926 stations, was sold, and eventually became the American Broadcasting Company (now ABC).

The Columbia Broadcasting System was started in 1927 in Philadelphia, and control was purchased two years later by the advertising manager of a cigar company, twenty-seven-year-old William S. Paley. He moved quickly to make the fledgling network competitive with the two established NBC networks.

A fourth network, Mutual, began in 1939 with WOR, then licensed in Newark, New Jersey, as its New York-area outlet. Mutual was the most free-wheeling of the original radio networks. It made up in marketing what it lacked in resources. Regional coverage was offered to advertisers who did not want to broadcast throughout the entire country. Mutual also played recorded programs, a practice then prohibited by NBC and CBS.

The New York-based flagship stations of the four networks have remained in constant operation. WEAF, from the NBC Red Network, is heard today in New York under the call letters WNBC-AM. The Blue Network Station in New York, WJZ, broadcasts today as WABC-AM. The *original* WABC is today's WCBS-AM, and WOR continues with its original call letters.

The Beginnings of FM

The principle of frequency modulation (FM) had been known long before its advantages for broadcasting became apparent in the late 1930s. (See Chapter 3 for an explanation of the physical differences between AM and FM.) In 1940, the Federal Communications Commission set apart thirty-five channels for commercial FM broadcasting and five for noncommercial, educational use. Transmission was to begin on January 1, 1941.

The FCC issued construction permits to fifteen stations simultaneously and ten more permits shortly thereafter. The first commercial FM station licensed by the FCC was WSM-FM, Nashville, which operated from May 21, 1941 until 1951. Though all radio station construction was frozen during the war years, more than forty prewar FM stations were operational in that period; there were about 400,000 FM receivers that could pick up their signals.

By 1948, there were more than a thousand FM stations licensed. In that year, NBC produced the first simulcast. The "Firestone Concert of the Air" was simultaneously carried on AM and FM radio—and on television.

Advertising, Sponsors, and Commercials

Just before Christmas in 1921, Vincent Lopez and his orchestra, playing from the Grill Room of the Hotel Pennsylvania in New York, were featured on the first remote dance band pickup. During the broadcast over radio station WJZ, Lopez engaged in a little self-advertising. He asked listeners to call for reservations at the Pennsylvania Grill to see his band play. The flood of incoming telephone calls knocked out one of midtown Manhattan's major telephone exchanges. The radio medium, it appeared, had the capacity to motivate listeners to action.

On August 28, 1922, the Queensboro Corporation, developer of Jackson Heights in Long Island City, New York, paid WEAF, then owned by AT&T, for ten minutes of time to broadcast information about its properties. The entire program was a commercial, radio's first. It began:

Let me enjoin upon you as you value your health and your hopes and your home happiness, to get away from the solid masses of brick, where the meager opening admitting a slant of sunlight is mockingly called a light shaft, and where children grow up starved for a run over a patch of grass and the sight of a tree. . . .Friends, you owe it to yourself and your family to leave the congested city and enjoy what nature intended you to enjoy. Visit our new apartment homes in Hawthorne Court, Jackson Heights, where you may enjoy life in a friendly environment.

The program was the first of what became a fifteen-minute series. Soon after, Tidewater Oil and the American Express Company bought time for similar undertakings, and then the New York department store, Gimbel Brothers, sponsored the first modern radio program utilizing singers and musicians. The program, observed by the public, was broadcast from a studio in the store using WEAF's technicians and talent. Browning King, a clothing store, became the first company to underwrite the exclusive presentation of a program. By December 1922, there were thirteen program sponsors on WEAF. At Christmas the station's owner joined the group. Carols sung by two thousand employees of American Telephone & Telegraph were heard on radio receivers in the New York area. It was easier for a sponsor to broadcast an indirect "talk" on WEAF, as the Queensboro Corporation did, then to run *commercials*. AT&T had a long list of restrictions. Not only was the offering of merchandise samples prohibited, packages or containers could not be described as to size, shape, or color. Prices could not be mentioned and "plugs" were out.

Nonetheless, businesses recognized the potential. Gillette ran talks on fashions in beards and cleanliness—and safety razors. Other companies sponsored similar "public service" messages. A lecture on dental hygiene provided, and paid for, by a toothpaste company was turned down, however, because the station felt its listeners would find the subject distasteful.

Advertisers wanted an association with entertainment, however, and WEAF and other pioneer radio stations finally agreed to sponsorships as long as no direct commercial messages were broadcast. The era of *association* was born.

In the early 1920s, the Ipana Troubadours barely mentioned toothpaste and the Cliquot Club Eskimos only hinted that a soft drink company was paying for their broadcast time. The A&P Gypsies didn't sell groceries, and the announcer who introduced the Browning King Orchestra made no reference to the fact that Browning King purveyed clothing. American Tobacco Company's "Lucky Strike Radio Show" didn't push cigarettes and the Goodrich Silvertown Orchestra, featuring the renowned Silver Masked Tenor, didn't overtly sell tires. Sponsor mention was formal and understated.

One of the few program commercials that has survived from that early era was for Perfect Circle piston rings.

> Again it is the pleasure of the Perfect Circle Company, manufacturers of Perfect Circle piston rings, to present Charlie Davis and his famous Indiana Public Stage Orchestra. These programs of the best in popular music are especially arranged for your entertainment by Mr. Davis and the Perfect Circle Company. The orchestra greets you tonight with.... Whenever you buy anything, whether for your personal use or for your home or for your car, there is that unmistakable feeling of satisfaction in the knowledge that it is a standard product, widely and favorably known. Perfect Circle piston rings are the standard of the automotive industry, used by more than 80 percent of America's car manufacturers in all or a large part of their production. Your comments on these Perfect Circle programs will be appreciated both by Mr. Davis and the Perfect Circle Company.

In 1923, radio's first regular comedy show featured the songs and snappy patter of Billy Jones and Ernie Hare who were known, over the ensuing years, as the Happiness Boys (for the Happiness Candy Stores), the Taystee Loafers, and the Best Food Boys. When they finally became the Interwoven Pair later in the decade, they were able to build a little sell into their musical introduction.

> How do ya do, everybody, how do ya do?
> Gee, it's great to say "Hello!" to all of you!
> I'm Billy Jones.
> I'm Ernie Hare.
> We're the Interwoven Pair.
> How do ya doodle-doodle-doodle-doodle-oo!
> Sock, socks...
> We're Billy Jones and Ernie Hare.
> We're the Interwoven pair.

Until the complete structure of radio changed with the emergence of television, advertisers remained associated with programs. The list is lengthy and includes "The Gold Dust Twins," "The Atwater Kent Program," "The Voice of Firestone," "The Fleischmann Yeast Hour," "The March of Time," "The Horn and Hardart Children's Hour," "The Cities Service Concert," "The Maxwell House Showboat," "The Longine Symphonette," "The Lux Radio Theatre," "The Chase and Sanborn Hour," "Bob Hope's Pepsodent Show," and "The Texaco Firechief" (which starred Ed Wynn and was the first comedy show to play before a studio audience).

The restrictive advertising practices of WEAF and AT&T were not universally followed. Many stations let it be known that if a sponsor wanted to describe his product and mention its price, there would be no objections raised. It wasn't too long before NBC noticed what was going on and the walls tumbled down for the entire radio industry. Indirect advertising was abandoned by most sponsors and, in many instances, they went—blatantly— in the opposite direction. By 1927, more than $4 million was being spent on advertising messages that were described as "insistent, demanding, and unsparing." By 1928, this figure had leaped to $10.5 million and to $40 million by 1930.

The power of the human voice had opened a myriad of possibilities, from the emulation of pitchmen and barkers to endorsement by all types of celebrities. Advertisers and their agencies quickly recognized that the new, intensely personal medium, unlike male-oriented newspapers, had a special appeal for women and children. Radio brought advertising directly into the home and the concept that drama, comedy, concerts, opera, news, and sports reached the radio listeners through the largess of companies who wanted to sell them something was readily accepted.

Radio's mass appeal allowed it to become the principle advertising medium for routinely used, low-priced products—cigarettes, candy, cosmetics, toothpaste, canned foods, cereals, mouthwashes, soft drinks, and patent medicines. Commercials for these frequently purchased categories, heard week after week, provided continuing purchase reminders.

At the same time, manufacturers of durable goods, from automobiles to large and small appliances, found network radio particularly suited to their needs and they became the second major class of radio advertisers.

Life magazine conducted a survey in May 1943 and reported that 91.9 percent of the nation's families had a radio and by 1945 radio's largest customer, Procter & Gamble, was spending $11 million a year for time and an equal amount for talent.

A New Art Form—The Commercial

As radio progressed as a mass medium, it clung to the concept of association between program content and advertising. Shows were owned by the company that put them on the air not by the networks, as television programs are today. The opening theme of virtually every major radio program played on the relationship between the sponsor and the star. Typically, Jack Benny began each program with the familiar "Jell-O again!" and Burns and Allen did a commercial bit in each of their comedy shows

Strong and successful efforts were made to integrate the commercial messages into the program proper. Each show had its own announcer who, in addition to presenting "a message from our sponsor," was usually a straight man for the star, as was Harry Von Zell for Fred Allen.

ALLEN: Someone once said that the world stands aside to make way for the man who knows where he's going, and so tonight it gives me great pleasure to make way for a man who knows what he's talking about, Harry Von Zell.

HARRY: Don't ever neglect a cold. At the very first sign of a cold, get after it immediately with the faster help of sparkling—er, sparkling—what's the name?

ALLEN: Fred Allen, remember?

HARRY: No, no, no, no. The name of the... I'm awfully sorry. I can't remember the name of what it is that helps fight colds faster. It slipped my mind.

ALLEN: Well, it will come to you. Go ahead, Harry.

HARRY: Well, yes, yes, of course. Ladies and gentlemen, this famous product acts quickly yet it's exceptionally gentle and since the progress of a cold is very fast, the greater speed of—er, er— what it is I'm talking about is especially important in fighting your cold and that's not all, this—er—the name will come to me in a minute—it also helps nature counteract the acidity that so often accompanies a cold. And, ladies and gentlemen, you can check these facts with your own doctor.

ALLEN: You'd better check the name, too, ladies and gentlemen.

HARRY: Oh, Fred, you know what I'm talking about.

ALLEN: Why certainly, Harry, you're talking about America's outstanding saline laxative.

HARRY: That's it, Fred. The name is...

ALLEN: The name is—er, er — so many physicians recommend it...

HARRY: Yes, yes, and it helps fight colds faster but what is the name?

ALLEN: Oh, here's a pretty to-do. Wait, Harry, there must be somebody around here who knows. If there is, will you please tell us confidentially...

AUDIENCE: Sal Hepatica!

ALLEN: That's it, Sal Hepatica! Thank you, ladies and gentlemen.

One of the particular strengths of important daytime personalities like Arthur Godfrey was that they also did the commercials and artfully wove them into whatever else they were rambling on about.

Children's programs built promotional offers around their theme characters. You could get Jack Armstrong's Magnesium Parachute Ball by sending in Wheaties boxtops. There were decoder rings, magnifying glasses, lariats, badges of all types, periscope viewers, shake-up mugs, and countless other *absolutely essential* items offered by Tom Mix, the Lone Ranger, Sergeant Preston, Buck Rogers, Captain Midnight, and the like. All you had to do was just get Mom to buy the products they were hawking.

Virtually all advertising was live although transcribed (broadcasting jargon for "recorded") announcements existed as far back as 1932. In that year the production company of Kasper-Gordon Inc. pioneered fifteen-second transcribed dramatic commercials, and in 1933, it offered transcribed musical jingles and full-length commercials. Prerecorded spoken advertising messages were, nonetheless, the exception until the late 1930s, when the emergence of disc jockeys who played records created a need for commercials that could be spotted between musical selections and recorded spots began to gain acceptance.

The first national free-standing spot announcement—as opposed to an integrated spot—was sold to an advertiser by the Schwimmer and Scott Advertising Agency in 1935. Live announcements were intensely flexible and the practice was to change them constantly. That is the principle reason why pretelevision spoken radio commercials have not survived on their own to any substantial degree in the archives of advertising. There are, however, extensive libraries of old radio programs, all of which have commercials in them.

Testimonials were used by the earliest radio advertisers. Sports figures and entertainers lauded all kinds of consumer products. Tobacco companies were heavy users of testimonials for various cigarettes and cigars.

Sing It Again, Sam

Surviving in profusion from pretelevision radio are singing commercials and their first cousins, identifying jingles. Many of them had lives that spanned decades.

The roots of singing commercials go back almost a hundred years before the existence of radio. Nineteenth-century folk songs frequently referred to mercantile and industrial entities, such as this allusion to a railroad: "Oh, the Rock Island line is a mighty good road.... "

In 1883, the Studebaker Brothers added a few words to a traditional folk song and gave away sheet music that included these lyrics, "Wait for the wagon, *the Studebaker wagon;* wait for the wagon and we'll all take a ride."

Forty-three years later, the concept came to radio. On Christmas Eve of 1926, the Washburn-Crosby Company (now General Mills) used a barber shop quartet to introduce a catchy singing commercial on WCCO, Minneapolis, a powerful radio station that it then owned. The commerical started like this, "Have you tried Wheaties, the best breakfast food in the land?"

Specially written musical selections for radio advertising, which masked a sales message in entertainment form, were initially used as themes for programs. One of the earliest was used by the Tasty Yeast Company:

> Tasty Yeast is tempting to your appetite.
> Creamy, wholesome candy, try a luscious bite.
> Vitamins are hiding in this candy bar,
> Pep, vim, and vigor linger where they are.

From those beginnings until today, there have been singing commercials, jingles, and aural catch phrases beyond counting. Jell-O's "J-E-L-L-O" dates back to the early 30s. Other early and memorable efforts were

"Duz does everything"; Adler Shoes', "You can be taller than she is"; Chesterfield Cigarettes', "Sound off—for Chesterfield!"; Gillette's, "Look sharp—be sharp!"; Lucky Strike's, "Be happy, Go Lucky"; Arrid's, "Don't be half- safe"; "Halo Shampoo—Halo"; "Call for Philip Maw-riss!"; Chiquita Banana's, "You must never put bananas in the refrigerator—oh, no, no, no!"; and Singing Sam's deep base intoning, "Barbasol, Barbasol, no brush, no lather, no rub-in...."

The all-time heavyweight champion of singing commercials, however, was written by the team of Allen Kent and Herbert Austen Croom (Ginger) Johnson. An upstart cola drink was trying to slice away some of giant Coca-Cola's market. In 1939, Kent and Johnson attacked the problem of writing a musical commercial to encourage the sale of this twelve-ounce, five-cent bottle of cola by making a spirited adaptation of an English hunting song, "John Peel." It is unlikely that anyone who ever heard it has forgotten it.

> Pepsi-Cola hits the spot.
> Twelve full ounces, that's a lot.
> Twice as much for a nickel, too.
> Pepsi-Cola is the drink for you!
> Nickel, nickel, nickel, nickel,
> Trickle, trickle, trickle, trickle,
> Nickel, nickel, nickel, nickel.

The Pepsi-Cola Company bought the Kent–Johnson jingle, used it for decades, and still holds the copyright. The company was artful in how they used the new musical spot. Running the exact same announcement many times during a concentrated period is a contemporary advertising concept that dates back to the first saturation campaign built around this Pepsi commercial.

Singing commercials have had their problems. Some station managers felt they denigrated their stations' programming. In 1944, WQXR, the *New York Times'* classical radio station, summarily barred them, as did several other stations around the country. David Ogilvy, the doyen of the international advertising agency, Ogilvy & Mather, once proclaimed, "If you have nothing to say, sing it!" It's not known whether he ever heard the worst singing commercial that has ever ridden the airwaves. It reputedly was carried on a Canadian radio station and went like this:

> Dignity, peace, and more for your dollar,
> At Coopersmith's friendly Funeral Parlor.

The capacity to recall words and music over long stretches of time would have to be impressive, even to David Ogilvy.

Most early musical commercials were performed anonymously, but particularly after World War II, well-known performers whose names and style were readily identifiable began to sing advertising messages. Ethel Merman, for one, did a series of radio commercials for Continental Airlines in the 1950s. At the time, her then-husband owned the airline, but twenty years later, on her own, she was again doing very successful commercials. These were for Mailgram, and, it must be assumed, she sang them for the money. Long before Miss Merman was belting out spots, early in his career a red-haired ukelele-playing ex-sailor named Arthur Godfrey did a memorable musical commercial that ended with the phrase, "You can search every clime but at three for a dime, you can't beat a Cremo Cigar!"

All the old forms still exist today on radio and television—straight spoken commercials, testimonial commercials, singing commercials, dramatic commercials, and especially humorous commercials. They've been modernized and formularized, rocked, rolled, and synthesized, but the roots of all broadcast advertising go back to pretelevision radio.

The substantive metamorphosis in radio after the emergence of television did not particularly change radio *advertising*. It changed radio *programming*. The twin result was the development of sharply defined radio formats and a new role for radio networks.

3

How Radio Works

Most radio advertisers and their agencies don't give much thought to how radio works but it helps to understand some rudimentary technical concepts. The physical laws that govern radio and the regulation of those laws by the Federal Communications Commission can, and frequently should, affect advertising decisions.

AM and FM are usually thought of as referring to two different sets of dial positions, but the letters really do stand for something else.

Amplitude Modulation and Frequency Modulation*

AM means *amplitude modulation*. FM means *frequency modulation*. Each refers to the technical method used to superimpose sounds, such as music and speech, onto a radio wave. These sounds, when broadcast from a radio station, travel along the radio wave until they reach a radio receiver where they are removed and converted back to the original sounds produced by the broadcaster.

In AM broadcasting, sound is conveyed to the radio wave by varying the

---

*Source material from "AM & FM—What Do the Letters Really Stand For?" used by permission of McGavern Guild Radio.

wave's strength (amplitude). This is akin to varying the brightness of a light bulb through the use of a dimmer switch. The operating frequency of an AM station is expressed in kilohertz (KHz). A station broadcasting at 960 KHz has a frequency of 960,000 cycles per second. All AM stations operate on frequencies that are 10 KHz apart (960, 970, 980...).

In FM broadcasting, sound is conveyed to the radio wave by slightly changing the wave's frequency. This is similar to changing the color of light by passing it through various shades of tinted glass. The operating frequency of an FM station is expressed in megahertz (MHz). A station broadcasting at 96.7 MHz has a frequency of 96,700,000 cycles per second. All FM stations operate on frequencies that are 200 MHz apart (92.1, 92.3, 92.5...).

AM Sky Waves and Ground Waves

AM signals travel through both the air and the ground. There are radical differences in the distances that each type of signal can travel.

Sky waves travel through air and space. During daylight hours, they are absorbed by the earth's upper atmosphere. At night, however, the waves are reflected by the upper atmosphere so that they can strike the earth's surface at points hundreds and even thousands of miles from the transmitter. The signals of certain AM radio stations are routinely heard from great distances at night. More than half the AM stations in the country must drastically reduce power after the sun sets below the horizon in order to prevent signal interference among stations at night.

Ground waves make up the portion of an AM radio station's signal that actually passes through the ground. Local audiences hear AM radio stations mostly through signals carried by the groundwaves. The distance that the ground wave can travel is largely dependent upon the physical characteristics of the soil, rock, and water present in the particular locale. The ability of the earth's surface to carry a radio wave is known as its *ground conductivity.*

Areas with low ground conductivity will tend to restrict the transmission of radio waves and produce a small signal coverage area. Areas with high ground conductivity will permit the radio waves to pass freely through them and produce larger signal areas. The absolute transmitting power of a station, therefore, is not the only factor influencing the size of a station's coverage area.

Different frequencies vary in their innate ability to be transmitted through the ground thus dial position for an AM station is significant. Higher frequencies with comparable power will encounter more resistance than lower ones, and, therefore, the lower a station's operating frequency (i.e., dial position), the greater its signal area. A 5,000-watt station low on the dial may have as large a ground wave coverage area as a 50,000-watt station high on the dial.

Types of AM Stations

AM stations are classified by type. Class I stations—often referred to as *clear channel* stations—are intended to serve the largest possible area. In addition to their ground wave reception areas (typically extending 200 miles out), their extensive nighttime sky waves can blanket entire sections of the country. Class I stations operate twenty-four hours a day at 50,000 watts. Some of these stations may use directional antennas but they do not significantly affect coverage. (Licenses for clear channel stations are no longer issued by the FCC as all the available frequency positions were utilized by the 1930s.)

A I-A clear channel station, like WBBM, Chicago or WCCO, Minneapolis-St. Paul, is the dominant 50,000-watt station broadcasting on its assigned frequency in all of North America. Until recently, each I-A station had exclusive use of its frequency but this exclusivity is no longer protected by regulation.

A I-B channel station is one of two dominant radio stations on the continent broadcasting on its frequency. KNX, Los Angeles, for example, shares the 1070 dial position with another I-B station, CBA in Moncton, New Brunswick, Canada.

Class II stations operate on the same group frequencies as the clear channel stations but their signal areas are normally smaller and they may be required to reduce power at night in order not to interfere with the Class I stations' signals. KRBE, Houston, a 10,000-watt Class II station, shares the 1070 dial position with KNX and CBA among others. At night, however, it reduces its power to 5,000 watts in order to protect KNX's and CBA's dominant sky wave signals.

Class III and IV stations are regional and local stations serving narrow geographical areas. They operate on frequencies of 250 to 5,000 watts that have been reserved by the FCC for these classes of service.

Characteristics of FM Radio Signals

FM broadcast signals travel exclusively through the air and have difficulty "bending" around terrain features that lie between the transmitter and an FM receiver. FM signals are characterized as "line of sight" which means that there should not be any significant objects, such as mountains, along the theoretical line extending between the transmitter and the listener. Because their signals are not reflected by the upper atmosphere, all FM stations are licensed to operate full time and their signals, if unimpeded, extend equal distances in all directions.

An FM station's power alone will not determine the size of its signal area. Because of its line-of-sight characteristic, the higher the transmitting antenna, the greater the area that receives its signal. When the FCC licenses an FM station, it specifies both its power and its antenna height; antenna height is expressed in relation to the height of the geographical area where the antenna tower is situated. A 20-foot tower on top of a mountain is better than a 200-foot tower in a valley.

FM stations indicate differences in polarization (the plane on which the waves are oscillating) because each type of polarization is intended to enhance the reception of radios employing specific types of antennas.

Horizontal polarized signals can most easily be received with rooftop antennas. Whip antennas, found on most autos, are more sensitive to vertically polarized signals. Circular polarized signals (used by television which employs FM sound) can be received well by any type of antenna.

Unlike AM, lower frequency FM signals do not travel farther than higher frequency signals, thus dial position is not a factor in FM radio.

Classes of FM Stations

Class B and C stations have the largest coverage areas. In most densely populated areas, Class B stations are limited to a maximum power of 50,000 watts with antennas up to 500 feet above the ground. Their coverage normally extends outward for seventy-five miles.

In less populated areas, Class C stations operate with power up to 100,000 watts and antenna height up to 2,000 feet. Their coverage area is typically ninety miles.

Class A stations, serving specified local areas, have lower power and height.

Unique FM Features

Both AM and FM signals can be transmitted by satellite from the source of the transmission to an individual radio station for eventual broadcasting over its own frequency to the station's listeners (see Chapter 6, "The Role of Networks and Syndication"). But there are significant aspects of FM broadcasting that distinguish it from its AM counterpart. One is its widely used stereophonic transmission (though progress is being made with AM stereo). Another is its round signal coverage area, resulting from the absence of directional antenna.

Because AM radio depends on changes of amounts (i.e., amplitude) of energy, AM signals are vulnerable to electrical interference (heard as static). FM radio, dependent on changes in frequency, avoids static interference. FM can also produce sounds up to 15,000 cycles per second—so high a pitch that many people cannot hear it—compared to AM's 7,500 cycles per second. Such high frequencies are essential to high-fidelity sound reproduction which incorporates overtones.

An FM signal need only be twice as strong as a competing signal to override it; an AM signal must be twenty times as strong. Both signals must be quadrupled in strength to double the diameter of their signal coverage areas.

   AM or FM, high power or low, mono or stereo, good dial position or bad—without the programming that listeners want to hear, radio waves have all the communications characteristics of a blank sheet of paper. Only as a communications medium does radio have value to advertisers.

4

Ratings and the Numbers

The audience for radio, like all media audiences, is precisely and minutely measured. This is the dirty word: *ratings*.

Broadcast rating points are an expression of percentage of audience. Ratings are used as a time-buying tool and provide the basis for establishing systems that generate more substantial audience analyses, such as *reach and frequency*—a measurement that expresses how many persons are exposed to an advertising message and how often.

Although ratings are considered absolutely essential to the advertising and broadcasting communities, all kinds of games can and are played with ratings numbers.

Where Is H. L. Mencken When We Need Him?

H. L. Mencken said, "For every human problem, there is a neat, plain solution—and it is always wrong!" Advertising people have commented more specifically:

> I would like research specialists to admit that a broadcast rating is merely an *indication* of an audience...to begin to use some old-fashioned words like "approximately," "possibly," "perhaps," and "maybe." I would like them to be a little more humble. (Jack Geller, vice president/media director, Weiss & Geller, writing in *Broadcasting*)

> Media has become paralyzed by the desire "to be safe." Agencies

depend solely on numerical tools for the development of target audience and the selection of media types and vehicles. (Harold Levine, chairman of Levine, Huntley, Schmidt & Beaver, writing in *Advertising Age*)

When did judgment stop being used by the media planner? When did instinct vanish? When was it that we started relying almost totally on *numbers* to justify media strategy and tactics? (Jim Surmanek, senior vice president/executive media director, J. Walter Thompson/West, writing in *Marketing & Media Decisions*)

Although many marketing, advertising, and broadcasting professionals like Geller, Levine, and Surmanek view the numeric approach to broadcast time buying with the well-known jaundiced eye, it is a fact of life.

Radio ratings deal with numbers of people. They do not assess radio station believability, prestige, cost per sale, listener attitudes, commercial environment, commercial penetration, or advertising results.

A Few Definitions

You can't play the game if you don't understand who the players are and what they are saying.

Research Services

Arbitron (Arbitron Ratings Company)—Research organization owned by Control Data which measures individual markets for both radio and television. Considered the standard of the radio ratings industry with 3,100 agency subscribers. Arbitron had a virtual monopoly between the demise of Pulse Ratings in the late 1970s and the acceptance of Birch's radio measurements in the mid-1980s. Arbitron depends solely on seven-day, self-administered diaries for its radio data. It measures television audiences using diaries and meters.

Birch (Birch Radio)—A competitive individual market radio rating service established in 1978. In contrast to Arbitron's diaries, Birch's methodology is based on telephone interviews about the previous day's radio listening. More than 1,400 advertisers and agencies now subscribe to Birch, and the number is growing.

Radio's All Dimension Audience Research (RADAR®)—Biannual measurement of national radio usage as well as the listenership of twenty radio networks, produced by Statistical Research, Inc. RADAR® uses seven consecutive-day telephone interviews for its information.

Nielsen (A. C. Nielsen Company)—The nation's largest market research organization. Nielsen does not measure radio. Its most widely quoted broadcast study is the Nielsen Television Index, the standard measurement for network television. The Nielsen Station Index measures local television audiences. Nielsen also produces the Nielsen Food and Drug Index, a product study that is widely used by advertisers and agencies. When Nielsen got into the television measurement business, the company correctly assumed that its television data would be trusted because its product indices were so highly regarded by the major package goods advertisers. In late 1986, Nielsen began switching over its thirty-year-old television diary methodology to the "people meter," a remote control device that records what show is being watched and which family members are watching. This switch created a furor in the agency and network communities because of the disparity in audience numbers between the two systems. The people meters showed a lower level of TV viewing than the traditional diaries. Agencies, seeing an opportunity to negotiate lower TV prices, were pleased, but the television networks were up in arms. Radio broadcasters sided with the agencies in this imbroglio.

AGB (Audits of Great Britain)—British-owned people meter research company now attracting business in the United States as an alternative to Nielsen. AGB does not measure radio.

Survey Areas

Metro Survey Area (MSA)—Audience researchers' designation of a market's metropolitan area that usually conforms to the U.S. Office of Management and Budget's Metropolitan Statistical Area, though not always. *Sales and Marketing Management* magazine, an accepted source for tabulating government data analysis, reports that based on the 1980 Census there are 315 metro areas in the U.S. The metro is the smallest measured area, and, for some radio stations, may represent as little as half of their audience. This lowest common denominator is the most frequently utilized by media people when evaluating a radio market. Such action is perfectly logical if the advertiser is a supermarket chain whose stores all fall within the boundaries of the metro area. It is not logical for advertisers of national products whose sales are not restricted to the MSA. The signals of many low-powered radio stations cover only the metro area and some, only parts of it. When metro ratings are used for station evaluation, these low-powered stations frequently appear to be performing better than they are.

Total Survey Area (TSA)—The coverage area surrounding a metro market whose radio listenership is measured by Arbitron. The TSA is determined by radio penetration of the extended area based on coverage studies and actual reports of listening (Arbitron diaries). Because TSAs are not exclusive, the same radio station may be rated in more than one TSA. When Arbitron analyzed thirty radio markets of various sizes recently, it found that the TSA audience ranged from 3 to 174 percent larger than the metro audience. Despite this obvious strength, about 90 percent of all requests for radio availabilities ask for the MSA and only 10 percent for the TSA. For some markets, the TSA and metro are virtually identical (e.g., this is the case in San Diego, California). But in other markets such as Los Angeles, the ge-

Figure 4-1.   **Los Angeles Metro, ADI, and TSA**

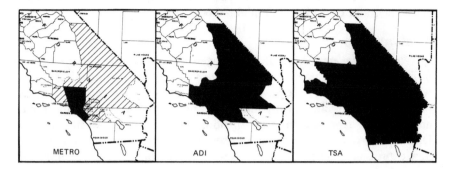

ographical difference between the MSA and TSA is enormous. Northern San Diego County, almost 150 miles away, is included in the Los Angeles TSA.

Area of Dominant Influence (ADI)—Arbitron's term for the exclusive geographical area covered by a specific market's television signal. Every county in the United States is assigned to an ADI and they do not overlap. There are 205 ADIs. They are usually larger than the MSA and almost always smaller than the TSA. Although ADI is a television entity, Arbitron provides radio ratings for ADIs so that radio can be compared with television in the same geographical area. Theoretically, a metro radio rating cannot be compared to a television ADI rating, but you would end up with a goodly chunk of money if you picked up a dollar bill every time the comparison is made. (See Figure 4-1.)

Designated Market Area (DMA)—Nielsen's equivalent of Arbitron's ADI.

General Terms

Response Rate—For Arbitron Radio, the number of persons returning a usable diary detailing their listening or viewing during a specified time period as a percentage of all persons twelve years of age or older who have received diaries. Arbitron is constantly striving to increase its response rate percentages which averaged 43.5 percent for 1987. The low percentage, however, does not invalidate the findings. For Birch, the percentage of respondents interviewed against the number of phone calls made is the response rate. It averages about 62 percent in the top 100 markets.

Demographics—Descriptions of groups categorized by their vital and social statistics. The most widely used demographic cited by broadcast researchers is age/sex, an extremely broad grouping, for example, Men 25-54.

Dayparts—Designated time periods during a twenty-four-hour broadcast day. These differ sharply for radio and television and vary slightly from radio station to station. The radio dayparts as reported by the rating services are Morning Drivetime (6:00 A.M.–10:00 A.M.), Daytime (10:00 A.M.–3:00 P.M.), Afternoon Drivetime (3:00 P.M.–7:00 P.M.), Nighttime (7:00 P.M.– midnight), and Overnight (midnight–6:00 A.M.).

Measurements

Rating—An expression of percentage of audience capable of watching or listening. Ten rating points means 10 percent of the potential population regardless of the tune-in level. In order for a rating to have meaning, it must be qualified demographically and geographically. Television rating points are normally expressed in terms of homes or households within ADIs or DMAs for programs or portions of programs. Age/sex television ratings are now expressed in terms of people as well as households. Radio ratings have always been expressed in age/sex demographic terms for metro or ADI geographical areas, and may be either for average quarter hour (AQH) or cumulative audience (Cume), which differ substantially (see page 33 following). You are comparing apples and oranges when attempting to make a direct comparison between household television ratings and people radio ratings.

Gross Rating Points (GRPs)—The total of all rating points achieved by an advertising schedule or group of schedules. One hundred gross rating points for Adults 25–54 does not, however, mean that 100 percent of this group has been reached. It means that an *aggregate* of 100 percent has been reached. Theoretically it would be possible to reach the same 1 percent of the audience one hundred times and achieve 100 gross rating points.

Share—The percentage of households actually watching a television program or people listening to a radio station. In describing the composition of an audience, rating and share are frequently cited in tandem, for example at a given time, station XYZ had a 15 rating and a 25 share. Translation: Fifteen percent of the population were tuned to station XYZ. This 15 percent represented 25 percent of people who were listening to the radio during the measured time period.

Frequency—The average number of times individuals or homes are exposed to an advertising message.

Radio Frequency—The number of times the average listener is exposed to a given schedule of commercial announcements within a specific interval of time. If the media truism, "Radio is a frequency medium," is intended to mean that frequency can be achieved fairly easily using radio, it is true. If, as is frequently the case, it is meant to signify that radio cannot cover a wide audience, it is nonsense.

Frequency Distribution—The level of frequency delivered to various portions of a total audience. It is a critical measurement of exposure. The *average* frequency for a ten-announcement schedule might be 4.5 announcements over a week's time, but no listener actually hears 4.5 announcements. Some may hear only one. Others might hear all ten. The rest will fall somewhere in between. Assume an advertiser has determined his message requires a minimum of three exposures to motivate a consumer. The frequency distribution provides an analysis of the true effectiveness of the advertising by indicating how many listeners were reached three or more times and how many were reached less than three times.

Reach—The number of different people or homes exposed to a media schedule within a given period of time.

Radio Reach—The number of different people who listen to one or more commercial announcements in a given schedule on one or more radio stations. Reach is a measurement of unduplicated radio audience and is generally expressed as a percentage. Reach can be computed for a schedule on one radio station or for a schedule on a group of radio stations, in combination. Reach can be computed with present technology for any age/sex demographic group. Despite its reputation for being a frequency medium, radio can typically reach 75–80 percent of almost any target in a single day, and as many or more people in a week as television can. A reach of over 60 percent can be attained with schedules on relatively few radio stations.

Reach and Frequency—A combination of the two estimates, based on standard formulas, expressed for a given schedule or schedules.

Average Quarter Hour Listeners (AQH)—The number of people listening to a radio station for a minimum of five minutes within a given quarter-hour period. It is a nonexclusive measurement. The same listeners may be counted in each quarter hour. It is a measurement of average listening, not audience.

Cumulative Audience (Cume)—The number of different people who listen to a radio station during a specified period of time. Unlike AQH, it is a measurement of audience, not listening levels. The "cume" audience of a radio station from 6:00 A.M. to midnight Monday through Sunday is the equivalent of a magazine's total readership. Two radio stations running identical schedules can develop an equal number of gross rating points but substantially different reach numbers because of the difference in cumulative audience. This occurs because the station with the larger cume adds more new listeners as a schedule progresses.

Exclusive Cumulative Listeners—The number of different people who listen only to one radio station during a measured period. That number would be the single station's "exclusive cume." Most New Yorkers, for example, regularly tune into two to three radio stations, but on weekday mornings in New York about 380,000 adults listen only to WCBS/Newsradio. There is no alternative for an advertiser who wishes to reach this exclusive portion of WCBS's audience but to advertise on this station.

Unduplicated Audience—The portion of one radio station's audience that is not shared with another radio station or stations. According to Arbitron, among 35–64-year-old adult listeners to WCBS-FM in New York, only 9 percent also listen to WOR. WCBS-FM's unduplicated audience against WOR is 91 percent.

Gross Impressions—The average number of persons, expressed as AQH listeners, reached by each commercial multiplied by the number of announcements in a commercial radio schedule. It is a boxcar number. Schedules with substantially different reach and frequencies can end up with equal numbers of gross impressions.

Cost per Rating Point—The average cost of purchasing one rating point or 1 percent of a broadcast audience or audiences. A statistical tool developed for television but now also heavily used in radio buying. Its primary function is to arrive at a relationship between audience levels and costs. For example, the average CPRP in a given market for Women 25–49 might be $100 while the same demographic's CPRP for a specific station might be $125. Without considering other factors, this could lead to a simplistic conclusion that the station is overpriced. This tool is too frequently used as a buyer's crutch.

Cost per Thousand (CPM)—In radio, a relationship between a station's AQH audience and the cost per announcement expressed as the cost of delivering 1,000 gross impressions. In television, the cost for the delivery of 1,000 homes or people by a television program. Though less widely used, it is a more precise broadcast audience measurement than cost per rating point because it is not affected by rounding up or rounding down of fractions. Cost per thousand is the standard efficiency expression for newspapers and magazines, that is, the cost to reach a thousand readers or subscribers.

Households Using Television (HUT)—The percentage of households using television sets at a given time of day expressed as a percentage of the universe of homes with television sets rather than the total population. A subdefinition is PUT—persons using television.

Persons Using Radio (PUR)—The number of persons using radio at a given time expressed as a percentage of all persons having radios. PUR is a rarely cited measurement.

Quintiles—Fifths of a media audience. In television, for example, viewers may be categorized as being in the "highest viewing," or first, quintile, or the "lowest viewing," or fifth, quintile. Researchers like Simmons and Mediamark (see Chapter 16) break down national media audiences into quintiles.

The Ubiquitous Computer

Though Arbitron, Birch, and Nielsen still produce printed rating books, which have some limited use, virtually all radio numbers are generated by proprietary computer systems. Mathematical models are programmed to utilize the ratings data to produce complicated extensions and variations of the numbers and everyone, sellers and buyers alike, depend on computerized reports for their analyses.

The computer software programs measure and compare individual and multiple station audience rankings, hour-by-hour audiences, trends, percentage changes, dayparts, multiple dayparts, and a variety of other groupings by market and age/sex demographics for metro, total survey area, and ADI. They will analyze schedules, compute costs, develop reach and frequency percentages, and compare various data.

Some programs, called optimizers, allow the buyer to set in quantitative goals expressed in rating points, reach and frequency, and so forth. Then the computer calculates and indicates which stations and schedules to buy in order to achieve them.

Some computer systems, such as Marketron, Telmar, and IMS, can be purchased by any station, sales organization, or advertising agency that subscribes to the basic data source. Several large agency subscribers to Arbitron, for example, have computer access to Marketron by modem and do their own analyses. Most computerized rating data, however, is generated by radio sellers, either radio stations or sales representative firms, both as a service to their customers and as a sales tool. Some of the larger broadcast sales companies, among them CBS Radio Representatives and Katz Radio, have produced formulas and systems that they use exclusively.

Audience numbers determine ratings. Ratings are the basis of factors like cost per rating point, which are used by buyers to evaluate pricing. Sellers must similarly calculate the effect of ratings on their rates. Audience, ratings, and pricing are like horses on a carousel—they keep chasing each other's tails.

5

The Significance of Format

Programming is the single most important factor in establishing a station's image and building its audience. A station's programming motivates listeners to tune in, tune out, or switch stations. In radio, programming is synonymous with format.

When target audiences are described solely in terms of age/sex demographics, advertisers usually rely on ratings. Ratings, however, are not sufficient when targets are defined as those people most likely to respond to the advertising message. Numbers cannot define the level of the listener's receptivity. Beyond numbers, there is the need for environment.

Without recognizing the significance of program environment, that is, format, radio cannot be used intelligently as an advertising medium. As a principle, media strategists clearly understand that format and demographics are interrelated because the format of a station determines the audience. Format, like editorial environment in a magazine, *should* be considered before going to a quantitative evaluation.

Just as *People Magazine* is unlikely to appeal to the subscriber to the *Harvard Business Review,* the hard rock aficionado rarely tunes in to a classical music station. Each radio format appeals to different individuals. Moreover, people listen to these radio formats in different ways. For an advertising message to penetrate and be effective, an advertiser should understand and be guided by these differences.

Unless the commercial is intended to reach everyone in a broad age/sex demographic group—and there are major national advertisers who have this need—buying radio time using boxcar numbers doesn't make much sense. Environment should be the first consideration in selecting radio stations, just as it is in buying space in magazines. Computers aren't customarily advertised in *Field & Stream* nor are ads for running shoes seen frequently in *Fortune*.

In the real world of media buying, however, infinitely more attention is given to ratings than to the evaluation of audience quality by format (see Chapter 10). A significant reason why formats attract less attention than they should is because there are so many of them. Sorting out all the format nuances is tremendously complicated; its difficulty gives radio time buyers a strong rationale for simply analyzing the age/sex ratings numbers. The economy factor rears its head. Most experienced buyers are capable of making evaluations based on format as well as ratings, but in many situations, they just do not have the time.

It is far simpler to depend on the mechanistic and simplistic ratings-tell-all-reasoning. This implies that a given format attracts a certain age/sex audience and that qualitative characteristics can be deduced from quantitative age/sex ratings numbers.

It is difficult to obtain a precise breakdown of every radio station in the United States by format because format changes occur constantly. The authoritative Radio Information Center in New York monitors the formats of more than 8,500 radio stations (see Table 5-1). Country and Adult Contemporary were the two most prevalent formats in mid-1987.

Of the total, approximately 45 percent are AM stations and 55 percent FM stations. FM dominance in both station numbers and listening represents an important historical change since the mid-1970s. The fall 1987 RADAR (Vol. 1, No. 36) showed that among all radio listening, AM listening of persons 12 or older was at 25.4 percent, down from 41 percent in 1981 and 58.5 percent in 1976.

This dramatic trend is a result of the move by many radio listeners away from traditional AM formats—news, talk, and information stations as well as Middle-of-the-Road (MOR) and big band music. A variety of sharply focused music formats, broadcast on the FM band with its superior sound fidelity, have carried away these listeners. This substantial loss of audience and the revenue the departed listeners represent has created a critical situation for many AM radio station operators. (See Table 5-2.)

In the last few years, emphasis has been placed on enhancing AM radio's audio quality. AM stereo is now available and other engineering moves are being made to upgrade AM sound.

For many listeners, however, audio quality is not the determinant in their choice of FM rather than AM stations. Stephen G. Apel, a researcher with Arbitron Ratings Company, directed a study in conjunction with the

Table 5-1. Commercial Radio Stations in the U.S. by Format*

Rank	Format	Number of Stations
1.	Country	2,464
2.	Adult/Soft Contemporary	2,345
3.	Rock/Contemporary Hit Radio (CHR)	798
4.	Middle of the Road (MOR)/Nostalgia/Standards	702
5.	Religion	549
6.	Easy Listening	363
7.	Album-Oriented Rock (AOR)	312
8.	Golden Oldies	260
9.	News/Talk	169
10.	Black/Rhythm & Blues	162
11.	Urban Contemporary	125
12.	Spanish	123
13.	Variety/Diversified	122
14.	All-News	44
15.	Ethnic	33
16.	Classical	27
17.	Jazz	18

Source: Radio Information Center. Used by permission.
*Breakdown of 8,921 radio stations in United States as of July 1987 by principal formats, ranked by number of stations. Total does not include 260 stations with unknown formats.

Annenberg School of Communications of the University of Pennsylvania, that found radio listeners believe there are substantial differences between the types of programs offered on the AM and FM dials.

Writing in *Broadcasting* in early 1988, Apel stated,

> Listeners hold strongly to the notion that FM radio is the place to find music programming, while AM radio tends to be the place for news, information and talk.
> Some listeners appreciate the reality-based programming that's clustered on AM stations. But these people represent a minority. *The majority of listeners turn radio on to hear music....* The perception that music is generally missing from the AM dial is behind much of the avoidance of AM radio....The notion that AM stations don't play music that's popular is responsible for alienating many listeners, especially those below age 35... [who] can't find any music they like on AM radio....Audio quality issues are secondary.

Table 5–2. Percentage of Stations by Format in Top 100 Markets (New York to Colorado Springs)*

Format	All Stations Percentage	Rank	AM Stations Percentage	Rank	FM Stations Percentage	Rank
Country	27.8	1	31.7	1	23.1	2
Adult Contemporary	23.9	2	22.7	2	25.3	1
Rock/CHR	10.3	3	4.1	6	17.7	3
MOR/Nostalgia	8.5	4	12.7	3	3.3	7
Religion	5.9	5	7.6	4	3.9	6
Easy Listening	4.0	6	1.4	10	7.2	4
AOR	3.6	7	.8	13	7.0	5
Oldies	3.6	7	5.3	5	1.6	9
Black/Jazz	2.0	9	2.4	8	1.6	9
Soft Contemporary	1.7	10	.8	13	2.9	8
News/Talk	1.4	11	3.1	7	.2	15
Spanish	1.4	11	2.1	9	.5	14
Urban Contemporary	1.3	13	1.3	12	1.4	11
Variety	1.2	14	1.5	11	1.0	13
Classical	.7	15	.2	16	1.2	12
All-News	.5	16	.8	13	.1	16

Source: Radio Information Center. Used by permission.
*Percentages as of February 1988.

The Structure of Formats

In general terms, radio breaks down into foreground formats, principally news, talk, and religion; a whole spectrum of pure music formats; and a few formats where personalities, talk, comedy, and commentary share the broadcast day.

Within the relatively broad music categories are a proliferation of sub-categories. The term *Country* for example, is a catchall for a group of narrowly programmed formats. There is "real" country, "pop" country, "progressive" country, "modern" country, bluegrass, the Nashville sound, country blues, country gospel, and other splinter formats. The only variety of country music that's barely being played these days is "real" western, or cowboy music. (There are easily as many variations in the contemporary music formats that range from Contemporary Hit Music to Golden Oldies.)

If the ratings don't reach a satisfactory level, it is a relatively simple task to adjust or completely change a music format. It happens frequently. These format changes complicate the radio selection process for an advertiser or agency, leading to the frequently warranted complaint that national spot and local radio are difficult to buy which, in turn, drives time buyers to ratings for evaluation.

Program directors contend there is a precise reason why every listener tunes to a radio station, and that every successful format fills some need or desire of its listeners. The closer a programmer can identify that reason and satisfy the listener's desires, the more successfully his station will attract an audience. The more tightly a music format is positioned, the more likely it is to stand apart from its competitors.

Programmers monitor their product minutely and vigilantly guard against any broadcast intrusion that might destroy what they consider to be the purity of a format. They are concerned with negatives as well as positives and constantly ponder what program elements might provoke a listener to leave.

An ABC Radio study done in 1981 concluded that programming elements are, by far, the most important factors in formulating a station's image and causing listeners to tune in, tune out, or switch stations. Even offensive commercials, or, worse yet, too many commercials have a relatively minor impact when compared to negative programming. There is no evidence to indicate that these findings aren't valid today.

There are some music stations that change formats in specific dayparts in order to attract an incremental audience during low-rated time periods. The Adult Contemporary format, as an example, is normally aimed at the 25 to 34 year olds and the Jazz format at 25 to 54 year olds. Until mid-1987, KIFM, an Adult Contemporary station in San Diego, programmed jazz from 6:00 P.M. to 6:00 A.M. every night and all weekend. To provide a bridge between its daytime and evening formats, KIFM played a few jazz selections each hour throughout the day. The strategy worked incredibly well; in a sense, too well. The jazz audience numbers grew so large that KIFM's management decided to go all jazz.

A substantial number of stations, primarily on the AM dial, that run a variety of formats throughout the week, set aside Sunday mornings for religious broadcasts. This is a throwback to the earlier days of radio when virtually every station reserved Sunday morning for church services.

There are a number of exceptions to format purity that occur on the AM band. Play-by-play sports is the most notable. It makes little difference what the regular format of a station is, radio sports is competing in a ballgame of its own. When major sports events like big league baseball, college and professional football, or basketball are on the air, the audience composition changes. A Talk radio station like KABC in Los Angeles attracts a mass of additional listeners when Vin Scully does play-by-play broadcasts of the Los Angeles Dodgers. By the same token, many of the station's regular listeners, who are not baseball fans, go elsewhere on the dial.

For two decades, the CBS All-News station in Los Angeles, KNX-AM, has carried a food news program from 10:00 A.M. to 11:00 A.M. every morning. During this one-hour show the station accepts calls from listeners. The program is a Los Angeles institution, but its audience is not the traditional KNX All-News audience. The station has resisted any other call-in programming and will not consider other program features that stray from classic All-News.

The Dodgers on KABC and the KNX "Food News" return profits to their stations. Commercials on these shows cost more than regular spots and the high audience levels these special programs attract inflate the stations' overall ratings. Higher ratings, however obtained, mean higher rates for everything the stations sell.

How People Listen

People respond differently to varying radio formats. Rarely does one tune in to a News or a Talk radio station except to listen. Try to hold a conversation in a room when an announcer on an All-News radio station is holding forth. With a music format, however, a person may listen attentively, may have it on merely to provide background sound, or may bounce between the two extremes.

Some years ago a research organization called Motivation Analysis measured radio listeners who were paying full attention to what they were hearing 60–100 percent of the time. News and talk formats scored 65 percent while music formats averaged 39 percent. There is no reason to think these relationships have changed materially. When music stations feature strong on-air personalities, the lines between foreground and music formats blur.

Music, however, has a universal appeal. Virtually everyone younger than 50 years of age was drawn to radio initially to hear music. Music listening on radio, which usually begins around age 12 or 13, combines an escape from the real world with an emotional tie to the performers. A strong attachment to the music and artists that an individual grows up with almost always stays with a person for a lifetime. Recognizing the power of these nostalgic feelings is a significant key to targeting specific age groups through music.

How people listen is a factor for advertisers to consider. If the buyer analyzing a spectrum of radio stations before placing orders computed only the number of persons in the target group tuned-in, but paid no attention to how they were listening, the wrong stations could easily be selected. For the selective advertiser, all formats are not created equal. The listener-is-a-listener rating numbers approach does not hold up.

If a format commands an especially cohesive audience—those persons who loyally listen to Black, Classical, Jazz, All-News, or News/Talk stations—and that is the audience the advertiser wants to reach, the prudent course is to place schedules on those stations. The same listeners almost always listen to other stations as well, but when they change stations, there are so many choices—particularly among the other music formats—that they become "fractionalized" and picking up a fractionalized audience is expensive and difficult.

The same format can attract a different kind of listener in different parts of the country. The country music devotee in the Northeast has traditionally been blue collar. In the Southwest, however, the format attracts listeners from all demographic groups, from the Oklahoma oil field worker to the Texas bank president, and virtually every small town in the region has several Country stations.

In contrast, All-News stations will almost always be located in big metropolitan centers where the news audience segment is sufficiently large to warrant the operation. That's why there are almost 2,500 Country stations and fewer than 50 All-News stations in the entire country. Jazz, Classical, Black, and Ethnic are other formats that need a strong population base in order to attract enough listeners.

The Foreground Formats

News and the All-News Format

There is a sound reason why there are so few All-News radio stations. News stations are expensive to establish and run, requiring fully staffed newsrooms and elaborate communications facilities. The high operational costs of All-News radio stations almost always forces them to set a higher cost per rating point for commercial time than the prevailing market average. It is not coincidence that two large companies, CBS and Westinghouse, dominate the format.

News stations build audiences slowly. It can take between two and three years to get a news station established, particularly in an area that already has one, while a music station can gain acceptance for a changed format in as little as three months.

Despite the fall-off in overall AM listening, All-News stations have maintained their share of audience. Although local news is considered the primary attraction, each All-News station is affiliated with a major radio network. The networks have continued to broaden their news coverage, features, and special reports; these changes have had a positive effect on their All-News affiliates.

When there are two All-News radio stations in a market, as there are in New York and Los Angeles, there is only a slight overlapping of audience. In magazine terms, if you read *Time,* there is a 75 percent chance you don't read *Newsweek.* An anomaly of radio time buying frequently occurs when buyers order a schedule on one All-News station in a two-station market and erroneously conclude they have "covered the format."

It also has become increasingly difficult to find newscasts on the mass audience FM music stations. Until 1981, the Federal Communications Commission required all radio stations to devote a certain percentage of broadcast time to news and public affairs programming. Deregulation eliminated those requirements and most FM music station managers swiftly dropped or severely cut back news and news-related features.

Reducing news staffs raised station profits but, more significantly, carrying uninterrupted music lured a larger, entertainment-seeking audience. Most radio programmers see news and music as two distinct, incompatible formats, and many music programmers believe that even a little news is a liability. One light rock station general manager was quoted as saying, "We have shortened our newscasts and we no longer have editorial or documentaries.... When listeners come to us, it is for entertainment. They know where they can go if they want news."

News and other foreground formats are listened to more intently and more seriously than radio formats whose sole purpose is to entertain. Here is an example. Nursing is considered a blue-collar occupation. Demographic breakouts indicate that the audiences of All-News radio stations are strongly skewed to white-collar occupational groups. Nonetheless, a major hospital in Los Angeles discovered its recruitment commercials for nurses drew more responses from a news station than they did from highly rated popular music stations.

Job hunting is serious business and the commercials were more effective in the environment of a news format despite the fact that relatively fewer nurses were in the news station audience. Conversely, a commercial announcing a big rock concert would be less effective on the All-News station—even if many of the news station's listeners were prospective attendees—than it would be on a contemporary music station.

News stations have high cumulative audiences. They reach a great number of different people for relatively short periods of time. It is the idiosyncratic news freak who stays glued to an All-News station for hours on end. Most listeners tend to switch away when they hear the same news stories repeated. (Westinghouse All-News stations like KFWB, Los Angeles, and WINS, New York, promote themselves by saying, "Give us 22 minutes and we'll give you the world.") If, therefore, an advertiser's commercial ran every hour on an All-News station, it would be heard infrequently by a large number of *different* people rather than frequently by a lesser number of people. In media terms, heavy advertising schedules are likely to increase reach more significantly than frequency.

Talk and News/Talk

Over the last few years, the number of All-News radio stations dipped slightly, but in July 1987, stations with News/Talk formats stood at 169, up from 149 two years earlier. This format, heard almost entirely on AM radio, is successfully bucking the trend towards dominance of the FM band.

While an All-News format can be precisely defined, Talk and News/Talk definitions are blurrier. Some powerful radio stations, such as KABC, Los Angeles, and KGO, San Francisco, put a lot of emphasis on news during the heavy-listening morning drive time hours. After 9:00 A.M., however, they settle in with two-way talk programming and usually carry newscasts only twice an hour. Such stations categorize their formats as Talk or Telephone (two-way) Talk.

Other stations, like KCBS San Francisco, KTAR Phoenix, and KIRO Seattle, the leading news and information outlets in their communities, function throughout most of the day as All-News radio stations—except for the 10:00 A.M. to 3:00 P.M. period. During this middle-of-the-day stretch, they switch to the conventional talk format fare. Such stations are usually, and correctly, called News/Talk.

What is conventional Talk format fare?

The reality is that it has no limit. Interviews, discussions with studio guests and listeners, sports talk, politics, restaurant and food shows, therapy purveyors of every variety—medical, psychological, sexual—and anything else interestingly carried along by a dominant personality can and does work on a well-run Talk radio station. Even political bias can be advantageous. KABC balances liberal-minded Michael Jackson with strongly conservative Ray Breem and has the best of both worlds. Most radio authorities rate the on-air talent to be more important than the subject matter. Personalities drive the format. That fact becomes readily apparent when substitutes, no matter how qualified, take over for a veteran talk show host. The programs invariably go downhill.

Talk formats reflect regional differences. The discussion of issues of local importance is an obvious difference but there are also differences in style. On the two coasts, talk show hosts keep to a swift pace. Callers who are verbally dawdling are admonished to get to the point. By contrast, even in the largest cities in the middle of the country the mood is more relaxed and stretched out. Listen to talk shows in any city in Texas if you want to witness this phenomenon carried to the extreme. Callers will sometimes talk three or four minutes nonstop.

The Talk format listener is not an in-and-outer like the All-News listener. A strong talk show host, like Jackson, who is considered the best interviewer in the business, and who is on four hours a day, can hold large parts of his audience for the entire time he is on the air. The audiences for a topical interviewer, a therapist, and a sports talk host, however, are likely to be different. This makes buying time on a station with a Talk format a selective process. The beer advertiser wants the young sports audience. The arthritis pain remedy commercial works best when it reaches the topical interviewer's older listeners.

In media terms, successful Talk stations are able to maintain big average quarter hour listenership but tend to fall down in cumulative, or total, audience. Fewer people listen for longer periods of time.

Contemporary Music Formats

The Radio Information Center isolates six major contemporary music formats, but, as noted earlier, broadcasters and radio-wise media specialists consider subtle differences that break the six into perhaps three times as many subformats.

Contemporary music stations never stop thinking about the precise demography of their audiences. When a format is altered or even totally changed, the purpose is almost always to become more attractive to a targeted segment. While the ratings reflect only broad age/sex demographic classifications, the programming is increasingly aimed at small subgroups.

This approach was aptly illustrated in the mid-1980s when some analytic programmers concluded there was an opportunity to target people who were just slipping into their forties. That brought about the birth of the Soft Rock Transtar 41 format. When they went on the air with it, however, the audience it attracted turned out to be younger and some wag said it should have been called Transtar 32.

Every radio station whose audience is measured breaks down its numbers by age cells, and every competent media buyer analyzes these statistics. National sales representative firms, which maintain large and active research departments, examine national data as well as data for their own list of stations in order to establish listening norms for various age groups.

Table 5-3 was derived from an analysis by Katz Radio of 2,141 stations (917 AM and 1,224 FM) in 133 markets measured by Arbitron in fall 1987. Note that this analysis does not cite relative numbers of listeners but only percentage breakdowns of age cells within given formats. Also be warned: There is inconsistency in format designations among every organization breaking out radio data, but they all agree on the most important formats.

Table 5-4 shows each format's share of audience in the top 100 markets (New York to Colorado Springs). These multimarket average percentages will vary sharply from market to market but do demonstrate the relative quantitative importance of the various formats within the total radio spectrum.

Following the Baby Boomers

The post–World War II generation and rock and roll go hand in hand.

In the mid-1950s, two independent radio station operators, Todd Storrz and Gordon McLendon, ascertained what were the forty best-selling records across the country and started playing them over and over again. They soon found themselves drawing vast audiences to their stations. Top-40 is the landmark format of modern radio and the subsequent growth of the medium, both in revenue and number of stations, dates back to its development. By the 1960s, the baby boomers were listening to Top 40 Radio and they made it the country's leading format.

Contemporary Hit Radio

Contemporary Hit Radio (CHR), originated by WCAU-FM/Hit Radio (now WOGL-FM), Philadelphia, in 1981, is today's version of Top 40. Relatively few selections are played; in radio jargon, CHR features a short playlist. The music played is always new, rarely is a number more than six months old. There is frequent repetition. The current hot performers dominate. When Michael Jackson and Madonna were at the top of the charts,

Table 5-3.   **Adult Audience Composition by Format***

	Age Cells							Percentage of Audience		Types of Stations Surveyed
	12-17	18-24	25-34	35-44	45-54	55-64	65+	Male	Female	
Percentage of U.S. Population	10.7	13.9	21.6	16.7	11.7	11.3	14.1	48	52	
Popular Music Formats										
Adult Contemp.	3.7	12.8	32.1	25.6	11.3	6.5	8.2	43	57	92AM/197FM
Soft Contemp.	3.0	13.5	32.6	26.2	13.8	5.7	5.2	38	62	5AM/89FM
Contemp. Hit Radio	25.6	28.6	25.2	13.2	3.8	1.6	1.9	43	57	30AM/231FM
Album-Oriented Rock	9.2	35.8	41.7	10.7	1.4	1.5	.6	69	31	10AM/159FM
Urban Contemp.	16.7	25.0	27.1	15.5	7.1	4.4	4.2	43	57	24AM/64FM
Classic Rock	4.9	26.0	46.6	20.2	1.4	.6	1.3	65	35	2AM/33FM
Classic Hits	3.2	19.4	42.3	20.7	8.4	2.9	3.2	59	41	5AM/22FM
Golden Oldies	2.7	7.5	27.6	38.2	12.8	4.6	6.6	55	45	87AM/24FM
Easy Listening	.6	2.9	7.1	13.5	18.8	23.7	33.4	39	61	18AM/130FM
Country	1.8	8.0	16.4	20.0	20.6	17.1	16.1	49	51	140AM/168FM
Middle of the Road	.7	2.3	8.4	14.9	14.5	22.5	36.7	41	59	105AM
Big Band	.3	1.1	3.5	5.1	11.4	30.6	47.9	46	54	75AM/4FM
Jazz	1.3	6.7	34.6	23.2	24.6	6.5	3.2	53	47	4FM
New Age Jazz	4.1	11.5	41.4	27.9	9.8	2.8	2.4	56	44	1AM/16FM
New Wave	15.6	28.6	38.2	14.8	1.4	1.2	.3	51	49	6FM
Other Formats										
All-News	.5	1.6	11.4	16.4	14.6	22.2	33.4	53	47	16AM
News/Talk	.3	1.4	10.3	13.8	14.2	20.6	39.4	50	50	85AM
All Talk	.2	1.6	8.0	12.6	12.3	24.1	41.3	43	57	24AM
Classical	1.0	2.5	12.4	19.5	19.8	17.9	26.9	49	51	4AM/29FM
Black	7.4	16.9	22.0	18.5	13.6	10.3	11.4	41	59	66AM/12FM
Spanish	4.7	9.6	27.2	19.5	14.6	11.3	13.2	43	57	53AM/15FM
Religion	1.3	6.2	12.7	19.4	8.6	16.0	22.0	33	67	75AM/21FM

Source: Fall 1987 Arbitron as compiled by Katz Radio Research. Reprinted by permission of Katz Radio.
*Percentages based on Metropolitan Survey Area Average Quarter Hour ratings of all persons 12+ years of age for 2,141 radio stations in 133 measured markets.

Table 5-4.   Total Weekly Audience Shares by Format, Spring 1987

Format	Percentage of Audience*
Adult Contemporary	17.1
Contemporary Hit Radio/Rock	15.3
Album-Oriented Rock	11.6
Country	9.5
Easy Listening	9.4
News/Talk	6.7
Urban Contemporary	6.3
Soft Contemporary	3.9
Middle of the Road/Nostalgia	3.7
All-News	3.7
Black	3.2
Spanish	2.8
Golden Oldies	2.3
Religious	1.7
Classical	1.6
Variety	1.1

Source: Radio Information Center. Reprinted by permission.
*Percentages based on Spring 1987 Arbitron Monday–Sunday Average Quarter Hour ratings of all persons 12+ years of age in the metropolitan areas of the top 100 markets.

CHR stations seemed to be playing their latest hits every few minutes. The on-air personalities exude a high energy level; teenagers' parents have been known to call it "frantic."

CHR appeals to the 12-to 24-year-old age group and leans toward females. This accounts for the repetitive approach toward music selection. Programmers who have minutely scrutinized listening patterns are convinced that familiar music appeals to women.

As an advertising medium, CHR was overestimated in the early 1980s. Broadcasters looked at the heavy advertising directed toward teenagers in publications like *Seventeen,* read the research relating to teens' disposable income, and envied the outstanding success of pioneer CHR stations such as WCAU-FM in Philadelphia (now WOGL-FM), KIIS in Los Angeles, and WHTZ in New York. A number of major broadcast groups turned to the format, thus creating an extremely competitive climate. Eventually many of the broadcasters who had hopped on the bandwagon had to hop back off.

As a practical matter, it proved extremely difficult to wean print advertisers from the magazines assiduously read by teenage girls. At the same time, music videos zoomed in popularity with both sexes and the cable TV channels featuring them drained off a large hunk of teenage broadcast advertising dollars. Contemporary Hit Radio is still a solid format (see Table 5-4) but there is a limit to how many stations can be successful with it. Even among those, there is a strong temptation to modify the format just enough to attract more of the 25 to 34 year olds who are a more sought-after advertising target.

Album-Oriented Rock

Album-Oriented Rock (AOR) was the baby boomers' choice in the 1970s. Its primary appeal is now to 18-to-34-year-old males, and getting older. Along with Classic Rock, a subcategory of the same genre, it's one of the "Big Three" contemporary formats.

Longer album cuts, leaning toward the heavy metal sound, are heard on AOR stations. To connoisseurs, the music is more rock and less contemporary. AOR stations pioneered the concept of a lot more music strung together without interruption. Their on-air personalities are distinctive, "hip," and issue oriented. They are less hyper than those heard on CHR.

Of all the popular music formats, AOR is subject to the most consistent fine tuning as it perceives its market maturing. Classic rock—music that goes back a decade or more—peaked in 1986 and the playlists are being carefully examined. There is concern about building stronger personalities to combat the jukebox syndrome, but overall AOR's appeal is its distinctive musical sound.

Adult Contemporary

Adult Contemporary is the powerhouse old pro of the popular music formats, with its principal audience falling between 25 and 44 years of age, though a considerable number of 45 to 54 year olds tune in as well. Because the 25-to 54-year-old demographic segment is the one most sought after by advertisers, Adult Contemporary occupies a favored position in the music spectrum.

The relationship between Adult Contemporary and Contemporary Hit Radio, the kids' favorite, is apparent, but the AC format has longevity and stability. The personalities on AC have lower intensity levels, and the music playlist extends back three to five years or more rather than a mere six months.

As a category, Adult Contemporary is not as pristine as CHR and AOR. Many stations whose formats should fall under other classifications, notably Soft Contemporary and Classic Hits, prefer to call themselves Adult Contemporary because they perceive this giving them an advantage in competing for advertisers.

Golden Oldies

Golden Oldies is where the older baby boomers are today.

To an unsophisticated listener, a powerful Golden Oldies station, like WCBS-FM, New York, might sound like an Adult Contemporary radio station. The difference is the music. The playlist harks back to the 1950s, 1960s, and 1970s. This music has a strong appeal to both men and women in the 25- to 54-year-old group highly sought by advertisers.

Logically, the format attracts many of the same advertisers found on News and News/Talk stations—airlines, banks, financial institutions, automobile manufacturers, and the like—as well as many less staid advertisers.

Soft Contemporary

This is the niche that the creators of Transtar 41 sought to fill. The music on a Soft Contemporary station is current and is characterized by its blandness. It is neither loud nor offensive. The personalities on these stations are practically invisible.

Urban Contemporary/Black

Urban Contemporary is a format that has a very strong appeal to blacks and Hispanics and has been very successful in cities where there are large populations of both groups. Black is a format whose appeal is almost completely to that group. Almost 75 percent of the Urban Contemporary audience is 34 years old or younger while less than 50 percent of the Black audience is that young.

The differences between Urban Contemporary and Adult Contemporary are found in the playlist and the on-air personalities. Some stations with the Urban Contemporary format describe themselves as Progressive Contemporary to establish the perception that their audience is a balanced one. Blacks and Hispanics on their own, however, have potent buying power and many advertisers want to reach them.

Although the Urban Contemporary's audience levels tend to be flat, it had one meteoric period. In the late 1970s, WKTU, New York, introduced a format called Disco. The music played was contemporary dance music with a strong black influence and it took off immediately. From a 1.2 percent share of the New York metro audience in April/May 1978, WKTU jumped to 11.3 percent by October/November 1978. This swift move made it the highest rated radio station in the largest market; stations in large cities all over the country started copying WKTU. Disco had a happy four-year run before it slipped quietly back into the larger Urban Contemporary category.

This phenomenon—the swift rise and fall of a new format—has occurred before in the radio business and will certainly occur again. New formats with bona fide attraction generate high ratings almost immediately. There are a great number of music listeners who seek a new experience and will sample innovative formats. (In the spring 1987 Arbitron, an Urban Contemporary station in Chicago, WGCI-FM, emerged as that city's highest rated station, displacing the perennial leader, WGN, the Chicago Tribune Company's MOR/Personality station. In radio circles, this was high drama.)

The problem is to sustain the high audience levels over an extended period of time. This is a more difficult task and the tendency is for station management, in its euphoria, to stick with the programming that brought such rapid success and to ignore the inevitable imitation by other stations. But format stagnation is invariably the wrong course. Major music formats are always evolving and this evolution demands continuing investment. Six months after WKTU had its 11.3 percent share in New York, another station copied the Disco format and went head to head with WKTU. WKTU's audience share dropped to 7.6 percent and it kept plummeting. Disco, as a format, did not change with the times and paid the price.

Successful Urban Contemporary programmers believe personalities are essential to complement the music and that its audience wants information about the music it's hearing. Urban Contemporary artists as a group are a fascinating bunch, as their videos demonstrate, and the format is as far from elevator music as you can get.

New Age Music

On Valentine's Day of 1987 KMET-FM, Los Angeles—a radio station that two decades earlier was an AOR pioneer—switched its call letters to KTWV and introduced "The Wave." The Wave combined light jazz, soft rock, and so-called new age music with virtually no commentary. The result was contemporary background music, going substantially beyond Soft Contemporary, that has been called "audio Valium," "yuppie elevator," and "hot tub" music. It became an instant success in Southern California and KTWV is now syndicating its programming to other stations through the Satellite Music Network.

New age music is mostly mellow, melodic, and instrumental with a heavy electronic influence. It originated with small, independent record companies that heretofore received scant attention from the large record retailers and no attention at all from commercial radio. Programmers now see it as an alternative to AOR and Adult Contemporary formats with an appeal to an urban, affluent 25–54-year-old market.

The jury is not in on new age music. It may become the Easy Listening/ Beautiful Music format for the baby boom generation; or the dreaded boredom factor may do in "The Wave" and its followers.

Easy Listening and Beautiful Music

Easy Listening and Beautiful Music are almost interchangeable terms, though programmers of the two formats would argue the point. Although Beautiful Music stations are likely to feature more vocals, both formats are designed to play continuous, nonintrusive, pleasant music.

In recent years, many stations have deserted Easy Listening, with the result that one or two stations dominate the format in most major markets. More than half of their audience is 55 years old or older and three-quarters of the listeners are past the age of 45. Awareness of the importance of these age groups is steadily increasing. The American population is aging and older families have the greatest amount of discretionary income at their disposal. The blandness of the programming, however, reduces intrusiveness, and though commercials are clustered, many advertisers are unhappy with the Muzak quality of the format. The format's programmers argue that the absence of all talk, except the clustered commercials, makes the advertising messages stand out.

Country

As noted earlier, Country is a broad designation for a variety of formats employed by almost 2,500 radio stations. In earlier days, the appeal of country music was almost totally to rural and blue-collar groups in the South and Southwest, and national advertisers shunned stations that played it. This negative stereotype has been changing, fast.

Today Country stations command large audiences in major metropolitan centers in all regions of the country. The format, the music, and the artists that sing and play it have moved into the mainstream of American culture. The crossover has worked two ways. Country artists like Willie Nelson have successfully performed and recorded standard popular music, while the likes of Frank Sinatra and Barbra Streisand have produced hits by dipping into the country repertoire.

Country formats still appeal to the rural, blue-collar group. There is a growing recognition, however, that the audience now extends far beyond this core and the attitude toward the format of national advertisers and big advertising agencies has steadily been shifting.

The people involved with country music—radio stations, recording companies, sales representatives and even some advertising agencies—are banded together in the Country Music Association. This organization works for the acceptance of country music as American and not merely regional music, and for the continued well-being of the radio stations that play it.

Middle of the Road/Big Band/Nostalgia

These formats featuring old-line artists and bands are almost totally on the AM band and they hold a small, declining share of the radio audience. The figure was under 4 percent by the fall of 1987.

Middle of the Road (MOR) has been described as the last vestige of pre-television radio—something for everyone. It is characterized by heavy dependence on personalities, the almost total absence of contemporary music, and a harking back to another era. Despite the trend away from this generalized programming, there are still some powerhouse radio stations categorized as MOR.

The Big Band format is MOR with a less eclectic selection of music.

Jazz

There are very few stations playing only jazz, but those stations that do, like KKGO in Los Angeles and KIFM in San Diego, are reporting a steady climb in advertising sales and increasing ratings numbers. A substantial portion of the audience, which is numerically small, is qualitatively high level.

Jazz has been enjoying a resurgence of popularity as a result of new audio technology as well as the advance in both age and income of the population. As a result, some jazz is being integrated into other music formats.

Classical

It's been said that Classical radio stations play oldies that go back 300 years. Because of the noncontemporary nature of the music, most broadcasters view it as an esoteric format. Its total audience is very small but very good. Its cost is invariably high when judged by standard media criteria.

Important classical stations, WQXR, New York, or KFAC, Los Angeles, for example, don't sell their numbers. They sell their programming, personalities, and features. These stations are aural cultural centers of their communities and they strive to build ongoing relationships with major corporate advertisers who wish to be part of this environment. (Within the format, commercial Classical stations compete for audience with a substantial number of not-for-profit radio stations that play fine music during parts of the broadcast day.)

Qualitative surveys have shown Classical station audiences to be stable, loyal, and responsive. Their listeners, most of whom fall into higher income groups, tend to listen attentively just as people attending a concert would. They feel a genuine kinship to the stations and can be motivated by advertising messages they hear on them.

With it all, a revolution is shaking up the Classical format. Many stations are now using strident promotional methods typical of contemporary music stations in order to increase audiences and their advertising revenues. Stations have directed announcers to talk less, be warmer, and to cut back on pedantic commentaries. Classical managers are looking at their stations as *radio stations* that play classical music rather than a special breed that only certain listeners are comfortable with.

Although this new approach undoubtedly has contributed to the 30 percent rise in audience from 1985 to 1987 reported by Simmons, it has also infuriated traditional listeners.

Religion

According to the National Religious Broadcasters Association, over the past twenty years, Christian radio stations have been growing at the astounding rate of one new station per week and, at the end of 1987, their listening audience was calculated to be close to seventy-five million adults. Unlike the sharply targeted music formats, the Religion category is an umbrella format. There are both commercial and noncommercial stations that primarily broadcast religious programming.

Among the commercial group, there has been an increasing separation between "traditional" Religion and "Contemporary Christian" formats. The traditional stations have relied primarily on block sales of long-form religious programs, while the younger contemporary format places a greater emphasis on spot sales.

Since 1983, mostly conservative Christian groups have filed for two out of three of all applications for low frequency noncommercial FM stations, and by mid-1987, these religious broadcasters held one-fifth of the 1,367 existing licenses and construction permits.

In addition to locally produced programs, Christian networks and syndicators are major sources of programming for both categories of stations. Fund raising is prevalent on Religion stations as it is on Religion television.

Diversified

Formats that simply defy categorization are called Diversified. For lack of a better description, they are frequently lumped together and called Variety.

Spanish Language Radio

Spanish language radio cannot accurately be called a format. It is an important range of formats that can include anything from News/Talk to Mexican Country bound together by a common language.

More radio stations than ever before are broadcasting in Spanish full time. Of the 123 stations classified by the Radio Information Center as "Spanish," the majority broadcast all of their programming in Spanish. Their number is twice what it was in 1986. *Hispanic Marketing* estimates the Spanish radio market to be $130 million.

There are 20 million Hispanics in the United States; their purchasing power is estimated at $34 billion. This Latin population, however, is concentrated in only 30 ADIs and the incidence of Spanish language stations reflects this. Miami, whose population is 50 percent Hispanic, has eight Spanish stations. Houston has seven. Greater Los Angeles has five with two more on the way. New York, with 2 1/2 million Latinos representing 20 percent of its population, has only four Spanish stations. Many smaller cities with substantial Latin populations have one or two stations.

Hispanic radio advertising is swiftly moving into the mainstream, reflecting a change in traditional cultural values. Today young, educated Hispanic women are the driving force in the marketplace. In addition to the Spanish language advertising agencies, major conventional agencies—especially those with package goods accounts—spend heavily to reach these women. Rates, which traditionally have been low, are rising as more advertisers move in. (Drive times on Spanish language stations are not priced as high as they are on English language stations because so many Hispanics in the work force use public transportation.)

Reflecting the increased importance of the target market, the giant representative firms, Katz and Interep, have formed specialized divisions to sell Spanish language radio in competition with the established Spanish radio representatives, Caballero and Lotus.

In markets with only one or two stations, the programming is essentially Spanish MOR—something for everybody. In larger markets, stations concentrate on narrower demographic groups within the Spanish-speaking population. Music playlists differ by region. Some stations call themselves Contemporary Spanish; some, traditional. In the Southwest, formats are broken down to "Ranchera" (Mexican country), "Nortena," "Chicano," "Regional," "Mariachi," and "International." In the Northeast and Southeast, the music is more tropical with a preference for "Salsa." In areas with many stations, formats reflect the general radio spectrum. There are, for example, Spanish language News/Talk and Easy Listening stations in Miami.

There is heavy sports programming directed to men over weekends on Spanish radio including soccer from Latin America and Europe, major league baseball from the United States, American football, boxing, and specials like the Pan-American Games.

The older stations, playing Ranchera and Nortena music and carrying heavy sports schedules, tend to be on the AM dial. The newer FM stations usually have a narrower focus with more targeted formats and a more modern broadcasting approach. In cities like San Antonio where Hispanics are well assimilated, music crossovers are common. A Michael Jackson cut will be slipped between Julio Iglesias and Jose Jose selections. Crossover happens rarely in New York, though, where the first and second generation listeners don't want to hear anything but Latin music and Spanish-speaking personalities. To the dismay of both Spanish and English purists, there are some stations carrying bilingual, street-talking disc jockeys.

With the Hispanic population continuing to grow as a result of continued immigration, and as the major marketers place increased emphasis on the Hispanic market segment, the future for Spanish language radio is bright.

National Public Radio Affiliates

The frequencies between 87.9 and 91.9 on the FM band are reserved for noncommercial radio stations. Many noncommercial stations, especially those operated by state and municipal universities and colleges, receive programming from National Public Radio. NPR's outstanding morning and afternoon news programs, "Morning Edition" and "All Things Considered," have steadily been siphoning serious listeners from commercial stations during the highly coveted drive time periods.

Noncommercial stations frequently repeat portions of the two-hour NPR broadcasts and thus often completely fill the 6:00 A.M. to 9:00 A.M. and the 4:00 P.M. to 7:00 P.M. time slots with these superbly produced news and commentary programs. The NPR listener, though broader based, resembles the Classical listener—professional, well educated, and upper income.

Formats and Radio Networks

A substantial percentage of commercial radio stations broadcasting today have a network affiliation or acquire programming from networks and syndicators. Today a station's network affiliation or syndicated programming has a direct relationship to its format. Strong stations are wooed by networks and syndicators who offer newscasts, features, and programs designed especially for specific formats.

In pretelevision radio, the exact opposite was true. A station's personality and importance depended largely on its network affiliation and the wooing was done by the stations. Despite this changed role from radio's "Golden Age," the modern station/format/network/syndicator relationship has pointed significance for radio advertisers.

6

The Role of Networks and Syndication

Network n **1:** *a fabric or structure of cords or wires that cross at regular intervals and are knotted or secured at the crossings* **2:** *a system of lines or channels resembling a network* **3:** *an interconnected or interrelated chain, group or system* **4 a:** *a group of radio or television stations linked by wire or radio relay* **4 b:** *a radio or television company that produces programs for broadcast over such a network.*
—Webster's Ninth New Collegiate Dictionary

Then and Now

Those old enough to remember the days before television may cherish sentimental memories about "The Golden Age of Radio." Weekly evening programs starred great performers such as Jack Benny, Fred Allen, Edgar Bergen and Charlie McCarthy, Al Jolson, Bing Crosby, and Rudy Vallee. Dramatic shows—"The Lone Ranger," "The Green Hornet," "The Shadow," "Mr. First Nighter," and others—were eagerly awaited in virtually every home in America. Comedy series like "Amos 'n Andy," which began in 1928, were on five nights a week. The "Lux Radio Theater" headlined Hollywood stars in radio plays and "Major Bowes Original Amateur Hour" attracted the star-struck, would-be-famous of every genre. In the daytime, personalities like Arthur Godfrey and Don McNeil were daily visitors, as were soap operas, children's shows, and newscasts.

Almost all of the memorable pretelevision radio programming was provided by one of the major radio networks. They operated like television networks do today with network programming absorbing large and desirable chunks of the broadcast day. In 1945, almost half of all radio programming was originated by four radio networks (CBS, NBC, ABC, and Mutual). Network compensation to their affiliated stations often comprised as much as one-third of the local stations' income and a network affiliation was one of a station's most valuable assets.

The networks themselves owned only 29 of the 901 radio stations broadcasting in 1945, but these stations were in the largest cities and accounted for more than one-third of the radio industry's total revenue.

The principle of radio networking in the pretelevision era was quite simple. The networks produced expensive programs with big stars that attracted big audiences. Local stations received the networks' programs free and were given a modest share of the revenue from commercials within the programs that were sold by the networks. Because network programming attracted large numbers of listeners, local stations could command more money for the local commercials they ran before and after network offerings.

By the mid-sixties all of this had changed. Television completely preempted radio's role as the universal medium and locally produced music formats—Top 40, Country, Beautiful Music, and so forth—took over station domination from the radio networks. The four major radio networks were now only providing hourly newscasts, occasional sportscasts, informational features, and a modest amount of play-by-play sports. There was little revenue available to compensate the stations and the networks bartered their services in exchange for time on their affiliates. A network would provide national newscasts and features to a station at no cost, generating its income from network commercials it sold within these newscasts and features. By 1965, less than 1,000 of the 5,300 radio stations on the air were affiliated with networks.

In 1969, ABC made a momentous decision. The network split its single network into four separate services. ABC Contemporary sought affiliates among Top 40 format stations; ABC Entertainment affiliated with Middle-of-the-Road stations; ABC-FM, with stations playing Album-Oriented Rock; and ABC Information, with News and Talk stations. This was the practical start of demographic radio networking. Program material emanating from the network was designed to appeal to listeners who tuned to a specific kind of radio.

By 1970, there were almost 7,000 radio stations in the United States, an increase of 28 percent in five years. As the stations concentrated on specific audience niches, networks narrowed their programming focus. Syndication producers also began creating longer, specialized programming with precise formats in mind. The networks responded to this new competition with their own longer shows, thus forever blurring the line between networks and syndicators.

At the same time that networks began seriously targeting particular audiences and longer shows were being developed by syndicators, the great technological leap to satellite transmission was occurring.

Until 1975, the traditional networks delivered their programming to affiliates only by telephone relay transmission. Line charges, assessed by AT&T, were a continuing cost that had to be borne by the affiliate, the network, or shared by both. When immediacy wasn't a factor, tapes of programs were physically shipped to stations. Most syndicators sent their material this way.

From 1975 to 1983, there was a gradual transition from telephone relay to satellite transmission. Satellites were first used by National Public Radio and the Mutual Broadcasting System to deliver programming to their affiliates. ABC, CBS, and NBC eventually switched over and satellite services in time went far beyond basic program delivery.

With the advent of satellite transmission, a radio station had only to make a one-time investment in a down-link dish while the network or syndicator bought transponder time on one of the commercial satellites and up-linked its transmission. The station turned its dish to the right position and picked up its programming through the air. Delivery from network to affiliate ceased to be a problem. Practically every radio station in the country now had the capability of picking up program material of uniformly high quality without additional cost. In the era of telephone relay transmission, the quality of network sound in smaller cities could be atrocious, but now a centrally produced program delivered by satellite sounded as good in Brattleboro, Vermont, as it did in Boston.

Concurrent deregulation on the part of the Federal Communications Commission had an enormous effect on the networks and syndicators. When the FCC ruled in 1981 that it was no longer necessary for local stations to run news and public service programming, it changed forever the relationship between networks and their affiliates. In the regulated era, many stations affiliated with networks in order to satisfy the news and public service programming requirements. To obtain what they had to have, stations also were forced to take network programming they didn't want.

With deregulation, local stations were able to demand the kind of programming they wanted from the networks. The syndicators in particular took swift advantage of the new ground rules and developed scores of new programs designed specifically for individual formats. The conventional networks were least affected because their AM radio affiliates in most cases continued with news coverage, but the networks and syndicators serving stations with music formats had to adjust to a buyers' market.

Overall, however, deregulation's effect on networks and syndicators has been strongly positive. This is borne out by their increasing share of the total radio pie in the years since the FCC relaxed its control over broadcasters.

The Conventional Networks—
News, Features, and Sports

With the exception of a few major play-by-play sporting events—the All Star Game, League Playoffs, and the World Series being the most prominent—conventional radio networks rarely take over blocks of continuous broadcast time during weekday daytime hours. Typical offerings to their affiliates from ABC Information, CBS Radio Network, Mutual Radio Network, and NBC Radio Network are hourly national newscasts, sportscasts, commentaries, business reports, and a variety of short features. A hefty amount of weekend and evening play-by-play sports, including the Super Bowl and Monday Night NFL football, is provided.

In addition to regular newscasts and short features, networks whose affiliated stations have music formats may also syndicate three- or four-hour musical programs designed for specific audiences. These "long-form" network offerings generally run on weekends or late at night. Each program, in effect, has its own network. CBS Radio-Radio, whose regular network consists of approximately 160 FM contemporary music stations, provides long-form weekend musical shows to as many as 1,200 stations.

Similarly, conventional networks, when they carry sports, will augment their station lineups. Major events like the World Series and NFL Football are usually carried over more stations than the basic network.

A few radio superstars literally have networks of their own. Paul Harvey, who is ABC's highest priced star, is heard every day on more than 1,300 stations, many of them contracting with ABC only to broadcast Paul Harvey newscasts and commentaries, and an average of 5,834,000 listeners hear every commercial Harvey broadcasts. The "Larry King Show," a late evening talk show carried by Mutual, has a substantially different lineup of stations than the network proper.

Some network offerings, however, are carried by fewer stations than in the network proper. CBS Radio's major league baseball "Game of the Week," a Saturday play-by-play sports feature, is typical of an optional program that is declined by a substantial number of affiliates.

Syndication

Program syndicators like Westwood One, the dominant company in the field, provide contemporary music and personality programming to stations without including any conventional news reports and short features. Westwood One produces more than thirty different programs, ranging from short entertainment features that run on weekdays to concerts that last up to three hours. Typical programs have titles like "Off the Record," "Rock Chronicles," "Star Trak," "Future Hits," "National Music Survey," and

"American Dance Traxx." Thirty-eight hundred radio stations clear some Westwood One programming which they receive without charge in return for airing national commercials.

Additionally, Westwood One owns the Mutual Radio Network which it acquired in 1985, as well as the granddaddy of all radio networks, the NBC Radio Network, which it bought from the General Electric Company in mid-1987 for $50 million.

Other major syndicators include the conventional networks, United Stations Radio Networks and a number of independents. The networks have a big advantage over the independents because they have their affiliated stations as a potential syndication base. An unimpressive station lineup in the top fifty ADIs will discourage most national advertisers.

Turnkey Services

There are also *turnkey* services that provide total programming for radio stations. A station has nothing to do but slip in local commercials. One of the largest suppliers of this kind of service is Satellite Music Network. They deliver complete program services, including news, sports, and features, in eight different musical formats twenty-four hours a day, seven days a week, in return for a monthly fee and two commercial minutes per hour which they sell nationally.

Transtar Radio Networks which, like Satellite Music Network, offers six twenty-four-hour formats, also syndicates CNN Radio's news service, an adjunct of Ted Turner's Cable News Network. In 1987, Transtar added a new service aimed for a mature audience called "AM Only" which features artists like Frank Sinatra, Johnny Mathis, and Andy Williams.

There are presently more than sixty networks and syndicated programs available to radio stations. The active radio networks in 1988, according to the Radio Network Association, were the following:

ABC Contemporary Network	Mutual Sports
ABC Direction Network	National Black Network
ABC Entertainment Network	NBC Radio Entertainment
ABC-FM Network	NBC Radio Network
ABC Information Network	NBC The Source
ABC Paul Harvey	NBC TalkNet
ABC Rock Radio Network	Satellite Music Networks
ABC Special Programming	Sheridan Broadcasting Network
ABC TalkRadio Network	Transtar Radio Networks
CBS Radio Network	United Stations Radio Network
CBS Radio Programs	One and Two
CBS Radio-Radio	United Stations Radio Networks
Mutual Broadcasting System	RadioShows
Mutual PM Network	Westwood One Radio Networks

Stepping Down from Television

Because network radio covers the country, it has been the principal radio beneficiary of rising television costs. When a national advertiser believes that TV costs have become prohibitive, the logical step down is network radio. Conversely, the step up from regional television is frequently network radio.

Some multiproduct network television advertisers, such as IBM, choose network radio for their more narrowly targeted products. For many years, IBM advertised its personal computers, products with a broad appeal, on television. At the same time, IBM used network radio for its line of printers, the market for printers being limited to those persons who already owned a computer or were about to buy one. In early 1987, when IBM introduced its second generation of personal computers, the IBM Personal System PS/2, it used heavy radio network schedules in addition to television and print. IBM reasoned that these more sophisticated machines could be a step-up buy for present computer users. This market segment is efficiently covered by those radio networks whose affiliated stations appeal to business decision makers.

Radio network buying even has similarities to television buying. It is thought of as an "upfront" vehicle, planned further in advance than spot radio and usually committed to for longer periods of time. The commitment is to the *total national delivery* of a demographic audience by the network's affiliates. The commitment to deliver this total audience, however, does not guarantee an equivalent audience delivery in each market.

Advantages to a National Advertiser

An advertiser who wants economical national coverage is logically attracted to the networks. A single advertising message can be carried by a network to markets all over the country at very low cost. The price of a commercial on a major national radio network is approximately the same as buying fifteen to twenty markets on a spot basis.

For thirty-second announcements, both local and national spot advertisers are customarily charged 80 percent of the cost of a sixty-second commercial. Network advertisers pay only 50 percent. This pricing differential works to the advantage of the networks, and it has made the thirty-second unit the standard for network commercials.

Networks deliver targeted audiences nationally. A beer advertiser can reach a national audience of predominantly male sports fans by sponsoring play-by-play sports; a business equipment manufacturer can communicate with executives by running commercials during drive time on-the-hour news broadcasts; package goods marketers can talk to a predominantly female audience by buying network schedules that run in the middle of the day.

The radio networks have all been working on techniques that will allow them to split the country for their advertisers much as the television networks do. With the increasing use of satellite transmission, this option will almost certainly be offered over the next few years. When it is, the radio networks will provide even greater opportunities to advertisers.

Syndicated Programs and the National Advertiser

Syndicators also aim at special target audiences. If a pickup truck marketer wants to reach a country music listener, he can advertise on syndicated programs like Westwood One's "Live from Gilley's" or United Stations' "Country Six Pack." If a jeans manufacturer wants to talk to young adults nationally, he might select "Off the Record" from Westwood One or "Casey's at 40" from ABC. The cost of delivering these audience segments is comparatively low.

Of all radio program material available, syndicated programs—and play-by-play sports—have the greatest kinship to television *programming*. Loyal listeners seek out a favorite program regardless of what station is carrying it.

Most long-form producers try very hard to satisfy their national advertisers (as do local stations when selling the spots allocated to them in syndicated programs for local advertisers). Opening and closing announcements, called billboards, and promotional spots may be included in the basic package to heighten client identification with the program.

Syndicated pricing must be efficient in media terms to attract advertisers. Long-form program buys can complement conventional network schedules by increasing frequency and reach and by bringing total per thousand audience costs down.

On-air merchandising support, such as contests or promotions involving local tie-ins, is rarely possible to arrange on conventional radio networks, but is practical on syndicated shows. Prize contests and other audience participation promotions can be designed for a particular program or personality, thus increasing the show's value to a national advertiser.

Weaknesses of Network Radio

As with all media, network radio is not without its weaknesses. Clearances—that is, agreement by affiliated stations to run network programming and commercials at a given time—are a major problem. A radio station's revenue from network advertising is a fraction of what it receives from local and national spot time sales. This creates a management dilemma. The station would ideally like to carry only the network programming it feels builds station audience. It would prefer not to carry other less attractive network offerings because it doesn't want to swap high-revenue commercial time for low-revenue commercial time.

Almost every CBS Radio Network affiliate wants "CBS News on the

Hour," but many of them are less enthusiastic about news commentaries, health features and other non-news features. Many stations push this kind of network programming into low-audience time periods. When commercial time is in short supply, they may not run it at all.

There is a reverse of this situation involving a narrow minority of network features. A few features are so desirable that affiliates want to run them more than once. Many CBS affiliates used to run Walter Cronkite's daily radio commentary twice, once upon receiving it in the early afternoon and then again in the early evening. The accompanying network commercial, however, would run only during the first broadcast. A local announcement would run during the second broadcast. More recently on CBS, commercial announcements were handled this way on Charles Osgood's "Osgood File" features.

Networks used to get cranky when this kind of thing happened. Until 1987, like most other conventional networks, the CBS Radio Network's network/affiliate contract granted stations the right to only one program usage. Starting in 1988, CBS revamped its program format. The most significant change was running Osgood four times a day and allowing individual stations to tack on a local announcement to each network offering. Affiliate stations were now legally able to sell commercials on the popular Osgood shows at local rates.

At the same time, the on-the-hour newscasts were structured so that individual stations who did not want to carry the full six minutes provided by the network could drop out at preset earlier junctures.

A prevalent practice called *wild-spotting* (also called *spot extraction*) occurs on virtually every network. It is also common on syndicated shows. Wild-spotting works this way. An affiliated station running a network news show at 8:00 A.M. does not run the network commercials that are transmitted with the program. Instead it replaces the network spots, usually back-to-back thirty-second announcements, with a local or spot sixty-second announcement which it has sold at a bonus price because the advertiser is promised positioning within the network news broadcast. The station receives substantially more money for this replacement spot than it gets for the network commercials. The station then "wild-spots" the two network commercials by running them at some other less desirable time within the 6:00 A.M. to 10:00 A.M. morning drive time.

Wild-spotting, in many situations, is not technically prohibited. Some radio network contracts only call for the advertiser's commercial to run on their affiliated stations within certain dayparts, but not necessarily within prescribed network programming. Not knowing when commercials are running, or even if they will run, makes advertisers and agencies terribly insecure.

One of the advertising disadvantages of present-day network radio is its lack of creative flexibility. A centrally transmitted, identical commercial is heard on every affiliated station, whether it runs in the network program-ming or is wild-spotted. There usually is no opportunity for adapting the message to the individual market and thus one of the medium's great strengths is lost.

In competing against the cost-efficient networks, the representative firms that sell national spot radio make two salient points. One is that with spot radio, national commercial messages may be tailored to individual mar-kets by using dealer tags or other localizing devices.

The second—and more fundamental argument—is that in any spot market, an advertiser with a diverse product appeal or a varying distribution system is able to pick stations, schedules, formats, and dayparts that best de-liver customers. When utilizing a radio network, he or she must accept the network's affiliates, and, in any given market, the affiliate may not be the best station for the advertiser.

This points up a significant difference between network radio and net-work television. For television network affiliates, prime time is totally domi-nated by the networks. The TV networks acquire and schedule the programming, determine how many commercial minutes will be sold, set the advertising rates, release time for local sales, and pay the affiliated sta-tions for running the network offerings.

Because television is a program-driven medium, when an advertiser buys time on a popular network show, he or she may assume that although the audience level will not be the same everywhere, it will not fluctuate wildly from one market to the next. Because the television network's dictates prevail, the show runs at the designated time in each market. It is because of the network that viewers tune to a certain television channel.

Although network and syndicated radio can be audience builders for a radio station, it is the local, day-in, day-out programming that is the pri-mary attraction for the station's listeners. The station is top dog; the radio network with which it is affiliated is more like a wagging tail. Except for spe-cialized programming, such as the World Series on the conventional net-works, and certain long-form syndicated shows on music stations, listeners hear the network programming, and commercials, because they chose to tune to that station, not because they opted to listen to a specific radio net-work.

With the great proliferation of radio networks, sharp competition has developed for affiliates. Frequently a network may not be able to sign up the most popular, highest rated station within the format it seeks. If in Chicago, X Network settles for the second- or third-best station for its affiliate, X Network's advertisers get the second- or third-best station in Chicago.

Heavy radio network advertisers are able to balance delivery across the country by buying a number of radio networks and combining the audiences in their calculations. The one-network advertiser, however, must be pre-pared to accept an erratic pattern of listener levels in different markets.

Accountability to advertisers is a particularly serious network responsibility. Network affiliate relations executives are charged with seeing that stations comply with their contractual agreements to run network programming and commercials. This chore requires constant monitoring; network commercials are a local station's lowest priority. It sometimes takes months before an advertiser knows exactly when and where his network commercial ran.

If radio stations have such little regard for networks, why do they affiliate? Major network affiliates usually feel that some network programming, such as hourly national newscasts, are essential to complete the station's broadcasting spectrum. Many other stations affiliate with lesser networks only for the money that affiliation brings them. They are paid by the networks or syndicators who require an outlet in their market.

Stations also affiliate with networks or accept long-form syndicated programs in order to fill time and to pick up some revenue for periods that are hard to sell to local or spot advertisers. The stations are able to air expensive shows they could not afford to produce on their own. Long-form programming is also used to keep staff costs low at times when audience levels are reduced such as holidays, overnight, late night, early morning, and parts of weekends.

The Future

While radio executives, who tend to look inward, compare network radio's growth to spot radio's decline, the choice for advertisers is between *national* radio—networks and syndicated programming—and other national advertising. There is minimal overlap between the top ten radio network advertisers and the top ten spot radio advertisers, but almost every major radio network advertiser is also an important advertiser in national print or television or both.

Network radio is an economical, easy to buy, efficient way to reach a targeted national audience with a commercial message. Network radio sales organizations are among the most sophisticated in the industry—they deal with major national advertisers who are themselves extremely knowledgeable. Networks and syndicators stand to benefit most from present and anticipated technological advances that will make it practical for them to accept regional advertising. They are adversely affected by their present inability to accommodate this growing regional marketing trend. All projections indicate that network radio will, from its small base, continue to be the fastest growing radio segment.

7

How Radio Reaches Target Markets

Today's marketplace has become so complex [that] "mass communication" as we now use the term may soon pass from the American scene....We must look increasingly for matching media that will enable us to reach carefully targeted, emerging markets.
—Donald E. Peterson, president, Ford Motor Company

If you're not thinking segments, you're not thinking.
—Theodore Levitt, *The Marketing Imagination*

Florence Skelly, one of the founders of the prestigious research organization Yankelovich Skelly & White, contends that "niche" marketing is in. A market niche is even smaller than a market segment. It calls for shooting arrows, not buckshot.

Segmenting with radio is the marketing application of *format differentiation*. Because individuals with different demographic characteristics listen to different kinds of radio stations, just as they read different kinds of magazines, advertisers can deliver their sales messages to preselected groups of prospects.

More than forty years after the emergence of television, there are radio industry leaders who contend that when faced with the growth of TV, radio *consciously* aimed for smaller, specialized, more homogeneous audiences.

Communications historians are prone to cite this as mere reaction. The fact, nonetheless, is that different tastes and interests are indeed best served by a diversity of programming. Radio programming today is directed not to broad audiences but to market segments. The advertiser's specialized audience, whether it be working women, blacks, teenagers, farmers, or top management, can be approached with precise focus.

The Segmented Market Concept

Mass marketing is declining in America. Segmented marketing is accelerating. Professor Levitt says, "To think segments means you have to think about what drives customers, customer groups and the choices that are or might be available to them. To think segments means to think *beyond* what's obviously out there to see."

Most products and services can be successfully marketed to a portion of the total American population of over 220 million people. Trying to reach everyone is frequently a poor and costly strategy.

Many marketers are now zeroing in on the best prospects, and in virtually every industry, products and services are being created for narrow slivers of the population. Automobiles are no longer designed for universal use but instead are intended to appeal to relatively small portions of the total market. The Honda Acura was introduced in 1986 specifically to attract the young, high-achiever group, the segment BMW has traditionally captured.

Package goods producers recognized that the eating needs and habits of various subgroups differed widely. As a result, they began marketing exotic frozen foods in small containers to appeal to young, single, working men and women. On the other extreme of the demographic spectrum, frozen dinners with low sodium, low cholesterol, and so forth were introduced to serve the needs of the growing older population.

Airlines have long acknowledged that 20 percent of their passengers represent 80 percent of their business. There are big benefits for the airlines in identifying and advertising directly to that particular 20 percent.

The tremendous growth of direct mail and catalog selling is a manifestation of segmented marketing built around the accurate identification of the potential customer. Major catalog houses, like L. L. Bean or Lands End, sell their lists or portions of their lists to other direct sellers for extraordinarily large amounts of money.

The flood of specialized magazines spawned in the last two decades further attests to the extreme value of interest groups.

A respected media strategist, Herb Maneloveg, writing in *Marketing Communications* summed up the situation neatly:

> The American public is no longer a homogeneous society. We are entering a segmented marketing world. The public has started to question the commercial messages that all look alike and offer

little meaningful differences in sales points.... There is a growing need to learn how to redirect messages against more targeted,
more select audiences.... Place the emphasis where it should
be—on the marketplace, the individual consumer who buys and
on the product to be sold. That's where future sales success lies.

Different Strokes

Target segmentation beyond broad age/sex demographics is not a factor for
everyone. A leading manufacturer of pasta products in Southern California
asked how many Los Angeles radio stations he would have to buy in order to
affect a measurable change in his sales volume. The best estimate was at
least eight to ten stations. His products are bought by virtually all households. He has the best distribution in his marketing area of the product category. His profit is measured in pennies, and additional advertising would
have to develop substantial additional sales to pay off.

Narrow targeting does not shape the pasta manufacturer's advertising
strategy and he is typical of a substantial group of package goods marketers.
Crest Toothpaste or Campbell's Soup certainly have important subsegments
within their large universe of users but their overall strategy must be based
on reaching huge chunks of the market. For them, radio is indeed a hand-
maiden of television.

These advertisers can afford to select media based on their efficient capability to cover broad age/sex groups, such as the pasta manufacturer's target which is Women 25–54. Buying advertising time "by the numbers"
works for them, whether they are buying television or radio.

Not every advertiser, however, has a wide target market. Numerically,
advertisers who seek to communicate with more rigidly defined demographic customer groups are in the great majority. When schedules are required to reach these narrower consumer concentrations, radio is able to
focus the advertising on the particular specialized audiences.

Radio's lower costs and greater targetability match up well with the
needs of many advertisers. For them, the shotgun approach is too costly.
Their marketing strategy calls for pinpointed targeting. Radio's ability to
reach tightly defined segments dramatically enhances its value.

For most advertisers, whether they are national marketers or local retailers, it makes more sense to develop advertising that has acceptable frequency against *a portion* of a broad market than to try to reach everyone
who might possibly buy. Radio has the unique capability of zeroing in on the
best prospects—whether they are baby boomers or senior citizens.

Why are there 5.6 radio sets in the average household? Because each
household contains individuals with different needs, tastes, and interests
who represent different market segments and who listen to different kinds of
radio.

There are market segments beyond counting, but here is a brief examination of some prominent ones.

The Affluent Over-Fifty Market

The huge post–World War II generation, whose average age is now moving into the forties, is the most publicized target group. Marketers have been minutely tracking this group since the late 1940s. Quite recently, however, these baby boomers' parents began attracting a lot of attention.

The great financial worth of the over-fifty market has become increasingly evident. Half the discretionary income in the U.S. is in households headed by people older than age fifty. They are no longer saddled with the expense of supporting and educating their children. The husband is usually at his earning peak and frequently the wife has returned to the workplace.

The estimated total income of those over fifty is $500 billion. This affluent, mature segment now numbers 61 million people and is expected to grow to 68 million by 1995. A subsegment, persons from 55 to 64 years of age, has the highest per capita income and the most discretionary income of any age group. Significantly, average life expectancy, which was at 73.7 years in 1980, is steadily rising.

Perceptions of the buying habits of older consumers are also changing. Older buyers had a reputation for brand loyalty because they were mistakenly thought to be set in their ways. Now that they are being directly targeted, this myth is being debunked. The fact is that discretionary income is an important key to brand switching.

The advertising community traditionally has been biased against older consumers, but recent research has been changing this attitude. In a study commissioned by CBS from Information Resources, Inc., brand purchase patterns were tracked in more than 7,800 households. The results released by CBS Research in 1984 suggested there may be "good reason to question whether the young are truly more experimental. In fact, in this study older consumers were as dynamic in their brand selections as younger consumers."

In 1975, the most frequently requested age demographic by radio advertisers was 25–39. By 1980, it had moved to 25–49. By 1987, it was 25–54. For a number of years, a volunteer radio industry group, "The 35 Plus Committee," has supported an educational campaign stressing the value of directing advertising to those older than 55 years of age.

Within the older age groups are some superior subgroups; top management is one. In 1984, *Dun's Business Month* surveyed the chief executive officers of the 237 largest U.S. companies and reported that only 6.5 percent of the CEOs were under 51. The publication also noted that there were as many CEOs over 65 as there were under 50.

An interesting group of older Americans are grandparents. There are about 49 million of them and most aren't doddering old codgers. More than 60 percent are under 65. They are healthier, more active, and better educated than they used to be. They have money, which they spend on themselves and on their grandchildren, and leisure time.

Because all radio audiences are measured by age, it is easy to identify the radio formats that are most listened to by older Americans. They are All-News, News/Talk, Classical, Easy Listening, Country, Middle of the Road, and Religion.

The Shrinking Household

The U. S. Census Bureau reported that the average size of households declined from 4.0 per household in the 1970s to 2.69 per household in 1983. Single person households accounted for 27 percent of all households and the number is increasing as marriage rates decline. Husband and wife households made up 58 percent of the total. Nearly one in five working wives earned more than their husbands and one in ten earned 80 percent or more of what their husbands earned.

Affluent childless married couples and affluent singles are big business for movies, live entertainment, restaurants, travel, and clothing. Significantly, they spend far less time in front of a television screen than their counterparts who stay at home with their children. But they are above average in their radio listening.

Down on the Farm

The Department of Agriculture estimates there are 300,000 Class 1A farmers, 470,000 Class 1 farmers, and 310,000 Class 2 farmers in the United States. They account for 90 percent of all farm income or more than $140 billion in agricultural sales.

The farmer is a regular listener who depends on his radio for weather forecasts; commodity prices; official agricultural announcements; and news of equipment, pesticides, animal health matters, and so forth. Many farmers have radios in the tractors as well as in their homes and trucks. Walkmen are popular, too. Many radio stations in agricultural centers provide special programming for this sharply defined market segment.

The Light Viewing Television Viewer

In the mid-80s, a magazine about television called *Panorama* came on the scene. Its editors took a lofty, intellectual approach toward the reportage of TV programming. It was a dismal failure and folded after a few issues. The principal reason cited for its demise was that the affluent, well-educated, professional/managerial people the magazine sought as subscribers were no more interested in reading about television than they were in watching it. They were typical of the lightest viewing television viewers.

Although all media audiences are statistically broken down into fifths or quintiles, it is with television that quintile analysis is most frequently used.

Table 7-1. Adult Television TV Viewers' Media Use—24 Hours

Medium	Light Viewers		Average/Heavy Viewers	
	Hours:Minutes	Percentage of Media Use	Hours:Minutes	Percentage of Media Use
Magazines	:22	8	:27	5
Television	:34	12	5:14	59
Newspapers	:42	15	:43	8
Radio	3:06	65	2:30	28
Total	**4:44**	**100**	**8:54**	**100**

Source: *Target Marketing and the Media,* produced by R. H. Bruskin Associates for the Radio Advertising Bureau. Reprinted by permission.

The demographic characteristics of the first or second quintiles—the highest TV-viewing audiences—differ dramatically from the demographic characteristics of the fourth or fifth quintiles—the lowest TV-viewing audiences.

Heavy viewers average almost five and a half hours of daily viewing and watch television every chance they get. Their decision is not *will* they watch but *what* they will watch. In comparative terms, it is easy to get an advertising message across to them. Advertisers actually worry about reaching them too often. A TV schedule of 80 gross rating points, if unwisely placed, might have commercials seen twice by the two highest TV-viewing quintiles and not seen at all by the three lowest TV-viewing quintiles.

For the lightest viewing two-fifths of the television audience, the viewing decision is based on selectivity. "I will watch television *only* if there is something I specifically want to watch." In the homes of these people, the TV set is off as much or more than it's on.

Thirty-seven percent of all adults are identified as light television viewers; they average 34 minutes of daily viewing and tend to be at the upper levels of education, income, and occupation. They are more likely to travel by air, more likely to use a major credit card, and more likely to own a late model car. (See Table 7-1.)

Since 1984, Simmons Market Research Bureau, on a commission from CBS, has conducted the InfoRadio Study, a comparative twenty-five-market media reach analysis. Among the demographic groups studied are professionals and managers who view little television.

In the 1987 survey of the twenty-five largest U.S. markets, Simmons measured the five-day cumulative audience reach of fifty InfoRadio stations (defined as stations people listen to for news and information) against professionals and managers in the fourth and fifth TV-viewing quintiles.

The findings indicated that for this low-viewing TV audience, the two radio stations per market average reach was 32 percent of adults, 42 percent of men, and 21 percent of women. This reach percentage against male professionals and managers is extraordinarily high, considering the low number of radio stations measured.

Wonderful Working Women

By 1990, there will be more than fifty-two million working women in the United States. This is an increase of 139 percent since 1960.

Working women are big radio fans and career mothers without partners are the heaviest listening women's segment. Over a twenty-four-hour period, working women spend about as much time with radio as they do with television. (See Tables 7-2, 7-3.)

According to Simmons, 91.4 percent of all working women are homemakers. Daytime television, which has historically targeted housewives, falls short with employed women who almost always have a radio in their cars. Frequently they have access to a radio at work, but rarely to a TV set.

Table 7-2.   Comparative Media Use by Working Women—Average Weekday

Time Period	Time Spent	Share of Time			
		Radio	Television	Newspapers	Magazines
Daytime 6:00 A.M.–6:00 P.M.	4:03	58	25	11	6
18 Hours 6:00 A.M.–12:00 midnight	6:42	42	43	8	7

Source: *Media Marketing for the 90's,* produced by R. H. Bruskin Associates for the Radio Advertising Bureau. Reprinted by permission.

Table 7-3. Comparative Media Reach against Working Women—Average Weekday

	Percentage Reached			
	Radio	Television	Newspapers	Magazines
Daytime 6:00 A.M.–6:00 P.M.	82	59	61	36
18 Hours 6:00 A.M.–12:00 midnight	84	85	70	46

Source: *Media Targeting for the 90's,* produced by R. H. Bruskin Associates for the Radio Advertising Bureau. Reprinted by permission.

Working women's interests, like working men's interests, vary widely. The radio listening habits of upscale working women, who buy more and higher priced products, tend to parallel the listening habits of upscale men.

The 1987 CBS/Simmons InfoRadio Study analyzed the media usage of professional/technical/managerial/administrative full-time working women in the twenty-five largest markets. The average of two radio stations per market reached 27.6 percent of this group over a week's time. Only one measured television program, the "Cosby Show," and one national magazine, TV Guide, exceeded 20 percent.

Involvement of Prime Prospects

Advertisers and agencies frequently place inadequate emphasis on the communications value of broadcast programming, that is, format in radio, when seeking out their prime prospects. The cost to define and locate a consumer market must be understood in both marketing and communications terms because age/sex demographics alone cannot measure involvement.

Target audience costs do not adequately measure programming's hold on a listener. When an advertiser can find his *precise consumer* through programming, that consumer is more valuable than others who simply fall within the conventional sex and age parameters. The homemaker who listens regularly to "The Food News Show" has considerably more potential to a food advertiser than a professional of the same age and sex who rarely prepares meals at home.

The application of this principle differs in the two broadcast media. In television, an advertiser's segment is unlikely to make up the entire audience of a television program. The cost of communicating with "the precise consumer" must, therefore, be the cost of delivering the message to the total audience, some of which will be wasted.

With radio, the audience is fractionalized to start with. A survey conducted for a major Chicago corporate advertiser indicated that 79 percent of the people in New York that this company considered influential could be reached with just two radio stations. This is not an atypical occurrence. An advertiser may reach and pay, predominately, for the fraction he wants— that portion of the public that is "the precise consumer" for his particular product or service—if planning and execution are prudent.

Segmentation by Daypart

Although format differentiation is radio's basic approach to target segmentation, there is also significant segmentation by time of day. Beyond the general and widely measured differences by daypart listening of broad age/sex demographic classifications, certain more narrowly defined groups regularly turn on their radios at specific times.

The obvious reason why the morning and afternoon drive time periods command the highest rates is that more and—in terms of education, income, and occupation—better listeners are tuned in.

The strength of All-News stations in these dayparts is in this much sought-after group—the majority are men in their late 30s, 40s, and 50s who earn substantial incomes and who are employed as professionals, managers, or in sales capacities. These are individuals who are interested in local and national news, sports results, weather, traffic, and the stock market. In most areas of the country, the only medium that delivers closing market prices is radio.

Working women, as a group, have unique daypart listening characteristics. In addition to tuning in at other times, they tend to be heavy nighttime radio listeners. One reason is they frequently handle their housekeeping chores in the evening. (See Table 7–4.)

Some have even narrowed the time period for working women to the late night hours. Peter F. McSpadden, formerly chief operating officer of Saatchi & Saatchi DFS Compton, stated that "late night radio could become a more effective way to reach working women than the historically efficient daytime television."

Many after-midnight listeners fall into other identifiable demographic categories. One is older men and women with irregular sleeping patterns; another is insomniacs, including a host of high-level executives. People who work at night comprise a large group of after-midnight listeners.

Late night radio advertising is inexpensive (some stations virtually give it away) despite the fact that 42.8 percent of all Americans past the age of twelve spend more than three "past midnight" hours a week listening to the radio.

Weekend radio, when subjected to cost-per-thousand or cost-per-rating-point analyses, almost always turns out to be a bargain. This is a reflection of lower demand on the part of advertisers for weekend time although many Americans, 80.1 percent of them, in fact, listen to their radios on Saturday and Sunday. The average weekend time spent listening is almost five and a half hours.

The Audience for Play-by-Play Sports

More than half the professional sports enthusiasts who consider themselves loyal fans *never attend a game!* Does everyone *watch* the Super Bowl and the World Series? Not exactly. In January 1987, 12 million adults *listened* to the Super Bowl on radio, and in October 1987, 50 million adults *listened* to the World Series on radio.

The power of sports broadcasting on radio is demonstrated by an anecdote from Len Lear's column, "Our Town," in the *Philadelphia Inquirer:*

> I was listening to a Sunday afternoon Phillies–Mets game on my
> car radio when I halted at a stoplight in northeast Philadelphia.

Table 7–4.   Percentage of Radio Listening by Location—
Persons 18 +

Time Period	Men			Women		
	Home	Cars	Other	Home	Cars	Other
7:00 P.M.–midnight Monday–Sunday	51.2	25.8	23.0	66.2	20.0	13.8
Midnight–6:00 A.M. Monday–Sunday	53.9	21.6	24.5	77.7	8.9	13.4
24 Hours Saturday–Sunday	49.3	28.6	22.1	65.5	20.7	13.8
24 Hours Monday–Sunday	36.2	30.0	33.8	55.6	19.7	24.7

Source: Percentages based on Fall 1987 RADAR® (Radio All-Dimension Audience Research) Reports. Copyright by Statistical Research, Inc., as analyzed by the Radio Advertising Bureau.

When the light turned green, there were at least three cars ahead of me. At that very instant, however, Phils pinch hitter, Joe Lefebvre, hit a dramatic three-run home run catapulting the Phillies from a 4–2 deficit to a 5–4 lead. When the cheering subsided, the traffic light turned red again. All of us on line grinned with the knowledge that we were indeed brothers under the skin. Not one car had moved on the green light and not one horn sounded!

The adult sports listener on radio substantially exceeds the national averages for income, education and occupation, as indicated by Simmons indices.

Advertisers who sponsor play-by-play sports on radio, however, get more than outstanding media efficiencies and large audiences. (See Table 7-5.) Some other benefits include the following:

- Prestigious association with a community institution
- Fan appreciation which translates into customer loyalty and goodwill
- Favorable selling climate for commercials
- Personalized selling by popular local sportscasters
- Exclusivity (usually there are no product conflicts)
- Commercial isolation (no clustering of spots)
- Excellent commercial frequency
- Abnormally high sponsor recall
- Above-average audience responsiveness
- Local merchandising tie-ins
- Special promotions
- Dealer participation

Table 7-5.   **Adult Listeners to Play-by-Play Sports on Radio**

	All Listeners		Household Income $50,000+		College Graduates		Professional/ Managerial	
	(000)	Index	(000)	Index	(000)	Index	(000)	Index
Baseball	19,052	100	3,876	145	4,475	137	4,409	148
Pro Football	10,922	100	2,233	146	2,706	144	2,561	150
College Football	9,643	100	2,051	153	2,746	166	2,413	160
College Basketball	7,219	100	1,528	151	1,995	161	1,611	143

Source: Simmons Market Research Bureau, *Study of Media and Markets,* 1986. Reprinted by permission.

A Limited Sales Objective

How much business is an advertiser capable of doing? This should be a major consideration when deciding how to advertise. A small package goods marketer with a limited production capacity might seek the exact same age/ sex demographic consumer as General Foods but need only to motivate a small fraction of the total group. An airline running two flights a day in and out of New York City draws from the same pool of prospects as the major trunk airlines who have hundreds of flights.

Budget limits and logical marketing should motivate an advertiser with a limited sales objective to reduce a broad target to a narrow one. Then advertising could be directed to the most promising segment. For the package goods marketer, this might be an upper income group or working women. For the airline, it might be business travelers.

Most advertisers who have a limited objective utilize newspapers and magazines. Because television is usually too costly for advertisers whose sales needs are modest, it is rarely a factor. When, however, radio is characterized, like television, as only a mass medium, it often is imprudently passed over in these situations.

Vertical Markets

In seeking to communicate directly to a specific target, it *is* possible to over-emphasize segmentation.

No advertiser, not even Procter & Gamble, thinks it has enough money. Many advertisers believe that to extract the greatest benefit from an inadequate budget, it is essential to communicate directly with precise vertical markets. Those holding this point of view favor dropping all mass media from consideration. Their accepted method for reaching narrowly defined vertical markets is to advertise in trade publications. Among many such advertisers, there is a widely held belief that this is the *only* way they can reach their prospects. That isn't so.

A consumer advertising foundation gives pinpointed vertical advertising credibility. If you marketed a proprietary data processing system to the drug trade, for example, your vertical target would be pharmaceutical manufacturers. The same pharmaceutical executives who read industry trade publications also read newspapers and consumer magazines, watch television, and listen to the radio. Moreover, the perceived value of the hypothetical computer system is enhanced when it is advertised in *Business Week, Time,* or on CBS All-News radio stations. It is likely that top management, unlike middle-management specialists, will be more heavily influenced by properly targeted general advertising than by trade publications.

Selectivity is still a major factor because within broader media, only certain magazines and certain radio formats will efficiently complement trade publications. A parallel situation exists when retailers or dealers pressure manufacturers to release all advertising funds for direct support efforts, that is, local advertising.

When brand advertising to the general consuming public is eliminated, a product's image can be substantially weakened. If a manufacturer's name appears only in a retailer's newspaper ad, the likelihood of generating sufficient brand awareness to spur sales is questionable.

An umbrella of general consumer advertising is extremely valuable. This umbrella does not require the manufacturer to employ costly television or magazines nor does it require exposure in all markets. It does require that the advertiser talk to a high percentage of prospective purchasers in his most important markets. The correctly selected radio formats and stations can reach the right consumer segment, thus supporting and complementing the retail advertising.

Segmentation through Cable Television

From its inception, cable television modeled its programming after radio; not after broad-scale television. This effort toward audience segmentation brought positive comment from journalists and other observers. What it did not bring, in most cases, was a lot of viewers. Many cable undertakings failed to attract large enough audiences to survive and of the advertiser-supported cable channels, only a few, notably Ted Turner's Cable News Network, ESPN, and USA Network, have broken into the black.

Cable television has had a measurable affect on the audience for commercial television. The three major TV networks have seen their shares slide over the last several years and cable is partially responsible. It has also pulled viewers from local commercial and public television stations.

Cable television's effect on radio did not turn out as the radio industry feared. Cable did not reduce radio's audience. It is not, as some called it in its early days, "radio with pictures." Cable *television* is television. It has every physical characteristic of commercial television except that reception is through wires rather than over the air. You still have to sit in front of the box to watch it.

What cable did do was cut into advertisers' radio budgets. Like radio, most cable channels are format driven and not program driven. Thus a beer company, for instance, seeking to influence young men, might pull dollars previously allocated to radio and use them on a cable sports network like ESPN. Format differentiation is an automatic segmenter, whether in radio, television, or magazines.

Taking radio budgets and using them for cable has not always turned out to be the wisest strategy. Trading a large radio audience for a smaller cable television audience might well be counterproductive. According to the 1986 Scarborough Study, an average of almost 150,000 adults listened to WBBM-AM's broadcast of every Chicago Black Hawk hockey game; there was more hockey listening on radio than there were *subscribers* to the six Chicago cable companies that televised Black Hawk hockey. This is not an isolated example.

Cable's lower prices did allow advertisers with budgets that were inadequate for commercial television, advertisers who in precable times might have considered radio, to become television advertisers. There may be a lot of vanity involved here, however, as the cost effectiveness of much cable usage is highly suspect.

One of radio's greatest strengths is its capacity to communicate with narrow portions of the population. In many instances where radio's use would be logical, however, it doesn't make the cut. The appeal of television is overpowering. Radio constantly struggles to escape the black, long, and—some would say—perfidious shadow cast by its younger but infinitely more powerful broadcast companion.

8

Television's Pervasive Influence

Television has an enormous influence on radio advertising. The overwhelming preference by advertisers and agencies to use television obviously affects the selection of media. Television accounts for 49 percent of all media billing of the 500 largest advertising agencies and radio only about 8 percent. This mandates that television buying techniques dominate broadcast buying. Finally, television affects strategic creative planning because most creative people want to work in television.

Creative Dominance

Of these three factors, the last is the most dramatic, visible, controversial, and pervasive. An advertising agency's most important asset is its creative product. In the 60s and early 70s, companies looked to agencies for marketing expertise, but today marketing managers in most major client companies are capable of setting and executing their own marketing strategies. In fact, most insist on it. Advertising is only one element in the total marketing effort. Within advertising, creativity dominates.

Still, many people on the media side of the business, both sellers and buyers, think that time and space are advertising. They aren't. Until ideas and words, performance and music, pictures and design, are molded into creative forms to fill the time and space, there is nothing. That is why creative people sit on top of the advertising pyramid—why Bill Bernbach is revered while Doyle and Dane are virtually forgotten, why David Ogilvy is a household word and Mather is unknown.

Because of this dominance, creative departments frequently overinfluence advertising solutions, in many instances to the disadvantage of their clients. The more "creative" the agency, the greater this influence. Top writers and art directors opt for television every chance they get. They are secure knowing that the advertiser who does not *want* to be on television probably has not been born. Certainly there are great numbers of advertisers who, for one reason or another, cannot be on television—cigarette advertisers are an example—but no one deprecates the medium.

Television is synonymous with creativity. Making minimovies is the ultimate advertising ego trip for creators and their clients. Attend any national advertising industry gathering. Examples of print advertising may receive token attention. Radio will scarcely be mentioned. But television reels never stop rolling.

A few years ago, at a Western Region Convention of the American Association of Advertising Agencies, during a creative panel titled, "I Wish I'd Done That," creative directors Kervin O'Reilly, of BBDO, and Hal Riney, then of Ogilvy & Mather, responded to the panel's general challenge by showing what they felt were outstanding television commercials. Neither displayed any print, radio, or outdoor. The third panelist, a creative director from Needham Harper & Steers, was unable to attend but he did send along the work he wished he had done. His selections were totally contained in a twenty-one-minute tape of TV spots.

Ken Roman, president of Ogilvy & Mather, was right on the mark when he said, "There are easier things in the world to do than getting top creative talent to write a radio commercial." The cold fact is that creative reputations are made primarily with television and secondarily with print advertising. Job hunters or switchers get big paying situations after showing their *reel* and their *book.* Few would deign to play a tape of radio commercials.

It's hard to blame them. Brilliant creative men and women, for whom salaries of $250,000 and up are not unusual, can neither receive this level of compensation nor attain star status among their peers by writing radio commercials. Their first reflex when analyzing virtually every advertising problem is to seek a television solution.

This reflex is a hurdle of tremendous proportion which works a significant hardship on people in the radio business. Ironically, it has also done a major disservice to the creative-dominated advertising agencies themselves. In large part, they have given up on their own capability of doing good radio and, by default, have allowed the most memorable radio advertising to be conceived and produced by outside radio specialists.

Media Selection

One of the outstanding television campaigns of recent years has been the Bartles & James Wine Cooler advertising created by Hal Riney & Partners for E. & J. Gallo.

In 1985, while the product and the advertising were both in formative stages, one of Gallo's media managers was in a meeting with the formidable Ernest Gallo, who tightly controls his company's marketing and advertising. The plan called for advertising Bartles & James on network television. The media manager pointed out that most people who bought wine coolers were young, so young, in fact, that there were industry concerns about under-age consumers drinking the stuff. Network television attracts older demographic groups. Other media, particularly radio, can be efficiently targeted to a younger market. Should the company, therefore, rethink the decision to promote Bartles & James on TV?

"Young man," Ernest Gallo is purported to have thundered. "We *always* advertise on television!"

In this situation, Mr. Gallo's instincts proved unerring. Whatever the waste circulation among nonprospects, the Bartles & James television commercials did everything that could be expected from an advertising campaign, thus demonstrating that great advertising can overshadow a questionable media strategy. If, however, exceptions prove rules, this is a striking exception. More often when television is selected illogically, the desired objectives of the advertiser are not achieved.

Another California table wine producer, far smaller than Gallo, was pressured to put its modest budget entirely into television in order to obtain distribution. After a well-known show business personality was hired to do the spots, the winery had just enough money left to buy some fringe television time in several of its most important markets.

The desired distribution was obtained. Unfortunately, with an inadequate budget for brand support advertising, the wine never moved from the retailer's shelves. In a few months, many retailers discontinued carrying the brand and the money spent on television was for the most part wasted.

Whether radio advertising would have achieved all of the winery's objectives is not the issue. Perhaps a combination of newspaper and radio would have been effective; television obviously was the wrong solution. When an advertiser craves television and his agency wants to make television commercials, it takes a most persuasive anti-TV advocate to move them down a different road.

Parallel case histories, some as extreme as this one and others less so, abound in a variety of consumer and industrial fields. Gallo and one or two others aside, the wine business is typical of a business that has difficulty in generating adequate budgets for television. When target markets tend to be segmented rather than universal, television, which is broadscale, can be wasteful. TV's power, though, manifests itself in myriad ways including the simplistic, "The client wants television."

A few years ago, still another California winery, owned for generations by an Italian-American family with tremendous wealth from land holdings, decided to market table wine under the family name. Previously, it only produced bulk wine that it sold to other wineries. The new brand was to be introduced in three markets. The marketing director, who had come from Gallo, and his advertising agency both saw the impracticality of television and proposed other advertising strategies to the company's owners. The proposals were rejected. The unembarrassed reason given was that the family members wanted friends and neighbors to see their television commercials. If Ernest Gallo could do it, they could do it.

Even in more conventional and businesslike marketing situations, the copycat syndrome emerges. A few years ago, when there were substantially fewer personal computers than there are today, it was rumored that Lotus Development, a leading computer software producer, was going to plunge heavily into television. The Lotus prospect was then only the IBM PC user, a fraction of a small universe. Both the computer and advertising communities were second guessing Lotus but despite a questionable Lotus media decision, every other major software company started making plans to get into television.

One knowledgeable executive in the data processing industry described the software business as one of "entrepreneurs and egos. If one goes on the tube, everybody will go on the tube." The software deluge on television didn't occur, but with no other medium—magazines, newspapers, or radio—would the same reaction have occurred. Television is the magnet that attracts everyone.

Even if emotion is discounted, product management people at national consumer product companies are often uninformed about radio. Many of them think of radio only as a local support and promotional medium. To sell them on the substitution or addition of radio to an advertising plan, whatever the merit, has inherent difficulties, and media people are frequently loathe to make the effort.

Butterfield Communications, in a 1986 study commissioned by the Stations Representatives Association, a national radio industry group, summarized the critical view of national advertisers. The study concluded that the respondents considered radio "a supporting vehicle, one-dimensional, fragmented, out of step with modern marketing," though valued for "targeting, merchandising opportunities, and localism."

Several years earlier, Ed Papazian, writing in *Marketing and Media Decisions*, postulated that the prejudices of marketing executives can be decisive in media selection. Although he credited agencies with playing an important role in media selection, he concluded that specific media—radio frequently but television never—are excluded from consideration because "the client isn't sold or because his hints and general attitude inhibit the agency from raising the subject again."

In fairness to clients who give scant consideration to radio, their feelings, lack of knowledge, or both are frequently shared by the highest echelon of agency account managers. Moreover, agency administrators are always happy to see television used because the high cost both of production and time bring in substantial commissions and fees. These attitudes make the task of the radio proponent even more difficult.

The gains that radio has been making can be attributed in part to television's own set of problems. These problems include greater audience fragmentation because of cable and the increased strength of independent TV stations, rising production costs, the fifteen-second spot with resultant on-air clutter, commercial zapping, movies played on VCRs cutting down TV viewing time, and, importantly, the diversion of media budgets into promotional budgets.

Television Buying Techniques

A presentation was made to sixty or seventy media planners and buyers at the Los Angeles office of one of the largest national advertising agencies. The mean age of the group fell well below thirty. Many of the younger people, most of whom were women, were in entry-level jobs which in agency media departments are low paying, detail oriented and pressure prone.

This question was asked, "How many of you have been involved with television buying?"

Almost every hand in the room went up.

The next question was, "How many of you have been involved with radio buying?"

Only three or four hands were raised.

In the media departments of large advertising agencies where television predominates, *everyone* is taught the rudiments of television buying and few are formally trained to buy radio.

For better or worse, quantitative evaluation of advertising has existed since the beginning of the industry. The circulation of newspapers and magazines has always been the determinant for pricing ads. Only with the advent of television, however, have "the numbers" become virtually omnipotent. Audience research companies' ratings are accepted as the universal standard of broadcast measurement and costs based on them are the norm.

Television is program driven and cost comparisons must be made, not between two competing TV channels, but between two competing shows. "Dallas" on CBS is compared to "Dynasty" on ABC. An NFL professional football game on NBC is stacked up against another game on CBS. Only numeric comparisons of audiences expressed in ratings have pricing validity.

The audience appeal of a television program is what attracts viewers.

The more successful the show, the greater the audience. The size of the estimated audience expressed as cost per point—which means the cost of achieving one gross rating point or reaching one percent of the advertiser's target demographic—is the basis for pricing. How many women between 25 and 49 years of age or men between 18 and 54, for example, will I reach at what cost? Television, in fact, usually guarantees *quantitative* audience levels to those advertisers who buy in advance of the season—the so-called upfront market—and will provide make-goods if these levels aren't reached. (A specific situation: The Super Bowl played between the Denver Broncos and the Washington Redskins in January 1988 did not attract the number of television viewers guaranteed by ABC. Make-good credits were immediately given to the advertisers.)

Back when television didn't exist and there was no such thing as a gross rating point, Ben Duffy was the president of Batten, Barton, Durstine & Osborne, then, as now, a major advertising agency. He used to tell a story about the inconsistencies of evaluating magazines using the numeric guide of cost-per-thousand readers (CPM).

True Story had a CPM of $.93 and *Good Housekeeping* had a CPM of $8.42. *Good Housekeeping,* however, was loaded with advertising while *True Story* ran very few ads and most of those were of low quality. In which magazine, Duffy would ask, would an advertiser be better off placing an ad?

The same logic could be applied when comparing two radio stations with totally different formats. Like the magazines, and unlike television stations, the comparison is not one of equivalents but of two qualitatively separate listening audiences.

The spillover of television cost-per-point evaluation and buying techniques to radio, however, frequently causes editorial or qualitative factors to be overlooked. This pervasive spillover first created and then opened an enormous can of beans. Buyers were allowed to analyze broad demographic groups numerically without having to consider that, like *True Story* and *Good Housekeeping,* a radio station's editorial content has a major effect on the qualitative subgroups making up its particular audience.

When buyers fail to understand the unique dynamics of radio, they are naturally comfortable with and supported by television's numeric approach. They are supported by the undeniable facts that television is the dominant advertising medium as well as the principal source of advertising expenditures and thus advertising agency income. They know television is unmatched in its capacity to generate reach and impact against mass audiences. And they are usually encouraged by their superiors to take a ratings point approach when buying radio.

The quantitative television buying approach, however, fails to consider what has been a basic difference between television and radio ratings—that television ratings until recently were usually expressed in terms of households while radio ratings can *only* be expressed in terms of people. Four members of the same household could all be listening to radios tuned to different stations, which is unmeasurable in household terms.

But cost-per-point buying, a procedure designed to meet needs created by television and substantially carried over to radio, does provide a simple answer to a complicated question. When television-trained buyers have to buy radio, they lean heavily on "the numbers" that they have learned to trust when buying TV. No matter how fervently the radio community might wish them to, the numbers are not going to go away. The hope is that they can be used as tools and not as crutches.

9

Determining Radio Rates

In general terms, all media pricing is based on audience, but there always has been a basic difference between the pricing of print media, magazines and newspapers, and broadcast media, television and radio.

Most major magazines and newspapers continually monitor their circulation figures and periodically issue printed sets of rates based on a guaranteed circulation level. Although complex and frequently confusing to a casual examiner, these rate schedules are usually the same for all advertisers. When a buyer negotiates with a publication, the standard negotiation is about such matters as ad position and merchandising support.

In late 1987, however, the traditional wall started to crack and a small number of prominent magazines—among them *McCall's* and the Time Inc. family of publications—agreed to negotiate rates with large advertisers. A significant trend may have started but almost all print media ads are still being bought at rate card prices.

In practical terms, there are no comparable rate cards in broadcast. Each buy is negotiated and the basic negotiation concerns price.

The Grid Rate Card

Almost all radio stations in major markets employ the *grid rate card,* a device which allows them to charge various prices for the same commercial time. A series of prices are established for all dayparts. Each set of prices is a grid and at any given time, a station may be operating on several different grids.

The relationships of the prices for the various dayparts within each grid are based primarily on audience levels and secondarily on varying levels of demand. If demand were not a factor, a pricing grid might look like this:

	Morning Drive	Daytime	Afternoon Drive	Evening	Weekend
Audience	300,000	100,000	200,000	50,000	100,000
Grid I—Sixty-second announcement	$300	100	200	50	100
Cost per thousand	$1.00	1.00	1.00	1.00	1.00

With most radio formats, demand for drive time announcements exceeds that for daytime announcements, and demand for daytime exceeds that for evening and weekend. To accommodate this, the grid might be adjusted to look like this:

	Morning Drive	Daytime	Afternoon Drive	Evening	Weekend
Audience	300,000	100,000	200,000	50,000	100,000
Grid I—Sixty-second announcement	$350	75	225	25	50
Cost per thousand	$1.17	.77	1.13	.50	.50

Another lower priced grid might look like this:

	Morning Drive	Daytime	Afternoon Drive	Evening	Weekend
Audience	300,000	100,000	200,000	50,000	100,000
Grid VIII—Sixty-second announcement	$200	50	125	20	30
Cost per thousand	$ .67	.50	.63	.40	.30

Why is there a need for multiple grids?

Commercial broadcast time is finite. There are only a certain number of commercials that may be sold. Since deregulation, this number is not established or monitored by the Federal Communications Commission as it once was, but is self-regulated by the stations themselves.

Pricing is dependent on audience. Audience is built through programming. Audience would be lost through the excessive interruption of programming by commercials and prices would fall, therefore stations seek the perfect balance of programming and commercials. The CBS All-News radio stations in New York, Chicago, Los Angeles, and San Francisco scheduled eighteen minutes of commercial time per hour under FCC regulation and presently run the same eighteen minutes under deregulation. Most stations with music formats carry 8–11 commercial minutes per hour.

The station's inventory or the number of unsold commercial slots is the most significant factor in determining what pricing grid will be quoted. If sales are weak, a lower grid will be quoted. If the station is almost sold out at the time the advertiser wants to be on the air, a higher grid will be quoted.

Grid selection is also affected by *what* the advertiser seeks to buy. Stations will quote more favorable grids to buyers of TAP or "Total Audience Plans" which normally are an equal dispersion of announcements over all or a number of dayparts. They will quote higher grids to buyers who seek spots only in the most highly demanded dayparts.

A radio station's inventory can be compared to seats on an airplane. If the customer will accept seats only in the first-class compartment (in radio terms, drive times), he must pay a premium for them. Furthermore, the empty seats in the back of the plane (other dayparts) then loom disproportionately large in the stock of unsold inventory. Because all the first-class seats are gone, these may have to be sold at bargain rates.

Conversely, when a station is totally sold out of drive time announcements but an advertiser says, in effect, he will pay whatever he must in order to be on the air, the station usually will accept the business. Radio learned how to do this from television. The price charged may be "off the card," that is, higher than the top grid. Other advertisers who bought drive time announcements at lower prices may have some of their spots pushed around or even missed in order to accommodate the higher priced order. Like television, the radio market today is an auction and the highest bidder usually prevails.

The radio station's sales manager is constantly juggling pricing and inventory to maintain a balance of salable spots and to assure the highest level of return to his management. Stations that are sold out for more than a week or two are thought to have priced their time too inexpensively. In a perfect world, they want to walk the shaky line between the highest possible rates and the maximum amount of business.

While teetering on this line, the sales manager must maintain a competitive position. Here is where negotiation enters the drama. A pure numbers negotiation customarily revolves around the cost per rating point (CPRP). The buyer may contend that the average market CPRP is lower than the station's CPRP, thus pressuring the station or its sales representative to quote lower rates in order to be included in the buy.

Dealing with Demographics

Sheer audience numbers or ratings points are not the sole factor in the give-and-take between buyer and seller and, in the real world, they are never considered in a vacuum. A buyer's target market is *always* defined in terms of age and sex. In submitting numbers or "efficiencies" to support a proposal, a radio salesperson only submits data relating to the specific segment of the market the buyer seeks, whether it be Adults 25–54, Women 18–34, Men 35 + , Teens, and so forth.

With magazines, the demography of the advertiser's target market is considered when *choosing* the magazines in which to advertise but historically this demography has had no affect on pricing. Except for the few magazines that have recently agreed to negotiated rates, the magazine rate card has been inflexible. In broadcast, however, the target demographic has always been a factor in the *pricing* negotiation.

To illustrate, assume that *Yachting* reaches an audience that is 80 percent men and 20 percent women. When an advertisement is placed in the magazine, however, the advertiser pays the same amount whether the target audience is male or female.

Now take a radio station whose audience breaks down in the same gender proportion. In the unlikely situation that an advertiser seeking to reach only women would buy this station (everything is hypothetically possible), he would almost certainly pay less for identical time than an advertiser seeking to talk to men.

Radio stations routinely price their commercial time based on the effective cost of reaching the advertiser's customer base. It is possible that the same advertising agency buying time on the same radio station for the same week could pay two different prices for two different advertisers. This is a continuing problem for buyers and sellers alike. An agency, knowing its lowest priced spots on station XYZ were $100 each for Client A, invariably pressures the station to maintain that price for its other clients despite differences in target audiences. The station contends that the agency is not entitled to use a pricing level based on a small target audience for advertisers with a larger potential within the station's audience. Thus are negotiating positions established.

The realities of the marketplace, however, are that an advertiser seeking only women would not advertise on a radio station whose audience is heavily male. Even if the advertiser wished to, it is unlikely that the station sales manager could drop his price level sufficiently to be competitive.

Real-life situations are customarily more complex. The accepted demographic for personal computers is Men 25–54. In advertising its Apple II computer at graduation time, Apple Computer chose to change its target to Adults 25–49, theorizing that mothers as well as fathers would be influential in gift purchases. All-News radio stations with predominantly male audiences, who were routinely included on Apple's advertising to the business community, found themselves hard-pressed to qualify for the graduation campaign. To do so, they had to lower the grid in order to be competitive against the adult demographic.

Special Availabilities

Special programming is packaged and priced separately. Ratings and audience levels are not the only factors considered. Play-by-play sports sponsorships, for example, almost always include a substantial amount of merchandising, such as free tickets, use of the radio station's hospitality suite, attendance at team luncheons, visits to training camps, and the like. The cost of this merchandising is figured into the cost of the sponsorship.

Sponsorship of features, like sports, weather, traffic and business, usually require a premium over normal spot costs and qualitatively superior programs, such as cooking shows that attract a definitive audience of homemakers, rarely are priced from grids. Contemporary music stations frequently offer sponsorships and special promotional mention for feature programming. Typical would be Cousin Brucie's Saturday night show on WCBS-FM, New York, which carries its own price schedule.

Syndicated features such as ABC's "American Top Forty," which is carried by almost five hundred stations, have commercial slots available for local sale and they almost always are sold at different rates than regular station spots.

Sports programming on networks, such as "Monday Night NFL Football," also includes a certain number of announcements for local sales and these are packaged and sold at premium prices.

Radio stations have been criticized—and in many cases, justifiably so—for competing *solely* on the criterion of price. Station sales managers and salespeople respond, however, by charging that most buyers *only* consider price when making purchase decisions. Price is the universal crutch. It is quantitative and subject to precise comparison. When sellers and buyers do battle, they joust with dollar bills.

10

Playing the Game of Buying and Selling

Devising a strategy for a radio advertising campaign and producing the commercials that carry the message are functions of *advertising*. Getting the commercials on the air—that is, buying and selling radio time—is *business*. At this point *real money* is being committed.

Strategic radio and tactical radio are often at odds. In many large advertising agencies, media people are out of the main flow. At the highest level, they tend to be *media* strategists but not *advertising* strategists. At lower levels, they may spend millions of dollars but not have the slightest influence on the direction of the campaign. Rarely do they hear the advertising until the commercials are on the air. As a profit center, the radio buying group is generally looked on as marginal because, when compared to the television group, too many people are responsible for spending too few dollars. Quality buying is always aimed for, but the emphasis is on speed and efficiency.

The generally accepted system of buying radio time is flawed. Quantitative measurements designed for television are too often uncritically adapted for radio. The system forces the buyer to see radio time as a commodity whose price is the only significant differential. It forces reliance on minute quantitative variances in audience data generated by rating systems that are less than totally reliable. It take absolutely no recognition of standard statistical error. Its presumption is that every radio listener is the same which is patently false.

Despite its shortcomings, the existing system functions. Media directors draw the big picture. Planners fill in the details. Between them, they lay out the guidelines, determine the target demographics, select the markets and allocate the budget. Then the media buyer takes over. She* is the key player in the negotiation game whose participants are salespeople from radio stations, radio networks and representative companies, the stations themselves, the agency, and the advertiser.

The buyer and the seller are partners in the true sense of the word. Their mutual accessibility is essential. Returning phone calls quickly is the norm on both sides because orders can be lost when that doesn't happen. The two talk almost exclusively with each other and maintain a continuing dialogue, even when they are not involved with a negotiation. The buyer must be familiar with the markets she is buying. Because the radio station spectrum is constantly changing, she relies on her close relationships with salespeople to keep herself up to date.

The buyer seeks a salesperson who understands her needs and isn't totally occupied heralding the strong points of his or her station. She seeks a creative salesperson who can suggest tie-ins and promotions that will enhance the value of the station's time.

Trust goes both ways. Time buying is a word-of-mouth business and what buyer and seller say to one another is binding. A verbal price quote is firm. A verbal order has all the legality of the confirming paperwork that will follow. Most radio contracts, which are often issued after the schedule has begun, are never signed.

When a football coach charts an offensive play on the blackboard, the theoretical outcome is always a touchdown. If the radio buying game is played out perfectly, every player should score. There should only be winners and if one player thinks he or she has lost, then there was a failure somewhere in the process.

The Buyer's Game

Before the starting whistle blows, the buyer must marshal a substantial amount of information normally given her by media planners. She needs to know:

- The flight dates—when the campaign is to begin and end
- The overall age/sex demographic target—for example, Adults 25–54
- Within the broad target, the primary emphasis—for example, 35–54

*Because most buyers are women, gender-specific pronouns are used throughout this discussion when referring to the buyer or the buyer's functions.

- And, if one exists, the secondary emphasis—for example, Women 25–34
- The important qualitative characteristics of the target—for example, upper income, college graduates, white-collar occupation
- The market list
- The overall or market-by-market budget
- The media weight goals expressed either in gross rating points or "reach and frequency," based on Arbitron or Birch, whichever rating service is used by the agency

Occasionally radio buys are made to a budget without consideration of weight goals. The buyer might be asked to make the best possible use of $50,000 in Los Angeles. Customarily, however, the buyer is given a budget and a goal for each market.

Despite all the gnashing of teeth and protestations to the contrary, cost per rating point radio buying is the standard practice of major advertising agencies and media buying services. It is the universal quantitative underpinning. Eighty percent of weight goals for radio buys are expressed in gross rating points (GRP). The common practice is to divide the budget by the GRP goal to come up with the average cost per point the buyer will be shooting for (e.g., $50,000 \div 500$ GRP's = $100 average cost per point).

At this stage of the game, she will solicit proposals from the radio stations she wants to consider. The plan she is working from may specify that certain formats are to be favored or that certain formats may not be considered. (Beer advertisers, for instance, will normally not place advertising on stations where there is a substantial teen audience. Although they know many teenagers drink beer, they are concerned about proponents of restrictions on alcoholic beverage advertising.) The buyer may determine that certain stations aren't qualified for consideration, but prejudging, if it is too severe, can be a disservice to the advertiser. Most experienced radio buyers are wary about cutting the prospect list down too drastically. Many, in fact, are resentful if the ground rules established by others—clients, account managers, media supervisors, and planners—restrict the ability to make what is believed to be the optimum buy. In most cases, the buyer is the person who will be held accountable for the cost efficiency of the schedule and the more inhibited she is in making a free selection, the more difficult it is for her to arrive at her desired average cost per rating point.

The buyer will tell the salesperson as much or as little as she deems wise. She will make a judgment as to what rating point cost the station is likely to come in at and probably will ask for a GRP cost about 10 percent over or under her real average GRP. She knows buying some stations that have low GRPs will allow her to buy others that are high. She also knows if she quotes too low a GRP cost overall, too many stations could meet it and she might be committed to more stations than she needs. One element is weighed against another. She's playing the game.

The Seller's Game

The radio salesperson is a harried middleman. On one hand, he or she (as many women as men are on the street selling radio time) must give the buyer the kind of schedule she wants at the lowest possible price. On the other hand, the salesperson must deliver every potential order to the station at the highest possible rates. These are basic conflicts.

Radio stations are intensely competitive. The industry is justly criticized for broadcasters' proclivity to speak ill of each other. Tremendous pressure is put on the salesperson to be included on a buy even if the station's audience isn't exactly what the advertiser wants.

A good salesperson, armed with information obtained from the buyer, must analyze the competitive situation and be concerned with four factors:

• The station's ratings and audience numbers
• Strengths or weaknesses of its format
• The station's audience composition
• Price

If, for example, the station delivers a large number of Adults 25–54, the salesperson may be able to work directly from a station ranker. This is a computer printout that ranks every station's audience for a given demographic group. (See Figures 10–1, 10–2.) The ranker may show the station has such a large share of the target audience that it would be difficult for the buyer not to include it.

Frequently this is not the case and pure reliance on the station's ranking may not be the best course. Perhaps the unique characteristics of the station should be emphasized. The qualitative profile of the format's audience may provide a rationale for being bought despite inadequate numbers. There may be programming features that are especially attractive to the particular advertiser.

A good salesperson will dissect the target demographic minutely and give particular attention to the subgroups that are to receive special emphasis. Some competitive stations that deliver a large number of total Adults 25–54 might be top heavy on one end or the other of the age span or weighted excessively toward men or women. The salesperson should be able to document the station's capability to round out the market. A tool to make this judgment is an audience composition breakdown, a computer-generated report that analyzes each station's total audience by narrow age/sex groupings. (See Figure 10–3.)

Coping with two rating services can be a headache for the salesperson. Until a few years ago, every advertising agency and nearly every radio station subscribed to Arbitron. Today a substantial number of agencies have switched to Birch but not all stations buy Birch's service. As the salesperson may not legally use ratings data unless the station is a subscriber—and this is policed vigilantly—making full-scale presentations to agencies who base

Figure 10–1.   **Computer Printout Showing Total Week Cumulative Audience of 25–54-Year-Old Adults for Forty Leading Los Angeles Radio Stations in Rank Order**

```
        CBS RADIO              REPORT SUMMARY        ARB ADULTS 25-54
        LOS ANGELES            CUME LISTENERS        6AM-MID  MON-SUN
                               TOTAL AREA
                             CUME(000)


     WINTER 87
  KIISF1,006.7
  KRTHF   968.2
  KOSTF   738.0
  KFWBA   671.8
  KNX A   639.2
  KBIGF   611.2
  KLSXF   607.7
  KLOSF   607.3
  KIQQF   572.8
  KABCA   539.1
  KPWRF   507.9
  KFI A   422.0
  KTWVF   415.1
  KNX F   376.7
  KJOIF   368.0
  KLVEF   321.8
  KFACF   301.5
  KRLAA   293.3
  KZLAF   288.1
  KTNQA   276.3
  KROQF   271.9
  KUTEF   268.1
  KKGOF   259.5
  KLACA   254.4
  KJLHF   245.7
  KRTHA   214.8
  KWKWA   214.1
  KMPCA   192.5
  KACEF   170.4
  KNOBF   139.3
  KALIA   139.0
  KDAYA   109.2
  KSKQA   107.2
  KEZYF   106.6
  KIEVA    88.7
  KGFJA    87.4
  KBRTA    86.8
  KFSGF    79.5
  KNACF    75.9
  KIISA    54.9
  XPRSA    28.0

   POP  6,273.0
 END OF TRANSACTION
```

Source: Winter 1987 Arbitron data produced by CBS Radio *RADCOM*. Used by permission.

buying on Birch is a major complication. When enough agencies are using Birch, however, the stations that are now holding out will have no choice but to subscribe to both rating services.

However the supporting information is obtained, the win-or-lose negotiation will take place over price. The salesperson is almost always negotiating two ways—with the buyer and with the station. When the salesperson was called by the buyer with the "availability," the station was queried about

Figure 10–2.   Computer Printout Showing Average Quarter Hour Listening by Daypart of 25–54-Year-Old Adults on Thirty Los Angeles Radio Stations Ranked by Average Total Week Listening

	CBS RADIO MARKET-LOS ANGELES M-S	MONDAY-FRIDAY				SATURDAY				SUNDAY			
	6-12	6-10	10-3	3-7	7-12	6-10	10-3	3-7	7-12	6-10	10-3	3-7	7-12
KIISF	610	1351	659	699	188	583	832	410	199	353	462	283	137
KRTHF	495	722	739	570	185	442	814	461	135	200	490	369	80
KOSTF	381	471	600	484	239	171	369	238	156	194	277	201	147
KLSXF	381	506	563	455	144	256	518	344	150	207	467	420	122
KPWRF	361	473	416	418	228	220	483	366	375	138	477	309	144
KTNQA	356	661	515	353	105	469	381	268	138	281	209	245	67
KIQQF	337	426	539	426	140	260	410	310	91	173	300	256	107
KTWVF	334	391	463	423	191	250	393	317	209	231	260	292	152
KBIGF	312	379	574	412	112	265	392	201	62	116	170	177	60
KLVEF	304	414	387	379	143	346	407	287	144	267	341	115	136
KABCA	302	570	341	333	217	304	187	167	126	164	153	155	104
KJOIF	261	381	432	295	66	288	413	151	81	177	241	127	77
KLOSF	257	361	340	321	96	199	374	244	126	220	208	272	104
KROQF	210	325	255	310	64	109	325	209	56	52	188	219	137
KNX A	188	410	165	255	128	202	66	72	50	110	67	56	55
KRTHA	178	187	217	246	70	186	365	251	43	51	297	179	61
KJLHF	177	195	174	196	148	129	275	284	126	42	146	321	127
KZLAF	175	287	217	214	83	186	299	124	85	65	142	28	38
KFWBA	173	417	172	228	52	210	93	85	44	148	48	116	37
KRLAA	171	247	233	196	89	177	242	120	56	101	163	130	23
KWKWA	130	159	145	137	106	219	159	150	87	65	152	95	49
KACEF	130	118	195	115	95	153	246	146	144	24	95	77	78
KLACA	122	185	138	128	84	101	103	107	101	29	237	74	31
KMPCA	116	126	88	172	132	95	142	60	64	56	143	94	5
KNX F	104	129	149	115	52	66	137	116	21	74	153	63	60
KKGOF	101	87	96	119	103	38	126	216	77	56	101	111	59
KFI A	100	251	67	152	59	114	29	27	10	25	36	69	24
KFACF	100	114	127	140	75	93	76	15	57	93	93	55	69
KALIA	97	143	134	69	81	79	145	54	71	63	119	24	0
KUTEF	93	136	105	151	34	114	119	101	26	36	43	38	34

ARB AUDIENCE ANALYSIS   SPRING 87   ADULTS 25-54   AVERAGE 1/4 HOUR(00)   AREA - METRO

END OF TRANSACTION

Source: Spring 1987 Arbitron data produced by CBS Radio *RADCOM*. Used by permission.

what prices to quote. If the advertiser was local, the station salesperson talked with the local sales manager. If the advertiser was placing a national spot buy, the sales rep called the national sales manager of the station involved.

The salesperson likes to be given a range of prices so that there is leeway in bargaining with the buyer, but usually the salesperson is given a specific grid. Each buy is priced separately even if several are being made by the same agency, though heavy utilization of a station by an agency will be a factor. Heavy utilization is sure to be one of the buyer's negotiation ploys. The station is also intensely interested in its share of the buy and will make concessions on price in return for a substantial part of the order.

The salesperson will put together a proposal, incorporating all the qualitative sales points and supported by all the rating data that can be pulled out of the computer system. "Creative" suggestions such as stacking announcements in various dayparts to overcome apparent weaknesses, choos-

Figure 10–3.   Computer Printout Showing Audience
Composition by Age of Forty Los Angeles Radio Stations
Ranked by Total Cumulative Audience of Adults 18+

```
C B S   R A D I O        %  COMPOSITION  ANALYSIS            CUMULATIVE
LOS ANGELES           ARBITRON      SPRING 87      TOTAL      6AM-MID  MON-SUN
BASE; % OF ADULTS   18+
                 A18-24  A25-34  A35-49  A50-54  A55-64  A65+           A18+
STATION    %       %       %       %       %       %                   (000)
KIISF    32.5    37.2    24.9     2.9     1.8     0.7                  1697.5
KRTHF    16.3    41.1    35.4     3.0     2.0     2.1                  1226.6
KABCA     3.4    15.7    25.3    10.1    20.1    25.4                  1202.3
KNX A     2.6    14.6    25.3     9.6    20.1    27.8                  1177.0
KOSTF    26.7    32.1    27.9     3.7     5.5     4.0                  1136.2
KPWRF    47.4    33.0    16.2     1.5     1.4     0.5                  1130.4
KFWBA     3.8    14.7    27.8     6.0    19.9    27.8                  1120.5
KBIGF    12.2    18.3    30.6     7.6    17.0    14.2                  1034.1
KLOSF    36.1    46.0    14.4     0.6     1.2     1.7                   945.3
KJOIF     3.6     8.9    23.3     8.6    26.2    29.3                   869.0
KMPCA     3.8     8.8    16.8    10.9    31.1    28.7                   796.1
KROQF    49.2    34.6    13.3     1.3     0.4     1.3                   779.2
KIQQF    14.1    27.8    37.8     7.0     6.5     6.7                   756.3
KLSXF    24.1    54.5    18.8     1.0     1.0     0.6                   754.4
KTWVF    14.5    38.3    35.9     4.8     4.3     2.1                   743.0
KFI A     6.7    19.8    32.0     6.7    16.8    18.0                   630.9
KLACA     7.7    21.2    28.5    13.5    17.0    12.1                   494.1
KLVEF    22.4    34.3    29.4     5.4     6.5     2.1                   487.2
KZLAF     8.6    19.0    39.7    10.2    13.1     9.5                   476.6
KFACF     2.8    12.8    32.6    11.0    22.7    18.2                   429.2
KNX F    13.1    42.5    28.9     2.0     5.9     7.7                   422.6
KTNQA    10.4    38.1    29.5     7.3     6.8     7.8                   420.9
KRTHA     9.8    18.7    49.6     5.8     7.9     8.1                   417.4
KJLHF    34.4    32.4    24.7     1.3     4.7     2.6                   411.5
KRLAA    10.1    34.3    38.9     7.0     5.8     4.0                   382.4
KKGOF     7.4    24.1    31.9     9.5    19.7     7.3                   321.6
KUTEF    22.6    41.5    29.9     1.9     3.1     1.0                   295.5
KACEF    27.6    39.6    21.3     2.1     5.3     4.1                   270.6
KWKWA    12.0    23.3    35.8     7.9     7.8    13.3                   259.3
KDAYA    42.4    25.9    16.6     2.4     8.8     3.8                   250.9
KNOBF    14.2    22.2    30.6    13.6    13.0     6.4                   246.2
KIEVA     2.7     4.4    20.4     9.5    25.6    37.5                   204.1
KALIA    14.5    32.7    29.6     4.5     9.9     8.9                   203.3
KNACF    60.2    26.0     5.2     3.8     3.8     1.0                   189.8
KGFJA    19.4    41.1    23.5     2.6     6.4     7.0                   164.9
KEZYF    43.7    39.9    15.0     0.6     0.7     0.0                   154.2
KKLAF     9.5    22.4    32.9    13.4    12.4     9.4                   150.8
KSKQA    18.3    34.1    25.6     8.0     4.8     9.2                   146.3
KBRTA     0.6    20.3    36.3    10.3    14.0    18.5                   126.8
KMAXF    25.0    29.3    27.4     7.3     6.6     4.5                   123.3
KFSGF    13.0    18.7    32.3     4.7     6.2    25.1                   116.5
KIISA    26.0    35.5    29.4     5.5     3.7     0.0                   111.9
KFACA     0.0    13.5    21.4     9.3    17.4    38.4                    90.6
KWIZF    27.9    36.9    25.0     1.5     8.8     0.0                    68.1
KWIZA    22.8    44.0    18.3     7.7     7.2     0.0                    37.7
POPULATION PERCENTAGES                                       BASE POPULATION
         15.9    25.2    26.7     6.0    11.7    14.5                 10828.4
NOTE; PERCENTAGES MAY NOT ADD UP TO 100% DUE TO ROUNDING.
END OF TRANSACTION
```

Source: Spring 1987 Arbitron data produced by CBS Radio *RADCOM*. Used by
permission.

ing certain program features, or highlighting promotions and tie-ins will be
part of the proposal. The object is to make it as easy as possible for the
buyer to include the station because stations that are hard to buy often don't
get bought. With everything now in hand, the salesperson makes the submission to the buyer.

Figure 10–4. Computer Printout Showing Sample Reach and Frequency Analysis

```
 2260MODE
 R070,003,T,A2554,287,    ,    ,  ,5,01,N,                                    1/1
       MON-FRI           SATURDAY              SUNDAY
 STA    COST 6-10 10-3 3-7 7-12 6-10 10-3 3-7 7-12 6-10 10-3 3-7 7-12 CMB  INDEX
 KNX A 5000   4    4   4    4    1    1    0    0    1    1    0    0  1,0,0
 KNX F 3500   4    4   4    4    1    1    0    0    1    1    0    0  1,0,0
 KBIGF 4800   4    4   4    4    1    1    0    0    1    1    0    0  1,0,0
             0    0   0    0    0    0    0    0    0    0    0    0  1,0,0
             0    0   0    0    0    0    0    0    0    0    0    0  1,0,0
             0    0   0    0    0    0    0    0    0    0    0    0  1,0,0
             0    0   0    0    0    0    0    0    0    0    0    0  1,0,0
             0    0   0    0    0    0    0    0    0    0    0    0  1,0,0
             0    0   0    0    0    0    0    0    0    0    0    0  1,0,0
        CBS RADIO           1 WEEK REACH AND FREQUENCY ANALYSIS|
 LOS ANGELES       ARBITRON ADULTS 25-54 (000) TOTAL  AREA  POP=
 ARBITRON               SPRING 87|                              6,273.0|

                                      AVG|
 STAT.  FORMAT COST    ANN  REACH%  REACH# FREQ    GIMP     GRP   CPM    CPRP|
 KNX A  NEWS   $5,000  20    4.1%   258.6  2.0    518.0     8.3  $9.65  $606.06
 KNX F  SFTAOR $3,500  20    2.1%   134.4  2.1    287.7     4.6 $12.17  $764.19
 KBIGF  ADL CO $4,800  20    5.0%   311.3  2.8    858.5    13.7  $5.59  $350.88
                                 TOTAL COMBO  1|
 TOTAL COST  NO ANN REACH%   REACH #  FREQ     GIMP     GRP     CPM   CPRP|
    $13,300     60   10.9%    681.2   2.4    1,664.2   26.5   $7.99  $501.51|

 END OF TRANSACTION|
```

Source: Sample analysis using Spring 1987 Arbitron data as produced by CBS Radio *RADCOM*. Used by permission.

Making the Buy

The various station representatives' proposals are like pieces in a jigsaw puzzle and now the buyer will start to put them together to create a sensible picture. She will eliminate the marginal stations and begin seriously to blend the schedules of the stations she wants to use.

On her computer or with computer runs requested from a sales representative, she will plot a number of alternatives and analyze each prospective schedule for its reach, frequency, and cost per rating point. (See Figure 10–4.)

The upper chart shows the stations, the schedule—twenty announcements a week spread over various dayparts—and the weekly costs. The lower chart, which is the one-week reach and frequency analysis proper, reads across as follows: station call letters; format (All News, Soft Adult-Oriented Rock, Adult Contemporary); weekly cost; number of announcements; percentage of the total survey area reached; number of different 25–54-year-old adults reached; the average number of times each listener is reached (frequency); gross impression (GIMP); gross rating points (GRP); cost-per-thousand listeners (CPM); cost per rating point (CPRP). The bottom line ("Total Combo 1") shows the same data combined for all three stations.

This analysis can be made for various station combinations and for multiple weeks.

After the ideal combined schedule has been plotted and assuming that it has achieved the buyer's weight goals, she will pick up the phone to place the orders. She will also call the representatives whose stations she is not buying to explain why they have been eliminated from consideration, thus giving them reasonable rationales to pass back to their disappointed principals.

Quite often, however, the buyer will not be able to obtain the weight she needs with the available budget. She will need more money and she has three ways to get it:

- From budgets for other markets
- From budgets for other media, for example, television, newspapers
- By negotiating with the sellers

Before going back to her superiors and requesting revisions in the budget, she will carry her price negotiations with the sellers to their outer limits. She's playing in the fourth quarter and the game's outcome is on the line.

The buyer will usually throw the problem back to the salesperson by saying the station's rates are too high and that without some adjustment, the station will not be selected.

The salesperson will always be loathe to simply drop rates. It would leave the station susceptible to the same pressure the next time around. The defense is to repackage the proposal. In conjunction with the station sales manager, the salesperson will change spots and dayparts around in order to come back with a schedule that may develop more gross rating points and give the appearance of lower rates.

Until the orders are placed, this kind of back-and-forth negotiation will continue. Buyer and seller will continue probing and evaluating. The buyer will calculate the upper limit she can spend. The salesperson will determine how low the station will go to be included. All of this will usually occur in a short time span because the buyer rarely has time to make more than one overall buying recommendation.

When the game ends, both teams should be singing victory songs.

Buying and Selling Radio Networks

The same principles govern the buying and selling of radio networks. There are just far fewer players for the buyer to engage. In the network version of the game, there are bigger overall audiences and more money on the line, but procedurally the buyer and seller both perceive a network as if it were a giant radio station.

Planning for many radio network buys begins earlier than planning for market-by-market buys. For some advertisers, schedules for an entire season or even a whole year are placed "up front," well in advance of broadcast dates. For others—radio network schedules for movies are a good example—buying often occurs as close as a week before the start date. RA-DAR®, rather than Arbitron and Birch, provides the audience numbers required by the buyer.

For some advertisers, the buyer may be interested only in numbers of listeners designated by age and sex. For others, qualitative and psychographic characteristics must be factored in. Whatever the case, the process customarily begins when the buyer calls network salespeople with a radio network availability.

Each salesperson determines what his network has available for sale and prepares a proposal. Depending on the nature of the buyer's request, announcements that run throughout the network's programming, called "scatter plans," or announcements that run only in certain program segments, "special avails," will be submitted.

Pricing for certain programs, the World Series, the NFL Super Bowl, and Paul Harvey are examples, is normally set in advance and whatever negotiation occurs revolves about matters other than cost.

The cost-per-point and price negotiation for network schedules that run through the programming, however, is similar to the spot market negotiation. The dollar amounts are simply larger. A considerable number of syndicated shows are also subject to price bargaining.

The buyer has one additional and vital function when constructing a network scatter plan schedule or buying a nationally syndicated show. Despite the fact that there is an overall national audience and cost-per-rating point goal, the audiences delivered in each major market should be individually evaluated. Radio networks, as noted in Chapter 6, do not deliver near-equal audiences in every market. A good affiliate delivers a large audience. A poor affiliate delivers a smaller number of listeners.

One large advertising agency that buys a considerable amount of network radio for movies checks the audience levels in from 50 to 75 separate markets. When holes appear in the schedule, spot radio overlays or unwired network buys are made to even out the coverage. Holes are less likely to appear when the buy includes several networks. The audiences of a number of stations in each market are being combined and where one network is weak, another is likely to be strong.

Because network clearances by affiliated stations cannot be precisely ascertained in advance, the advertiser's right to a postbroadcast analysis is frequently part of the buyer–seller negotiation. The buyer establishes a requirement that all individual station clearance records be provided for a given week. What week's schedule will be scrutinized in detail will not be known in advance by the network. If the analysis shows that the network has not delivered as contracted, there are penalties involved but more important, its poor clearance performance will be prejudicial when subsequent schedules are being considered.

Merchandising and promotion are also part of network packages. For substantial advertisers, a network may provide one of its leading personalities for a client's sales meeting, tickets for sporting events, in-store promotional material, premiums, prizes for contests, and the like.

A competent network buyer is careful to communicate with all the network salespeople, as she does when dealing with local and spot salespeople, when ready to place orders—both the winners and the losers—to explain how her decisions were made. Similarly, even if she feels a certain network is not likely to qualify for an upcoming schedule, she will usually call every network with every availability. Salespeople are extremely important resources and experienced buyers try hard to remain on the best possible terms with all of them.

Because network radio has always been an economical medium for a national advertiser, much of the competition for business has revolved around pure price. In recent years, however, networks who can document that their major market affiliates reached demographically and psychographically superior audiences have developed new advertisers by concentrating on listener quality. The CBS Radio Network has been especially effective in establishing new business-to-business advertisers by stressing its stations' qualitative attractiveness.

Buying and Selling Unwired Networks

The mechanics of buying and selling unwired networks are an amalgam of spot and network procedures. Depending on the advertiser's needs, the emphasis can be on one procedure or the other.

Because there are now only three important unwired players—Katz, Interep, and Supernet (the latter two both owned by the same megarep parent)—the buyer has very few salespeople to deal with and the relationships get quite chummy. Though the buyer is definitely in the driver's seat, each unwired network salesperson tries to persuade her to give him or her the initial opportunity to put together all the stations she needs for her buy. "Closeting" the competition, not giving other salespeople the opportunity to make a submission, is common in the unwired network business.

Though virtually every unwired buy is based on cost efficiency, there are no set rules for the game. Some buys are made on the basis of winner take all. In others, the buyer may look at the submissions and cherry-pick from all of them.

Except when filling in holes in a wired network buy, unwired networks are bought at either an even gross rating point level or a laddered GRP level. In the latter case, a buyer may specify that she wants fifty GRPs in the 100 largest markets and twenty-five GRPs in markets 101–200. The buyer will tell the salesperson how many GRPs she requires, desired frequency, sometimes specific stations or formats, and either a cost per point or bottom-line cost for the complete lineup of stations. She also sets the submission date. Most unwired buys come down quickly. Buys for movies, the major unwired advertiser category, may be specified and consummated in a few days.

Though the salesperson and the buyer have a complicated negotiation to cope with and though price is the foremost consideration, there is no cost saving to the advertiser with unwired networks. Although some skilled salespeople present the coalition of stations as if there were a saving, unwired networks are rarely more cost effective than spot radio and cannot come close in price competition with wired networks.

There are, however, enormous administrative savings. With each unwired network, the buyer deals with one sales representative, essentially places one schedule, gets one contract, and one invoice. It is relatively quick and easy.

The seller, however, is in a different situation. Each unwired network availability creates a mass of internal negotiations between the various components of the three major unwired networks. These unwired networks are built from the station lists of many representative firms, most but not all of which are divisions of the two giant megareps. The stations represented by CBS Radio Representatives, for example, are usually part of the Supernet network. Before the submission can be made, the unwired network salesperson must literally negotiate with the salespeople from all the components who present their various stations' proposals as they would to a buyer in a spot situation.

There is a legitimate internal competition to get stations on the submission list. Any one of the three unwired networks has a sufficient number of affiliated radio stations to deliver all the GRPs a buyer could want. The station selection is almost always made on the basis of efficiency, that is, the stations that come in at the lowest cost per point get on the list. The exceptions occur in cherry-picking situations where certain key stations may be specified. But price is the linchpin of unwired networks.

To the individual stations, being included on an unwired buy is no different than getting on a spot radio order. To the national sales representatives who make up the unwired amalgamations, however, there is an important additional advantage. It comes down to a question of who earns the sales commission. Regional buying agencies (see pp. 7, 103) are local buyers in markets where they maintain offices. When a regional buying advertising agency makes an unwired network buy, the order comes out of one location rather than out of several regional buying offices. Unwired thus turns a substantial number of *local* radio orders into *national* radio orders.

Media Buying Services

Most of the larger independent media buying services, which have proliferated in the last fifteen years, market their ability to buy more efficiently—that is, more cheaply—than advertising agencies. They do virtually no magazine or newspaper buying because with print media, there is little opportunity to deal with a range of prices and thus no opportunity to negotiate with sellers for lower rates.

Some, though not all, media buying services contract with their advertiser or agency clients to make broadcast buys at an agree-upon cost per point. If they are able to negotiate a lower cost per point with the media sellers, they retain that differential as part of their compensation. This circumstance strongly pressures the buying service to make cost consideration its highest priority and to rely almost exclusively on cost per point to make radio buys.

Regional Buying

Several giant advertising agencies and a few of the larger media buying services buy broadcast time regionally. J. Walter Thompson, Bozell Jacobs Kenyon & Eckhardt, and McCann-Erickson are prominent examples.

In a regional buying agency, the media plan, including goals, budgets, and demographic targets, is developed by the branch office that handles the account and then forwarded to buying offices in large cities throughout the country. If an account that is serviced in New York requires radio or television time in Chicago, buyers based in Chicago will negotiate and place the orders locally. Chicago-based buyers additionally would also buy time in Minneapolis, St. Louis, and other midwestern markets.

The rationale for regional buying is that it fosters the development of buying specialists who are concerned only with a handful of markets. They stay totally conversant with market and media conditions and, in theory, buy more economically and more effectively. Regional buying also increases the number of markets in which buyers can bypass national sales representatives and deal directly with the stations' local sales staffs. The advertising agencies that employ regional buying enthusiastically trumpet its benefits.

The purported weakness of centralized buying is that the buyer is distanced from the markets she has to buy. The weakness of regional buying is in the physical separation of media planning and media execution. Some regional buying agencies actually discourage buyers from talking with persons in the account and planning group. The buyer's line of communication is usually with her office's buying supervisor.

Though the planned cost per point characteristically is based on historical buying patterns executed by highly professional buyers, if the cost-per-point goal in a plan is unrealistic, a buyer situated thousands of miles from the planner is prone to make the buy fit the plan. A buyer who is regularly buying a market is loathe to buy it at a higher than normal cost per point—even to meet the qualitative specifications of the plan. Whether this occurrence best serves the needs of the advertiser is debatable.

Advertising agencies make an asset out of regional buying, especially when soliciting new accounts, but the system is imperfect. Because its intrinsic emphasis is quantitative, qualitative radio buying can suffer at the hands of regional buyers.

11

The Cost-per-Point Fallacy

When radio industry managers get together, one subject—the use of gross rating points to plan and buy radio schedules—is certain to be a subject of heated discussion. Blind reliance on the cost per rating point is a trap that reduces rather than improves the effectiveness of advertising on radio stations and even on qualitatively structured radio networks. Because television schedules are based on GRPs, using the same statistical base for planning radio is easy, precise—and wrong.*

With television, the viewer's loyalty is to programming, not to a TV station. At a program break, a station can lose all or most of its audience and quickly replace it with a different group. People are constantly tuning in and out of the various channels. In the course of a week, most viewers will be exposed to all of the network affiliates and some of the independents. A major television station will reach well over 90 percent of a market.

With radio, loyalty is to stations. Radio stations are like television programs. Because listeners listen to an average of less than three stations, the total audience is spread over a large number of stations and no single radio station will reach more than a fraction of the total market. Depending on format, listeners will stay with a single radio station for varying amounts of time. Talk, Ethnic, Classical, and Beautiful Music stations can hold listeners

*Some source material for this chapter provided by Robert Galen, Senior Vice President, Research, Radio Advertising Bureau. Used by permission.

**Figure 11-1. Computer Printout Showing Multiple Audience
Data Analyses Including Audience Turnover for Thirty
Los Angeles Radio Stations Ranked by Cumulative Audience***

```
                                  CBS RADIO
6AM-MID  MON-SUN        MULTIPLE AUDIENCE DATA ANALYSIS    POP MSA   4,558,000
ADULTS 25-54                      LOS ANGELES
ARBITRON  SPRING 87


STATIONS      MSA CUME          MSA AQH        MSA     TIME SPENT LIST.   AUDIENCE
            AUD(000) RANK     AUD(000) RANK    SHARE     HRS MINS         TURNOVER

KIISF         941.5    1        61.0   1       7.3%      8'   10''          15
KRTHF         750.2    2        49.5   2       5.9%      8'   19''          15
KOSTF         605.0    3        38.1   3       4.6%      7'   56''          16
KABCA         549.8    4        30.2  11       3.6%      6'   55''          18
KPWRF         537.0    5        36.1   5       4.3%      8'   28''          15
KLSXF         513.3    6        38.1   3       4.6%      9'   21''          13
KFWBA         496.7    7        17.3  19       2.1%      4'   23''          29
KTWVF         490.8    8        33.4   8       4.0%      8'   34''          15
KIQQF         489.1    9        33.7   7       4.0%      8'   41''          15
KBIGF         480.9   10        31.2   9       3.7%      8'   10''          15
KNX A         469.0   11        18.8  15       2.3%      5'    3''          25
KLOSF         433.4   12        25.7  13       3.1%      7'   28''          17
KROQF         357.5   13        21.0  14       2.5%      7'   24''          17
KJOIF         333.0   14        26.1  12       3.1%      9'   52''          13
KLVEF         320.2   15        30.4  10       3.6%     11'   58''          11
KTNQA         301.9   16        35.6   6       4.3%     14'   51''           8
KRTHA         288.3   17        17.8  16       2.1%      7'   47''          16
KRLAA         281.1   18        17.1  20       2.1%      7'   40''          16
KZLAF         275.6   19        17.5  18       2.1%      8'    0''          16
KLACA         272.1   20        12.2  23       1.5%      5'   39''          22
KMPCA         258.9   21        11.6  24       1.4%      5'   39''          22
KNX F         250.9   22        10.4  25       1.2%      5'   13''          24
KFI A         237.3   23        10.0  27       1.2%      5'   19''          24
KJLHF         233.4   24        17.7  17       2.1%      9'   33''          13
KFACF         209.3   25        10.0  27       1.2%      6'    1''          21
KUTEF         193.4   26         9.3  30       1.1%      6'    3''          21
KKGOF         180.5   27        10.1  26       1.2%      7'    3''          18
KWKWA         169.6   28        13.0  21       1.6%      9'   39''          13
KACEF         167.0   29        13.0  21       1.6%      9'   48''          13
KNOBF         155.1   30         5.8  34       0.7%      4'   43''          27
AQH PERSONS USING RADIO MSA:  18.3 %
MARKET CUME RATING MSA:       97.1 %
END OF TRANSACTION
```

Source: Spring 1987 Arbitron data produced by CBS Radio *RADCOM*. Used by
permission.
*Five audience measurements are displayed for 25–54-year-old adults in the Los
Angeles Metropolitan Survey Area: cumulative total week audience and ranking,
average quarter hour listening and ranking, average quarter hour share of
listening, average listener's time spent with station, and audience turnover.

for hours. An All-News station is likely to lose them in a much shorter period of time.

How long people listen affects the two dimensions of radio measurement: *average quarter hour*—an expression of how much time is spent with
radio—and *cumulative audience,* or total listeners. A station with high average quarter hours but low turnover might reach many fewer listeners than a
station with lower average quarter hours but high turnover. (See
Figure 11–1.)

Because a few television stations reach almost all of the population, an
advertiser with a good program dispersion can achieve excellent reach on a

multiple station TV buy. It can even be done with a well-crafted single station schedule. One hundred television GRPs—each point representing 1 percent of television homes—are capable of reaching a high percentage of all television homes. If 100 prime-time GRPs are bought in a series of markets, the achieved reach and frequency will be approximately the same for each market.

In budgeting for television, the initial determination is the cost per point. No matter if budget or weight drives the schedule, the procedure is relatively simple. If a GRP costs $50 and the advertiser has $5,000 to spend, he can afford 100 GRPs. If the weight goal is 200 GRPs, the schedule will cost $10,000.

One hundred GRPs on radio is unlikely to get a good reach against any broad-based demographic target. One hundred GRPs on a single radio station would net an alarmingly low reach and a very high frequency. Because each radio station's cumulative audience is different, no two stations' GRPs will contribute identical reach. The consistency of the measurement that works so well in television breaks down when applied to radio. (See Figure 11-2.)

The chart on page 107 shows two radio stations with identical average quarter hour ratings but with different cumulative audiences. Station A has a larger number of people tuning in but they listen for shorter periods. Station B has fewer listeners but they stay with the station for longer periods of time.

A forty-eight-announcement schedule run over four weeks develops a 16.7 percent reach on Station A and a 9.3 percent reach with Station B. With identical levels of GRPs—in this example, 91—Station A reaches 80 percent more different people than Station B.

To effectively buy radio, the determinant is the mathematical probability of reaching someone in a *given station's* audience. A person tuned in for long periods of time can be reached with a few commercial announcements. To reach someone who is listening for only a short period of time, a comparatively large number of spots are needed. Buying equal numbers of gross rating points and using GRPs as the statistical base distorts the process.

Note that reach × frequency = GRPs. For example:

20% reach × 5-time frequency = 100 GRPs
10% reach × 10-time frequency = 100 GRPs
5% reach × 20-time frequency = 100 GRPs

A well-planned radio campaign should be based on a reach and frequency goal against the target demographic. Depending on the advertising message being presented and the available budget, the reach and frequency goals will differ. The number of stations to be bought and the amount of spots to be run will vary.

With radio, the geographical coverage of the different stations must also be factored in because, unlike television stations where coverage patterns are

Figure 11–2.   **How Stations' Reach Differ**

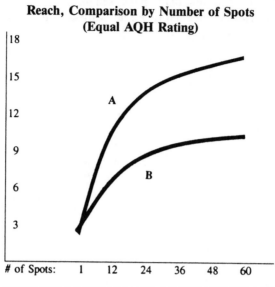

Reach, Comparison by Number of Spots
(Equal AQH Rating)

Market Reach At Varying Spot Levels						
Station	1	12	24	36	48	60
A	1.9	11.3	14.4	15.8	16.7	17.2
B	1.9	7.4	8.8	9.1	9.3	9.4

Source: Radio Advertising Bureau. Used by permission.

generally comparable, two radio stations in the same city can cover widely differing areas. Station rates are based on the total audience, not on just the metro audience, yet most radio buys are based on metro GRPs. This creates another distortion in the process.

Relying *principally* on cost per rating point to structure radio advertising campaigns is an ongoing folly.

When buying or selling time on radio and television or space in newspapers and magazines, it's easy to get completely enthralled by media considerations. Many buyers and sellers fail to recognize that media is not advertising. Unfilled time and blank pages sell nothing. It is the marriage of a creative product, a commercial or an ad, with a medium that makes the process work.

12

Creativity
Process and
Product

When advertising fails, it usually fails creatively. Advertising failures, nonetheless, are frequently blamed on the medium. But as it says in an old song, "It ain't whatcha do. It's the way how you do it."

An Empty Canvas

Vin Scully, who is considered the best baseball play-by-play broadcaster in the business, comparing his work on radio and television, said, "The freedom of radio is incredible. With television, you try to put captions on pictures that are already furnished. The director directs, the cameraman points, and you talk. Radio is like an empty canvas. You step into the booth and paint whatever you like."

The same blank canvas beckons to advertisers. The better the painting, the greater the rewards. Many advertising heavyweights believe that despite television and magazines' siren appeal to writers, radio offers the greatest opportunity for pure creative effort.

The late Archibald MacLeish once remarked that "the ear is half a poet," and will accept fantasies the other senses reject. A television screen and a printed page are absolutes, bounded by pragmatic sight. What is heard on the radio can be expanded by imagination into wondrous visions that exist only for the listener.

When a radio script has a disciplined creative structure, when a radio performance moves with an exacting sense of pacing, and when salesmanship and showmanship are balanced in a perfect partnership, the listener is uniquely drawn in. This happens no matter what the creative technique—humor, drama, music, straight announcement, or sound extravaganza.

But it's easier said than done.

Be Churchillian

How to start? A writer could hardly do better than to follow the five rules Winston Churchill enumerated for successful speechwriting.

1. Begin strongly.
2. Have one theme.
3. Use simple language.
4. Leave a picture in the listener's mind.
5. End dramatically.

Winnie may well have said it all. Creative directors, teachers of advertising, free-lance radio specialists, and successful radio writers, however, have produced useful checklists and guidelines beyond count for crafting effective radio commercials. Not every pronouncement can be applied to every commercial. And inspiration does count!

On Being Heard

If the listener pays no attention to a commercial, it might as well not have run. The dynamics of making certain a commercial is noticed vary for foreground and background radio stations because people listen to different kinds of radio stations in different ways. If someone is tuned to a news broadcast, it is a reasonable assumption—one backed by research—that this person is actually listening. The commercial, therefore, should immediately encourage the listener to continue listening. The more a commercial blends with the newscast, the more likely this is to happen.

On a music radio station, as on a television program, the commercial is likely to represent a sharp break from the programming. Here the commercial must instantly discourage the listener from mentally relaxing. The more dramatically the commercial jumps out at the listener, the less likely it is to be overlooked. Although a musical commercial on a music radio station assuredly could be missed by some listeners, if it's an outstanding spot, it still might be more effective than a spoken commercial. Why? Because this station's audience has tuned in to hear music.

On All-News or News/Talk stations, musical spots will absolutely stand out. They might also signal the listener to tune out mentally. A strong case can be made for designing commercials that don't break the mood.

There is no solution to the problem of "being heard," but most creative directors want a radio commercial to stand out. If you don't pull the listener into the commercial, if you're not heard, the advertising won't produce. Few advertisers produce different commercials for different radio formats.

(Anheuser-Busch is a prominent exception. Their radio commercials are tailored to ethnic groups, demographic segments, and station formats.) Most companies produce a single set of announcements that run on every station they schedule. With all-purpose commercials, opt for standing out.

Who Is Advertising?

If the advertiser isn't strongly identified, the commercial has to be a loser. There is so much confusion with name and brand identification in broadcast media, both radio and television, that every copywriter should be aware of this disturbing possibility. Confusion can exist whether the advertiser is a local furniture store or a leading national advertiser.

Generally, on radio, brand or name identification should be established early and often. Some writers contend that if you follow this dictum too faithfully, you will end up with a dull commercial. Certainly there have been superb radio commercials where the principle has been ignored. There have been many more commercials, however, where brand or name identification was sacrificed on the altar of creative dilettantism.

Is the Advertising Premise Valid?

Advertising works only if its underlying premise is valid. Some ghastly radio commercials have rung up incredible numbers on the cash register though outstanding commercials undoubtedly would have been even more effective. If a decision has to be made, however, between saying what has to be said or being patently "creative," the option should be made for saying what has to be said. The selling idea, some creative directors would say the *great* selling idea, must come first.

Don't Drown in a Sea of Features

A few years ago, a new financial newspaper began daily publication. It was weighted down with statistics and charts for the most part unavailable elsewhere—tools for the serious investor. To obtain subscribers, this financial journal advertised heavily in newspapers, magazines, direct mail, and radio.

The advertising copy in all media centered on the newspaper's unique numbers-oriented editorial features. There was little or no emphasis given to the value of these voluminous statistics, though the publication's management obviously believed the charts would make the reader a better, sharper, smarter, richer investor.

But that wasn't said in the commercials. The radio advertising would have been more productive if it concentrated on the *value* of all the numbers rather than the numbers themselves; if the commercials ended by saying to the listener, "Which means to you...."

Advertising bromides, like old soldiers, never die. One of the hoariest is that people do not buy electric drills because they want drills. They buy drills because they want holes.

In radio, where time is finite and comprehension must be swift, there is no point in asking a commercial to be a directory. A bald recitation of features without relationship to benefits is a prescription for failure.

Drawing Pictures

Charles Osgood, of CBS News, penned an answer in verse to a listener who wrote him saying radio isn't visual. It went, in part, like this:

You say that on the radio, there are no pictures there.
You say it's only for the ear, but I say *au contraire,*
There are fascinating pictures on the radio, you see,
That are far more picturesque than any on TV.

No television set that's made; no screen that you can find,
Can compare with a radio, the hitter of the mind.
For the pictures are so vivid, so spectacular and real,
There isn't any contest, or at least that's how I feel.

When possible, radio commercials should be written for the ear *and* the eye. One of the most memorable radio campaigns of recent years, the Stiller and Meara campaign for Blue Nun Wine, was created by copywriters *and* art directors. Jerry Della Femina, head of the agency that produced the commercials, described the process:

When we create a radio commercial, we invite the art directors—the visual people—to work right along with the copywriters [because] writing for radio is probably the most descriptive piece of work you can do. It gives you the chance. . .to stimulate the listener's imagination.

When a storyboard is prepared, as was the case with each Blue Nun spot,* its purpose is to make certain that the spoken words will evoke the desired visual image. The more memorable the visual image, the more effective the commercial.

STILLER: Good evening, miss. Will you be dining alone?

MEARA: (sob) Yes!

STILLER: What can I get you?

MEARA: Manicotti.

STILLER: Oh, I'm sorry, miss. We're all out.

MEARA: No, I mean Carmine Manicotti. He just broke our engagement. He had his mother call and tell me.

STILLER: Oh, the swine.

---

*Blue Nun commercial printed by permission of Schieffelin & Somerset Company.

MEARA: No, she was very sweet about it.

STILLER: No, I meant Carmine. Anyway, may I suggest the Surf 'n Turf tonight?

MEARA: Is that some new singles bar?

STILLER: No, the Surf 'n Turf is our delicious combination of lobster tail and filet mignon. Perhaps to raise your spirits a very special wine to go with it.

MEARA: Can I get a wine that goes with seafood and meat?

STILLER: Certainly. May I bring a little Blue Nun to your table?

MEARA: Oh, I'm sure she would be very sympathetic. But I'd much rather be alone.

STILLER: No, no, miss. Blue Nun is a wine. A delicious white wine that's correct with any dish. It goes as well with meat as it does with fish. And perhaps after dinner, cantelope?

MEARA: I don't see cantelope on the menu.

STILLER: No, that's me. Stanley Cantelope. I get off at eleven. Maybe we could go out on the town.

ANNCR.:   Blue Nun. The delicious white wine that's correct with any dish. Another Sichel Wine imported by Schieffelin and Company, New York.

Get the picture?

The Great Straight Commercial

An advertising trade publication runs a special radio section each year that includes scripts of ten commercials the editors consider best of the current crop. In any year, most will be two-voice dramatic humorous spots. Some will be elaborate musical productions. But you can make money betting that not one will be a single-voice straight commercial.

As a veteran judge of many award competitions, this author can categorically state that judges do not vote awards to straight spots. Winners have to sparkle. Humor sparkles the most. Music sparkles second. Nonetheless, thirty or sixty seconds of straight copy can be emotional, exciting, and provocative if a great reading is combined with strong, direct writing.

In 1986, the actor Eli Wallach did a series of commercials for the sugar industry.*

WALLACH: What's the matter with sugar? I'll tell you what's the matter. Nothing! Sugar's pure. Sugar's real. And I've got news for you, sugar has only sixteen calories a teaspoon. Only sixteen! Come on, you're not using one of those substitutes, are you?

---

*Sugar industry commercial printed by permission of the Sugar Association, Inc.

Don't you know there's not a single artificial ingredient in real sugar. Pure, sure, sixteen-calorie sugar. Because some things just can't be improved.

ANNCR.:   Sponsored by the Sugar Association, Incorporated.

The words on paper seem unremarkable but Wallach's distinctive voice and intelligent reading made the sincere, factual copy written by North Castle Partners pound across like great theater. There was a beautiful interaction of script and performance.

One of the first computer companies to address its advertising to business decision makers rather than computer technicians was Cado Computers (now Contel Cado). Around 1975, before the advent of the small, modestly priced microcomputer, a Southern California advertising agent named Rob Robinson pioneered the use of radio for Cado's business computers. His successful straight commercials were not exceptional but his choice of talent was magnificent. Cado's commercials were read by the late actor Richard Basehart. Basehart, who spoke in rich, commanding tones, made ordinary commercials extraordinary.

There's nothing wrong with an outstanding oration when you have the required elements—the right voice and the right copy. Churchill, Roosevelt, and Kennedy did all right without dramatic humor or music.

Live Radio—Beauty or Beast?

The live commercial has disappeared from the television screen but it's still as healthy as ever on radio. Radio can be, at the advertiser's option, the most flexible of media. Commercials can be revised in midschedule to accommodate changing market conditions. Response mechanisms, like telephone numbers or addresses, can be localized without re-recording. Messages can literally be written overnight and broadcast on very short notice.

With live talent, advertisers can economically accommodate demographic, ethnic, and regional differences. A Texas drawl in Houston, a broad New England "a" in Boston, and a southern inflection in Atlanta assuredly evoke empathy for the nonlocal advertiser.

Commercials done by station personalities or announcers are still a staple of local radio, but most advertising agencies with national and regional accounts shun live spots. They think that way about live commercials because they feel restricted to a single voice reading straight copy. Also they worry about consistency. On one station a live announcement could sound excellent and on another, terrible.

There are, however, instances where either timeliness, association, or economy are overriding considerations.

It was timely for a hot chocolate drink marketer to place a commercial schedule during the winter months on a Boston radio station. The live copy urged mothers to make sure their kids had consumed a hot mug of the stuff before going off to school. Each morning's announcement opened with a line stating what the temperature was in Boston that moment. It was topical and convincing, and it could only be done live.

Farmers Insurance Group, whose products are not sold in every state, wants to avoid innocuous all-purpose oral footnotes, such as "Not available in such-and-such states." Writing live announcements for use in specific states rather than the entire country, Farmers has been able to tailor its advertising messages to fit local needs. Because Farmers is a heavy play-by-play sports advertiser, the company feels it also benefits from the sports announcers reading its copy.

Radio is the fastest way of moving information. In 1981, when the air traffic controllers' strike created schedule havoc, almost every airline in the U.S. turned to live spot radio. When deregulation resulted in a competitive pricing frenzy, airlines couldn't tape commercials fast enough to keep fare information and discount offerings current. Live radio's lead times were even shorter than newspapers.

Radio is the only broadcast medium where live commercials are acceptable. This is a unique advantage. For example, advertisers who sponsor Paul Harvey would have it no other way. Harvey does the commercials and his association with his advertisers is as important as the copy itself. In practically every city in America, there are radio personalities whose implied endorsements are enormously valuable. Having them do live commercials makes sense.

There are categories of advertisers—direct response advertisers are a prime example—who must immediately evaluate results of ads and commercials. Their evaluation is used to fine-tune the copy and as a result, new versions of a basic commercial may be needed almost instantly. Live radio answers this need in an economical way.

Live radio has its place and its particular strengths should not be overlooked in the creative process because it is "poor man" radio. It is a creative option that is ignored by most advertisers and their agencies.

Oft-Forgotten Sound Effects

Sound effects, when they are logical and understood by the listener, help plant an image in the mind. Sound effects can even become the principal element of the commercial. Still, most writers overlook sound effects, concentrating on voices and music only.

Sound effects must be identified. Otherwise they may confuse the listener or be missed altogether. Old time radio writers handled this perfectly. Their dialogue always told the audience what they were hearing.

VOICE: The storm's getting mighty bad, paw.
SFX: *(rain on tin roof, wind, creaking)*

Almost thirty years ago, Stan Freberg originated his outrageous style of humorous commercial that became the role model for the genre. Freberg did not rely solely on clever dialogue. He understood and made heavy demands on sound effects. This commercial, produced for the Radio Advertising Bureau, is one of his most notable.*

MAN: Radio? Why should I advertise on radio? There's nothing to look at. No pictures.

FREBERG: Listen, you can do things on radio you couldn't possibly do on TV.

MAN: That'll be the day.

FREBERG: All right, watch this. (*clears voice*) OK, people, and now when I give you the cue, I want the 700-foot mountain of whipped cream to roll into Lake Michigan which has been drained and filled with hot chocolate. Then the Royal Canadian Air Force will fly overhead, towing a 10-ton maraschino cherry which will be dropped into the whipped cream to the cheering of 25,000 extras. All-l-l right, cue the mountain!

SXF: (*massive rumbling followed by a huge splash*)

FREBERG: Cue the air force!

SXF: (*drone of planes*)

FREBERG: Cue the maraschino cherry!

SFX: (*long whistle and dull splash*)

FREBERG: OK, 25,000 cheering extras!

SXF: (*enormous crowd roar*)

FREBERG: Now, you want to try that on television?

MAN: We-e-ell.

FREBERG: You see, radio's a very special medium because it stretches the imagination.

MAN: Doesn't television stretch the imagination?

FREBERG: Up to 21 inches, ye-e-es.

The Two Sides of Humor

When she was good, she was very, very good,
but when she was bad, she was horrid.
—Traditional Nursery Rhyme

Humor is wonderful and terrible.

---

*Stan Freberg commercial printed by permission of the Radio Advertising Bureau.

Humor is a serious business. Comedians and great comedy writers are rarely carefree people. For many, worrisome might be a better description. Too many copywriters, however, think knocking off humorous commercials is a piece of pie.

Good humorous commercials stand the test of time. Bad humorous commercials start to pall after the initial hearing. There are, nonetheless, an inordinate amount of awful, would-be-humorous spots running on the radio.

The unfunny funny spot does the most disservice to advertisers who are selling a serious product or service, one that involves making a serious purchase decision. Buying something that involves thousands or tens of thousands of dollars isn't frivolous and whether humor should even be considered is a fair question.

Many big advertising agencies have given up using their own people to do humorous radio and, in some shops, to do any radio at all. On this point, Ken Roman, of Ogilvy & Mather, said:

> When there is a radio campaign to be created, all the major agencies go to outside specialists.... And what do we buy? Most often, humor. We don't take radio seriously. Radio doesn't go on the reel or in the proof book, so we cop out and go to a comedian ...but is humor right for everything?

It's a legitimate question.

In many cases, humor is right. If there is little product differentiation, advertising can go a long way to create it. Humor is ideal for establishing that perception. Products that are sold in a supermarket—package goods, wine, beer, cleaning products, and so on—have made effective use of comedy. In recent years, automobiles, banks, and business services have moved cautiously to humorous radio.

The best humorous radio commercials are done by a small number of outside specialists—Dick Orkin (Dick Orkin's Radio Ranch); Bert Berdis, Jim Kirby, and Alan Barzman (Bert, Barz & Kirby); and Joy Golden (Joy Radio) are the most prominent. The grand old man of comedic commercials, Stan Freberg, whose work in the 1950s and '60s blazed the path for today's radio funny people, is still in the business, as are old time radio veterans, Bob Elliot and Ray Goulding (Bob & Ray). Chuck Blore (Chuck Blore & Don Richmond) does some comedy but is known mostly for his musical and dramatic spots. It would take a museum wall to hang all the awards this tiny group has garnered.

What sets these few people apart from the hundreds of copywriters and radio producers who try to emulate them is that they are genuinely gifted comedians and comedy writers. They understand humor and they devote their lives to it.

Like all great comedians, each has a distinctive style. In advertising terms, each has his or her own solution to advertising problems. When called in to do a radio campaign, they invariably fit their own type of humor to their client's problem. They all understand that you can't do a hilarious bit for fifty seconds and then just throw in the advertiser's name. The selling message must come through as a result of the humor.

Joy Golden's view is that people want to be entertained, not lectured to. Advertising, she feels, should not make you miserable. Dick Orkin contends because of the similarity between competitive products, the memorability of the commercial is what makes the difference.

But as a case in point, as great as they are, one Dick Orkin spot resembles another because Orkin invariably plays the leading role in his comic minidramas. When too much of his work is on the air at the same time, the potential exists for a traffic jam in the listener's head. His clients, however, don't complain. Orkin, a very funny man, believes his humor appeals both to the emotions and the imagination, and that's how he entices people to listen and to remember.*

SFX:	(car screeching to a halt)
POLICEMAN:	Pardon me, sir, would you step over to the patrol car, please?
MAN (Orkin):	Oh, hello, officer.
POLICEMAN:	Do you have business in this neighborhood, sir?
MAN:	Yes, I live four blocks from here. It's the brick colonial with the crack in the driveway.
POLICEMAN:	What are you doing out this time of night, sir?
MAN:	Well, I got all ready for bed, see, and darned if I didn't forget to pick up a copy of *Time* magazine at the newsstand today.
POLICEMAN:	What type of coat would you call that, sir?
MAN:	This is a hou-hou-house coat. You see, I spilled cocoa on mine and I just grabbed by wife's. I guess the puffy sleeves look a little silly. (embarrassed laugh)
POLICEMAN:	Do you want to get in the car, sir?
MAN:	(under his breath) In the car?
SFX:	(car door slams)
MAN:	See, I just don't go to bed without a *Time* movie review or something from the "Modern Living Section."
POLICEMAN:	Yes, sir.
MAN:	I tried reading something else but there isn't anything like *Time*. Do you know, officer, how many editorial awards *Time* magazine has won?
POLICEMAN:	No, sir.

Time magazine commercial printed by permission of Dick Orkin's Radio Ranch.

MAN:	And *Time* is so respected. I'm a firm believer along with Winston Churchill that you are, uh, what you read.
POLICEMAN:	Uh, huh.
MAN:	(*with tear in voice*) Oh, please don't send me up the river for wearing puffy sleeves.
SFX:	(*car coming to stop, door opens*)
POLICEMAN:	You're home, sir.
MAN:	I'm home. (*sob in voice until he realizes what policeman has said*) Oh, thank...God bl...(*clears throat*) OK, bye.
SFX:	(*car door slams*)
ANNCR.:	*Time* magazine, the most colorful coverage of the week.

The agency for Fromageries Bel's Laughing Cow Brand Cheese, TBWA, New York, gave Joy Golden the assignment of producing a radio campaign that would make this French import jump out of the supermarket deli case. The initial budget of $375,000 (which isn't much more than it costs to produce some thirty-second television commercials) had to cover time and creative. TBWA was able to advertise only in six major markets.

Joy Golden's first series was, in her words, "heavy ethnic," and she attributes its success not only to her deftly prepared scripts but to careful casting. "If you've got first-rate words coming out of second-rate vocal cords, you've got troubles." Her client's sales went up 52 percent nationwide after thirteen weeks of radio.

The second Laughing Cow series, "Valley Girl," won almost every creative award there was to win in 1986 and 1987. There were no sound effects and no music, just a racing, breathless reading.*

VALLEY GIRL:	OK so like I was sitting here eating a little round laughing cow in a red knit bag and counting how many pairs of shoes I owned when the phone rang. I said like hello. And this deep voice said like hi. And then like I totally freaked. I said this isn't the highway patrolman? He said yes it is. I said no it isn't. He said yes it is. So I said really? Then he said like what're you doing. I said eating a little laughing cow and counting my shoes. He said got any extras? I said they're too small for you. He said that's OK, I eat twenty of them. I said even the suede ones? He said oh no. I said officer, why don't you come over and have the laughing cow instead. Mild Mini Bonbel. Nippy Mini Babybel and smooth Mini Gouda. You know like really awesome and naturelle. Six delicious cheeses in little net bags.

---

*Laughing Cow commercial printed be permission of Joy Radio.

Each one wrapped in wax with a cute little zip thing. He said what's your address? I mean talk about an inquisitive mind, right? I said you want crackers, too? He said OK. So I said OK. So OK, OK? So *then* I said what should we do after we eat the cheese. He said I'll watch you count your shoes. I mean like I've had heavy relationships before, but like this is intense.

The cheese sales were intense, too.

Terrific Music

When music is part of a radio commercial, it should be *great* music because the music of a radio spot penetrates deep into the consciousness. This does not mean you need the New York Philharmonic Orchestra. A small combo, a seductive guitar, a single flute are all capable of providing terrific music. There are those who think that outstanding radio campaigns of the future will be based on the yet untapped potential of synthesizers.

Chuck Blore, whose body of commercials makes more use of music and sound than any other radio specialist, feels that sound is one of the most powerful but least-used broadcast tools.

Picturing Yourself

"Picture yourself at the wheel of your spanking new Stutz Bearcat cruising along an open, country road. The wind whips through your hair and the tangy scent of new-mown hay is flowering the air...."

Picturing *yourself.* It is one of radio's unique characteristics. Because the voice in the commercial is talking to *you,* asking *you* to visualize yourself in a certain situation, you do it without a thought.

When an actor is cast in a television commercial, personification is automatically limited to that actor. If you do not see yourself in the actor, the TV spot may lack conviction for you.

Plucking the Heartstrings

Television writers readily admit it's impossible to be cerebral in thirty seconds, no less fifteen. If a commercial is to be memorable, it must provoke an emotional response. Love me or, at least, like me. Buy me.

Radio writers, who usually have the luxury of sixty seconds, frequently overlook the challenge to pluck the heartstrings. Because radio is the only medium that does not demand the use of the eyes, the words can be more intimate and involving. They have more power to move emotionally.

Phil Dusenberry, the executive creative director of BBDO, put it this way:

Radio speaks with the one thing that attracts writers to the profession in the first place—words. Powerful, moving, persuasive collections, and stylization of words....Nothing treats the spoken work better than radio. Nothing caresses and massages the language or brings such sweet poetry to the consumer.

NW Ayer hit on a great line for AT&T Long Distance and the agency turned to Chuck Blore to do the "Reach Out and Touch Someone" radio. For more than eight years, Blore created a series of commercials that intimately involved the audience and evoked a strong emotional response.*

CATHIANNE:	Hello.
DANNY:	Oh, hi. You probably still remember me, Edward introduced us at the seminar...
CATHIANNE:	Oh, the guy with the nice beard.
DANNY:	I don't know whether it's nice...
CATHIANNE:	It's a gorgeous beard.
DANNY:	Well, thank you, uh, listen, I'm gonna, uh, be in the city next Tuesday and I was, y'know, wondering if we could sorta, y'know, get together for lunch?
CATHIANNE:	How 'bout dinner?
DANNY:	Dinner? Dinner! Dinner's a better idea. You could pick your favorite restaurant and...
CATHIANNE:	How 'bout my place? I'm my favorite cook.
DANNY:	Uh, your place. Right. Sure. That's great to me.
CATHIANNE:	Me too. It'll be fun.
DANNY:	Yeah...listen, I'll bring the wine.
CATHIANNE:	Perfect. I'll drink it.
BOTH:	(*laugh*)
DANNY:	Well, OK, then, I guess it's a date. I'll see you Tuesday.
CATHIANNE:	Tuesday. Great.
DANNY:	Actually, I just, uh, called to see how you were and y'know, Tuesday sounds fine!
SFX:	(*phone hangs up*)
DANNY:	(*yelling*) Tuesday....Ahhhh....She's gonna see me Tuesday. (fade)
SINGING:	Reach out, reach out and touch someone.

---

*AT&T commercial printed by permission of Chuck Blore & Don Richmond.

The honesty of the spots made people feel good about what they had heard and by osmosis feel good about the telephone company. Blore says, "If someone feels good about what you tell them, they will want to like your product even before they try it and they will try it because you got to them in the best possible way...with feeling."

Before the radio campaign began in 1974, AT&T's research disclosed that long distance telephone calls were primarily associated with expense. Even though rates had become quite moderate, making long distance calls was seen as a costly luxury.

The "Reach Out and Touch Someone" campaign changed the total perception of long distance phone calls. A long distance call became a way to be with someone you cared for.

The Cost of Words

The novelist E. L. Doctorow once said, "Sometimes I think films are about spending money. If I want you to experience rain, I have a wonderful tool— the word *rain*. It doesn't cost very much, and I can make it a cool rain or a warm misty rain coming down through a green forest. If my friend, Francis Ford Coppola, wants to make rain like that, it costs him $60,000 a minute."

Substitute the words "TV commercial" for "films." Relate what Doctorow has said to television creativity and radio creativity and the respective costs of each. With radio, the production costs are no more for great words than they are for pedestrian words.

The top radio specialists charge from $7,500 to $10,000 for creative, studio costs, and talent for a totally new commercial. Subsequent spots in a series normally cost less. If music is not a factor, the total can be reduced considerably. This is the upper limit for production expense, the possible exception involving the use of extraordinarily high-priced talent. The lower limit is no production cost at all for many live commercials.

Production costs are today's single biggest problem for television advertisers. An Association of National Advertisers report on the situation in 1985 showed that TV production costs had increased 99 percent in the preceding five years. With average costs exceeding $100,000 for a thirty-second commercial, elaborate commercials have run between $300,000 to $750,000 to produce. Whole radio campaigns, production *and* media, can be run for what it cost to produce one television commercial.

The attitude toward radio production expenditures is usually more relaxed than it is with television. Many advertisers are willing to spend a few thousand dollars more to get outstanding commercial radio production— the great music, the perfect talent— because the base cost level is so low. The Anheuser-Buschs of this world don't settle for broadly executed, all-purpose radio spots. Because the expense is modest, they produce a number of commercials, each designed to run on a certain kind of radio station and to influence a specific listener.

Hitting the Narrow Target

When a commercial is aimed at a slim target, there is an inherent danger. Unlike a mass-directed advertising message, if you miss a narrow target, *you miss it all.*

There are situations when it makes good creative sense to identify the group you want to talk to. Starting a commercial with "This is a message for corporate financial officers..." will be a turnoff for 99.9 percent of the audience. But it won't be for the 1/10 of 1 percent you want to reach.

Busting Through the Bureaucracy

It is not only the lower cost of production that encourages writers and producers to take creative chances with a radio campaign. There are usually fewer approval levels to cope with. Agency creative review boards tend not to subject every step to painful scrutiny. Clients are likely to take a less conservative view. The result can be fresh, innovative, and effective radio advertising.

But not always.

Agencies don't think their clients are always right but they do recognize the clients always sign the checks. They believe they know what will and will not be acceptable to their clients. They often make their judgments based on what will be acceptable to the safest of the safe-players. The safest of the safe-players are invariably in middle management jobs. The product manager at a big package goods company can be a killer if a rule shattering radio concept is being proposed.

Chuck Blore has dealt with this problem firsthand. Blore says:

> Regardless of the size of the budget, everybody in broadcast advertising wants to be safe. An idea that doesn't sound like a commercial is rejected half the time. If it sounds like a spot, then they say, "That's what my commercial should be like."...Refusing to give the listener the routine or the expected may be harder to get accepted, but once you do the response is so much greater.

John O'Toole, for many years chairman of Foote Cone & Belding, contended that the only way to create great advertising was to go to the top. The higher up advertising involvement goes in a client organization, he concluded, the better the advertising will be. To obtain an outstanding creative product, whatever the medium, top management must believe that advertising is an absolutely critical element. Then top management will not be inhibited by the fears of lower echelons and will take the risks that have to be taken.

Busting through the bureaucracy involves a risk of its own but there are instances when it is a creative responsibility.

Another Kind of Creativity

How can be as creative as *what*. Magazines have always traded on this. Note pop-ups, tipped samples, double covers, and inserts of all kinds. Radio commercials can be tagged or run with doughnuts (holes in the middle for live inserts), piggybacked with dealer announcements, carry live copy changes daily, and have centrally produced spots swiftly delivered all over the country by satellite transmission.

With radio, however, creative department participation almost always ends when the initial commercial production is finished. The media department's reach and frequencies and costs per point take over totally. How the commercial is used should be a concern—some might say, a responsibility—of its creators.

The purpose of running a full page newspaper ad is to make a major impact, to be sure an ad is seen by every reader of that day's paper. Perhaps an advertiser who needs to make a major impact should buy an extremely heavy radio schedule—as much as an announcement an hour for a week's time. This would guarantee that the commercials are heard by almost every listener of the station.

Perhaps some advertisers should follow up megabuck weekend television exposure with Monday–Tuesday radio schedules to provide direct dealer support. "You saw our half-million dollar TV spot on the Super Bowl telecast. Now here's how to do something about it."

The salient point is that creative people who freely suggest print space increments in which they want to work ("We need a two-page spread!") rarely consider how commercials will be utilized.

But they should.

TV without Pictures?

Radio frequently is used to complement a television advertising campaign. The concept of imagery transfer is practical and effective. When radio and television are artfully used in tandem to reach the same advertising objective, a listener can hear the audio spot and evoke the specific pictures of the TV commercial.

Even when an image transfer is being sought, the practice of simply lifting radio commercials directly from television sound tracks is a pallid method of creating radio announcements. When an advertiser's radio and television campaigns have differing objectives, lifting TV tracks can lead to outright disaster. Lou Centlivre, managing director of creative, Foote Cone & Belding, Chicago, commented, "I feel radio is the stepchild of campaigns really designed for TV.... The kids today don't know radio. They just take the sound off TV and expand it to a sixty[-second spot]."

When television-generation copywriters consider radio a second-class medium, they do a disservice to the advertisers who use it. According to Jim

Thompson, United Group head at Leo Burnett, United Airlines's formula used to be "to take a great music track from the TV commercials, punch a couple of holes in it for an announcer and call it radio."

There is increasing recognition that this is not the way to go. United changed its view several years ago after the agency developed a straightforward television campaign that did not include a rich music track. Commercials designed specifically for radio had to be created. In Thompson's words, "A new attitude developed about radio, a new excitement. Our best people were now working on radio."

Significantly, United enlarged the subjects they were covering with radio because the new work was of such high quality. Announcing prices and schedules had been radio's chore. Themes like the caring attitude of United's people and the scope of its service—heretofore covered only in sixty-second television spots and color spreads in magazines—began appearing in radio announcements.

Unless radio advertising is designed for radio, its creative potential will never be reached.

There have even been instances when radio was adapted for television— or so it appeared. In 1984, Shearson/American Express ran a television campaign called "Minds over Money." It used no pictures, just a series of words on a dark screen and a voice-over reading them aloud. At the time, *Business Week* reported that the spots were so successful that the company was substantially increasing its budget.

Who's Writing Radio

Most senior creative people in large national agencies do not want to work on radio advertising. An account supervisor at a New York agency was quoted in *Advertising Age.* He said, "I have asked my creative teams to explore the use of radio on behalf of a client's campaign. From the look on their collective faces, you would think I had grown a third eye."

This is a horrendous problem faced by the radio industry. Its corollary is that most radio writing in large agencies is, as one creative director noted, "always given to the rookies." No wonder a handful of outside specialists do most of the memorable work.

Ed McCabe, former president of Scali McCabe Sloves, is a member of the prestigious Copywriters Hall of Fame. His attitude about doing radio advertising was summarized by Phil Dougherty, the advertising columnist of the *New York Times,* who wrote:

> Of course, there are those high-priced and allegedly highly creative agency people who feel they are too important to do advertising for a medium like radio....For them, a word from Mr. McCabe: "These are certainly not creative people. These are mo-

rons who can't grasp this simple idea—the world is a far better place as a result of Michelangelo not having said, 'I don't do ceilings.' "

A study by Radio Recall Research documented that a *memorable* commercial increased average recall 300 percent. When radio is recommended, there is a responsibility shared by agency and client to shoot for memorability—to be certain that the best possible creative effort is put forth.

Bombing Out—The Creative Flip Side

Radio commercials do indeed play in the theater of the mind, but just as on Broadway, there are more bombs than hits. Many advertisers do not consider the potential negative effects of bad commercials.

Radio is the ultimate personal advertising medium. In most cases, the communication is between the advertiser and *a single person*. Although this is assuredly one of radio's great strengths, it can work against the advertiser whose commercial, for whatever reason, turns the listener off. It isn't necessary for the listener to switch stations. All he or she has to do is mentally tune out. And it happens far too often.

There are many reasons why listeners are turned off by a commercial announcement.

- *Subject Matter of No Interest to the Listener.* There is no real solution to this problem (e.g., a man hears a commercial for an exclusively female product). It does, however, point up the importance of quickly convincing the right listener when he or she *should* be interested. If you're trying to reach women, forget the men but make certain you have each woman's attention. The beginning of a radio commercial is critical.
- *Boring Commercial.* The yawn is the world's greatest sales inhibitor.
- *Badly Written Commercial.* There are a lot of negative reactions to badly written commercials but one of the worst is a lack of comprehension. The listener doesn't understand what the advertiser is trying to say. There is a simple way to eliminate this problem. Read the script or play the spot to several unbiased people before putting it on the air. Writers and producers know their subject so well that comprehension is something they may not even consider.
- *Overproduced Commercial.* Overproduction overwhelms content. The ensuing confusion is usually too much for the listener to fathom.
- *Overcomplicated Commercial.* An ad in any medium can do about one thing well. If you ask a radio commercial to do more, it will probably be too complicated and thus ineffective. Simplicity counts.
- *Strident Commercial.* The screaming syndrome. Strident commercials are irritating. If what the announcer is screaming about, however, hap-

pens to be something you're interested in buying, the commercial may still work. This is one of advertising's great anomalies.

- *Nonhumorous Humorous Commercial.* As noted earlier in this chapter, unfunny and silly commercials do not stand repetition.

- *Muddy Sound Differentiation.* A welter of voices that blend into aural mush make hard listening in heavy traffic. This happens all the time. Spots are evaluated under studio conditions where the slightest nuance of sound can be distinguished. But they are heard by *real* listeners when they are driving at high speed on a crowded, noisy highway.

- *Client as Talent.* Resist this! It is usually disastrous. There are very few Lee Iacoccas.

- *Exaggerated Claims.* Commercials that strain the listener's intelligence are almost always ineffective even in the rare situations when the exaggerated claims are true.

- *Imposition of the Advertiser's Moral Position.* Although the person on the receiving end of a commercial does expect to be exhorted to buy or do something, being preached at isn't in the contract. A financial institution in Southern California regularly runs prayers in its commercial time at Thanksgiving and Christmas. The management apparently thinks it is performing a public service when it is, in fact, creating substantial resentment among listeners who have not turned on their radios to hear even nondenominational religious programming. Never forget the environment. What's fine in one may be awful in another.

There is, unfortunately, a lot of bad advertising out there. There is bad television, bad print, and bad outdoor. And bad radio.

Advertisers and agencies may contend that "radio didn't work" after they have inflicted inferior creative efforts on the suffering audience. Radio stations can become extremely upset when they are forced to air bad spots. They are concerned about the dreaded tune-out—listeners punching buttons and switching stations because of a commercial so horrible they can't bear to listen to it.

Commercials work negatively as well as positively. Bad ones don't only *not* make sales. They *lose* sales for advertisers, lose audience for radio stations and even lose accounts for advertising agencies.

Successful advertising depends on skillfully coping with a number of forces. In the majority of situations, the creative solution—what is said—is the first among equals. How, when and where the creative work is displayed are the other essentials. When the blend is right, in radio as in other media, the results will be felicitous.

13

The Payoff
How Radio Sells

Advertising works.

Even bad advertising works if the product or service meets a consumer need. Most automobile dealer advertising is a testimonial to that fact. Good advertising works much better than bad and great advertising works even better yet.

It's surprising, however, how many advertisers don't *really* believe advertising works. They know they *must* advertise but the vaguely undisciplined process is disturbing to them. The manager who is comfortable only with rigidly defined quantitative guidelines and objectives sees advertising, with its curious mix of creativity and numbers, as the oddball marketing element.

When advertising is assessed, there is a prevalent feeling that waste is rampant. John Wanamaker, the New York department store mogul of the early twentieth century, reputedly said he knew 50 percent of his advertising dollars were wasted, he just didn't know which 50 percent.

It follows that if advertisers, and agencies, are prone to question whether the total process is legitimate, their basic question will be broken down into subquestions.

Do newspapers work?

Do magazines work?

Do outdoor boards work?

Does television work?

Does skywriting work?

Does radio work?

Not one of these questions has any validity. Media, whatever the type, offers only blank space or time. Only when the word "advertising" precedes the query is any sense made. Advertising is an interrelationship of a message and a medium. An increment of time never sold anything. What is heard or seen during that increment of time has to do the trick.

Does *radio advertising* work?

Of course. It works with incredible success when all or some requirements are met—when the commercial addresses a consumer need, the message is newsworthy, the creative level is acceptable/excellent/outstanding, the advertising objectives have been defined, the station or network selections are targeted correctly, and the weight is adequate.

Still, the medium must often confront skeptics. To veteran radio executives, there is probably no more disturbing pronouncement than the phrase, "Let's test radio." (Few advertisers or advertising agency executives ever say, "Let's test television.") If there is legitimate testing to be done, it is not the testing of the medium, but of the material being broadcast, the mix of stations and formats, scheduling and the weight.

Many advertisers have put sensational stuff on the radio and have been very successful. Although it never hurts, supercreativity is not the key element in every success story. Some radio advertisers merely said the right thing at the right time in a straightforward manner. Some have found innovative ways to capitalize on the medium's intrinsic capacity to personalize, segment, localize, and so on.

The late Arthur Godfrey, one of the great radio personalities and salespersons, said there are only two essential elements required to motivate the listener. They are, "Listen to what I'm saying and believe what I'm telling you."

The fact is: Good radio advertising gets results.

A Problem in Hawaii

Several years ago the tourism industry in Hawaii was caught in a slump. Tour operators, who book block space for groups months in advance, must release unwanted space thirty days prior to scheduled arrival date and more booked block space than normal was being cancelled. With occupancy declines of 10 to 20 percent, a Sheraton executive was quoted in *Business Week* as saying that Hawaii's middle-income tourism business had "fallen to pieces."

In most parts of the U.S., Hawaiian vacations are planned well in advance, but on the West Coast many upper-income people make an impulse decision to "go over to the Islands for a week." Sheraton, the largest hotel operator in Hawaii, ran radio commercials in every major West Coast city from San Diego to Seattle suggesting the idea of an island holiday. The appeal was to listeners who might otherwise not have considered such a vacation. Sheraton chose stations whose listeners included more affluent segments of the population because individual travel is more costly than group travel.

The radio advertising brought sufficient response to cover most of the rooms cancelled by tour operators. The time span between the day a listener called the Sheraton reservation center and the desired arrival date averaged nine days. Sheraton was able to schedule and run its radio spots in under thirty days—after it received block cancellations and knew how many rooms had to be booked quickly.

The Sheraton campaign was newsworthy for several reasons. It proved that radio has a capacity for planting a new idea in the minds of listeners: in this case, taking an individual trip to Hawaii on short notice. It also documented that radio has a strong capacity to induce action. The medium is not passive. Finally, it showed that from concept to execution, very little time is needed to put radio advertising on the air. Stations are used to receiving last minute orders so buying time was no problem. In Sheraton's case, its agency at that time, Fawcett McDermott Cavanagh, wrote and recorded the commercials in a Honolulu studio in a few days, but had even swifter action been required, the commercials could have been broadcast live.

Turning on a Dime

Speed was absolutely essential to another campaign that came out of Honolulu. This one was for the Hawaii Visitors Bureau.

During one winter in the early 80s, the eastern part of the United States experienced a string of storms. Residents battled heavy snowfalls and below-freezing temperatures for days on end. At that time, there were plenty of empty hotel rooms in Hawaii. On a Monday, the HVB, through its agency, Milici-Valenti/Doyle Dane Bernbach, decided to run radio commercials in the major cities on the eastern seaboard extolling the tropical temperatures of the Hawaiian Islands and suggesting that the freezing easterners hop on a Honolulu-bound airplane *right now.*

Radio time was bought by Doyle Dane Bernbach's Los Angeles office on Tuesday and the commercials were produced in Honolulu the same day. Tapes were shipped by air to the radio stations that night and the campaign was on the air Thursday morning in New York, Boston, Philadelphia, and Washington.

As a result of this Hawaii Visitors Bureau campaign, a lot of people happily swapped frost-reddened noses for sunburned ones.

Flying a Jordanian Airline

There is a healthy segment of the U.S. population that is unlikely to fly on an Arab-owned airline under any conditions, so Alia, the Royal Jordanian Airline, has always had unique marketing problems. Alia began flying from New York to Amman, Jordan, in 1977. In 1979, Houston was added as a gateway, and in 1981, Chicago.

Alia had a limited number of flights leaving Houston and Chicago. This led to tight budgetary restraints. As reported in *Television/Radio Age,* Boerner Advertising Associates, Alia's agency, reasoned that with a few major radio stations in each market, they could reach potential Alia passengers—mostly business travelers—in a wide area of the Southwest and the major midwestern population centers.

The first effort was made in Houston. Using KTRH, an All-News station, and KPRC, which has a News/Talk format, Alia's message was directed to businessmen and -women through announcements in morning and afternoon drive time, newsbreaks in other parts of the day, plus sponsorship of business news features. The agency reported, "The result was easily measurable. When the radio spots ran, the telephones lit up. Hardly anyone mentioned [our] print advertising."

When advertising began in Chicago, local newspapers were dropped and some television was added, but the backbone of the effort was All-News radio WBBM, and WGN, Chicago's high-rated personality station. Again, according to Boerner, "Every caller was asked how they found out about Alia's service. . . . Travel agents, tour wholesalers, and cargo agents had all seen or heard Alia's broadcast spots. The lesson was that radio. . . provides immediate and almost total access to Alia's various market segments."

Influencing Top Management

The highest level of management in business and finance, and corresponding high levels in government, are populated by people who don't watch much television. Respected studies, such as Simmons Market Research Bureau's *Study of Media and Markets,* show them at the bottom of the viewing barrel. Corporation presidents spend a lot more time reading newspapers and magazines and listening to the radio than they do watching the tube.

In 1987, the CBS/Simmons InfoRadio Study measured media habits of top management men in the twenty-five largest markets in the country (Table 13-1). It showed the following:

Table 13-1.   **Percentage of Television Viewing by 25–54-Year-Old Men in Top Management in the Top Twenty-Five Markets**

Program	Reach Percentage	Index
Sixty Minutes	20.7	106
CBS Evening News with Dan Rather	4.8	44
ABC Nightline with Ted Koppel	3.3	121
Major Golf Tournaments	7.4	100

Source: Simmons Market Research Bureau 1986. Reprinted by permission.

All of these programs have a reputation for being aimed at a qualitatively high-level audience but the indices indicate they're not doing particularly well with top managers. An index of 100 means that the percentage viewing is exactly equal to the percentage that demographic represents in the total population. If this is perplexing, don't feel badly. Even MBAs from Harvard, Stanford, and the Wharton School have problems understanding precisely how indices are developed. Just recognize that 100 is a dead-on average, numbers slightly above 100 don't mean much, numbers substantially above 100 are good, and numbers below 100 are bad. An index of 44 for the CBS Evening News is very bad; 121 for Ted Koppel is 21% better than average.

A company called TRW's target audience is top management. In 1974, TRW, Inc. started a long-range corporate campaign aimed at increasing the awareness of the corporation among a group described by Maureen Hartigan, TRW's corporate advertising manager, as "the shakers and movers in the business and financial world."

TRW doesn't sell anything that ordinary people can buy, other than its stock. Like all publicly owned corporations, however, its stock price is an extremely important business indicator and a low awareness of TRW among investors is not desirable.

Awareness was low. Until 1965, TRW had been known as Thomas Ramo Woodridge and invariably when large corporations change their names, there is a time lag before investors catch on. (When Swift & Company changed its name to Esmark, sales in its stock slipped so sharply that the company was dropped from the Dow Jones Index.) Research showed there was nothing, neither strong negatives nor positives, associated with the new name. TRW then took steps to do something about it by aiming advertising to the business and financial community.

TRW ran television and radio campaigns in ten cities populated by people the corporation considered important— Boston, Chicago, Cleveland (its headquarters), Detroit, Houston, Los Angeles, New York, Philadelphia, San Francisco, and Washington, D.C. There were seven control markets where no broadcast advertising was used. Ads also ran in a few business and consumer publications.

By 1980, the combined broadcast campaigns, which featured outstanding commercials, raised awareness among key executives in the ten cities to 90 percent. In comparing television and radio, Ms. Hartigan commented, "We believe radio offers the more immediate impact. . . [and] additional flexibility."

Tom Dawson, a former Radio Division vice president who spent thirty years at CBS, recalled a meeting with Robert D. Lundy, TRW's vice president for public relations and advertising. Speaking several years after the TRW campaign began, Lundy stated one of the most important ingredients in determining the success of TRW's advertising was what he called "executive playback." It had been, Lundy told Dawson, "very positive, very consistent and very strong. I've been on trips with our president when the radio

Table 13–2.   Comparative Media Reach Percentages and Indices against 25–54-Year-Old Men in Top Management in the Twenty-Five Largest Markets

Medium	Reach Percentage*	Index
Fifty InfoRadio Stations**	42.9	221
Television		
Sixty Minutes	20.7	106
CBS Evening News	4.8	44
ABC Nightline	3.3	121
Bill Cosby Show	24.9	112
Cheers	23.3	135
Moonlighting	13.5	112
College Basketball	12.0	88
Pro Football	30.2	97
Golf	7.4	100
Tennis	6.8	144
Magazines		
Business Week	9.7	235
Fortune	6.2	271
Wall Street Journal	12.8	356
Time	28.3	174
Newsweek	20.5	162
Sports Illustrated	20.6	129
Inc.	4.5	374

Source: Simmons Market Research Bureau 1986. Reprinted by permission.
*Radio reach is based on projected five-day cumulative audience; television reach is based on average half hour; magazine reach is based on average issue.
**InfoRadio consists of fifty radio stations in the first twenty-five markets defined as radio stations listened to for news and information but not exclusively All News or News/Talk formats.

advertising has been mentioned to him [by his peers] and it started a conversation on some product or growth area the company is trying to get into."

With 85 percent of TRW's broadcast dollars going into television and only 15 percent into radio, Dawson thought it impressive that the peer-level playback resulted from TRW's radio. It confirmed a large body of research. It's difficult to reach top level executives with television but they all listen to the radio. (See Table 13–2.)

Increased Sales

The first widescale application of electronic mail, Mailgram, was introduced by Western Union and the U.S. Postal Service in 1970. In the years when Mailgram was highly promoted, radio was its principle medium.

In the early 70s, testing for media effectiveness took place in six new markets over a thirteen-week period. Radio, television, and newspapers were used exclusively in two markets each. A balance of the three media was used in eight other markets. All the expenditures were at approximately the same level.

In the radio markets, volume went up 35 percent. In the television and newspaper markets, volume increased 27 percent and 19 percent respectively. The volume in the eight markets with a balanced media mix was up only 17 percent.

These results set the course for a heavy use of radio. Mailgram's agency, Trout & Reis, developed memorable commercials that featured such personalities as Don Knotts, Bob & Ray, and Rodney Dangerfield. The key copy line was, "Impact of a telegram at a fraction of the cost," and the underlying theme of the commercials was demonstration—demonstrating where and when the listener could use a Mailgram.

By 1980, there were five Mailgram messages being sent for every domestic telegram. In the ten year period from 1971 to 1980, Mailgram's annual revenue increased from $3 million to $95 million. Radio's share of the advertising budget increased from a hefty 42 percent in 1975 to an astonishing 77 percent in 1980.

Unfortunately, you cannot hear Mailgram radio commercials today because Mailgram is no longer advertised on radio. This raises a legitimate question: Why not?

According to Jack Trout, president of Trout & Reis, Mailgram's management made a strategy change in the early 1980s with which the agency did not agree. The original strategy stressed impact—the *impact of a telegram*. The revised strategy stressed speed—the fact that a Mailgram was always delivered the next morning. The agency argued without success that a strategy change was not called for because speed was assumed by consumers because of Mailgram's kinship to the telegram.

New radio commercials, these featuring Ethel Merman, emphasized overnight delivery—the *speed of a telegram*. A downhill slide began which eventually resulted in a virtual cessation of advertising, and a divorce between Mailgram and Trout & Reis. Advertising success stories sometimes turn into advertising nonsuccess stories. Even Ethel Merman, who was great in the Mailgram commercials, couldn't make everything come up roses.

All Wine Bottles Look Alike

Many marketers of premium wine still believe you have to show a picture of the bottle in the advertising. (How else would the brand be recognized?) They think label identification is essential prior to purchase, but they are wrong.

Almost all wine bottles and almost all wine labels look alike.

Even Gallo, the largest marketer in the United States, usually gets only a few facings for each individual wine. Smaller wineries are lucky if a specific varietal wine gets more than one facing. The result is that, except when passing hard-to-come-by bulk displays in a market or liquor store, the premium wine customer has to seek out the brand he or she desires.

In wine marketing, *name identification* is more important than label identification. Radio has a unique capability of heightening name identification.

Without doubt, the most successful advertising campaign that ever ran for a wine brand used the comedy team of Stiller and Meara on radio. The product was an undistinguished, sweetish German wine called Blue Nun; the outstanding, humorous commercials were created by Della Femina, Travisano & Partners. (See Chapter 12.) Previous advertising had all been "picture of the bottle" ads in magazines.

Before the great white wine explosion began in the late 1970s, only a sophisticated slice of the populace was knowledgeable about table wines. Most Americans were uncertain about what wine went with what food. The advertising strategy developed for Blue Nun positioned it as the wine you could drink with meat *or* fish. A hostess or host could serve it with anything. All fears were assuaged.

The first Blue Nun radio announcement ran in 1973 and the last in 1979. In that period, Jerry Stiller and Anne Meara did twenty-four Blue Nun commercials. So consistently did the agency stay on the strategic line that the last spots produced sound exactly like the earliest ones.

Blue Nun started off selling 70,000 cases a year and when Schiefflin decided to drop the radio in favor of an anemic television campaign in about 1980, sales were over 1,600,000 cases a year. The decision to get out of radio was heatedly opposed by the agency and the disagreement led to its loss of the account.

Jerry Della Femina still recalls the Blue Nun account fondly. "I can't think of a single campaign that did more for a client than Blue Nun. And it was all radio."

Breaking the Mold

Large companies frequently embark on corporate advertising campaigns to encourage investors to buy their shares. TRW's advertising, described earlier in this chapter, is a prominent example. A long-standing taboo, however, inhibited advertisers from coming out and saying, "Buy our stock. You'll make money."

A decade ago, a paper manufacturer called Great Northern Nekoosa decided to do just that in order to add vibrance, vitality, and a sense of immediacy to its continuing print advertising. A series of radio commercials directed to New York City's large investment community were produced by its agency, Lord Geller Federico Einstein. This is one of them.*

---

*This copyrighted commercial printed by permission of Great Northern Nekoosa Corporation.

SFX:	(*in the stock exchange: bell clanging, crowd roar*)
ANNCR.:	With so many companies vying for investor interest, it's possible for even big and respected companies to be overlooked. There is, for example, a paper-making company that many investors have never heard of, yet of the hundreds of papermakers in the United States, only four or five can match this company's two-million-ton capacity. During the last five years, this paper company's earnings per share have grown at an average annual rate of 30 percent. It has three operating divisions and each holds a leading market position. One division, for instance, makes and sells more ground wood printing paper for telephone books and mail-order catalogs than any other North American producer. With its strong earnings growth and solid competitive position, this paper company has every reason to expect a growing future. It is listed on the New York Stock Exchange under the symbol GNN. The name is Great Northern Nekoosa Corporation.
SFX:	(*crowd roar, bell clanging*)
ANNCR.:	A name for investors to remember.

A number of hurdles had to be cleared before these announcements could go on the air. Initially, the Securities and Exchange Commission had to agree that nothing false or misleading was being said. The SEC eventually gave its approval. Because the plan called for advertising only in New York and only on the few radio stations that securities analysts and large investors were likely to listen to, the initial order was placed on the CBS All-News station, WCBS-AM.

The agency reasoned that if the Great Northern Nekoosa copy was approved for broadcast by CBS's tough continuity clearance department, every other station on the schedule would run it. The CBS reaction, however, was a resounding, "No way!"

When asked why not, the CBS continuity clearance director replied that the commercial was obviously in violation of SEC regulations. Great Northern Nekoosa politely explained that the SEC had given its approval to the copy and unless CBS could show that in some way it violated Federal Communications Commission regulations, the advertising should be accepted. CBS's legal department was brought in and grudgingly concurred with the advertiser's position. The eight-week campaign went on the air.

The Great Northern Nekoosa commercials ran only in the mornings between 6:00 A.M. and 8:00 A.M. Wall Street executives are mostly commuters who get up early and who listen to the radio at home while dressing and having breakfast. They are also avid news followers because external events can sharply affect the financial markets.

The modest campaign was a smashing success. Not only was substantial activity in the market generated for Great Northern Nekoosa, the public relations effect for both the advertiser and its agency was astounding. An agency executive described what happened:

> It was absolutely incredible. Everybody and his brother got phone calls. They wanted to know who was doing this and how it was being done. For such a small amount of money, the response was incredible. We got phone calls. They got phone calls. Everybody was just fascinated with that campaign.

Although the radio advertising was not the only force at work, six weeks after the campaign ended, the index of Great Northern Nekoosa's stock price was considerably ahead of the Dow Jones index and the indices of the ten leading paper companies.

When you walk down a new road, every sensation is heightened. In radio as well as in other media, so much advertising is imitative that innovative, fresh, mold-breaking advertising is able to jump out and holler, "Hey, pay attention to me!" And when that happens, you get results.

Brother against Brother, Sort of

In 1984, a unique event of unparalleled impact occurred in the United States. *The* telephone company—that is, the 107-year-old Bell System—was broken into seven regional telephone companies. Old Ma Bell, AT&T, no longer had loving, supportive children spread about the country. Now she had competitors.

In the good old regulated days, AT&T itself never dealt with the consumer. The consumer talked to the local telephone company and the local company had only AT&T to go to. After deregulation, that all changed. In a marketing environment permeated with frustration, confusion, and uncertainty, AT&T itself had to go head-to-head against the regional operating companies to sell and lease consumers everything from individual instruments to complete business systems. The underlying task, as described by Richard D. Draper, advertising director of AT&T Information Systems, was "to change the customer's ingrained behavior of calling the local phone company for their telecommunications needs and convince them to call AT&T instead."

Radio was utilized for four reasons: it was efficient against the small business community; none of AT&T's principal competitors were making extensive use of radio on a nationwide basis; it allowed AT&T to maintain the strong, continuous presence that was deemed essential; and it provided the flexibility needed to focus on various products and systems.

AT&T's far-reaching television campaign, which used actor Cliff Robertson as the company's spokesman, was in the tradition of *the* telephone company, straightforward and serious. The Information Systems' radio campaign was directed to the small business community. Here staid AT&T moved in a totally different direction using a lighthearted approach. As Draper explained, "Humor could be applied to the problems being experienced by small business customers and to the solutions offered by AT&T." Dick Orkin's special brand of humor credibly humanized the giant corporation.

Today AT&T believes that most small business customers are likely to call them rather than the local Bell operating company for telephone products and services. Radio advertising played a major role in bringing about this change in attitude.

One or Two Stations

Creative media tactics can bring success to a radio advertiser. In both Houston and Chicago, radio was one of two media employed by Alia. (See page 131). This tends to be the norm. National advertisers rarely put all their dollars into one medium but this does not detract from radio's success quotient in this instance. The significance of Alia's case is that the two-station-per-market strategy was right on the button.

Many advertisers and agencies shrink from using radio this narrowly. They won't consider a radio campaign unless a "sufficient" reach and frequency can be achieved.

Have any campaigns consisted of advertising run only in a single magazine? Certainly. There are numbers of documented cases and they are not limited to special interest magazines. For example, it might be logical for a motorcycle helmet manufacturer with a small budget to run all his advertising in a single motorcycle publication. Many advertisers who seek broader markets, however, have run one-magazine campaigns in *Time, Business Week, Sports Illustrated,* and scores of other periodicals or one-newspaper campaigns in the *Wall Street Journal.* By advertising in a single periodical, the advertiser acknowledges that he is not reaching all his prospects. He is communicating with a selected segment of his prospects. It's a good strategy and radio is no stranger to it. One- and two-station campaigns are common on local radio and virtually every important station in a market can document some successes.

In Los Angeles, Accountants Overload and its subsidiary, Accountants Unlimited, are fifty-two-week advertisers on KNX. The companies provide temporary and permanent financial service employees to business. They seek to talk with top management, comptrollers, and personnel managers. Since they started in business in 1977, they have successfully done this by placing virtually their total schedule on this powerful CBS All-News radio station.

In Chicago, Laventhal & Horwath, a leading accounting and consulting firm, was the first major company in its field to advertise on radio. To attract entrepreneurial clients, they offered a tax brochure exclusively on WBBM, another All-News station. They averaged more than a hundred requests per day during the time their schedule ran in 1986–87.

Michael Jackson, a polished and articulate talk show host on KABC, Los Angeles, picked up a trick from Arthur Godfrey. Jackson incorporates his personal endorsement when he does the commercials for many of his sponsors in his clipped English accent. Hamburger Hamlet, a highly successful and distinctive restaurant chain, has placed its entire budget for the past decade in the hands of Michael Jackson, as has Glabman's, a small chain of family-owned furniture stores.

A number of multimarket advertisers have used radio in this limited fashion as well. National advertisers such as Rolm Telephone, Prime Computers, Neutrogena T-Gel Shampoo, and Viadent Toothpaste have placed entire radio budgets on a single radio network. Rolm and Prime's commercials, addressed to chief executive officers and chief financial officers, were heard only on CBS Radio Network affiliates. Neutrogena and Viadent's messages are still running on the 1,300 ABC affiliates that carry Paul Harvey. Because their commercials are carried by only one network, they are all one-station advertisers in individual markets.

An advertiser does not have to cover the entire universe to get a satisfactory return from his investment. There will be a lot more one- and two-station success stories when there is a greater acceptance that radio, like magazines, is a segmented medium. The art is in matching the station to the advertiser's target market.

From Little Acorns and the Virtue of Consistency

When Philadelphia-based Automatic Data Processing was expanding its data processing service bureaus in the early 1970s, its first move in a new city was to buy an existing data-service company and change the name to ADP. Then the company would begin to build its computerized payroll and personnel record business by sending direct mail to the city's business community.

This is exactly what ADP did when it moved into San Francisco in about 1974 except that the hitherto successful formula was not uncovering clients. The direct mail was not pulling. In San Francisco, the Bank of America's Business Services division had been selling the bank's excess computer capacity for a number of years. It dominated the outside data processing payroll business that ADP sought. When San Francisco business executives received mailings from Automatic Data Processing, a company virtually none of them had ever heard of, the mailings routinely ended up in the wastebasket.

ADP was persuaded by an enterprising local radio salesman to buy one announcement a day, five a week—so few that virtually no radio station would accept such an order today— on a financial market report featuring Ray Hutchinson.

For several decades, Hutchinson broadcast every weekday from the Pacific Coast Stock Exchange in San Francisco on KCBS. Virtually every San Franciscan who had an interest in the securities markets and the world of commerce was acquainted with Ray Hutchinson. When business people began hearing about Automatic Data Processing on Ray Hutchinson's market reports, they stopped throwing away their direct mail and instead began to respond to it. The imprimatur of an accepted radio authority provided the needed bona fides for this new entrant into the tightly knit San Francisco business community.

After this toe-in-the-water introduction, ADP embraced radio with considerable enthusiasm and today is a large national radio advertiser. Twice a year, in the spring and in the fall, ADP runs radio schedules addressed to small- and medium-sized business decision makers in a large number of major markets. ADP's director of communications, Stan Livacz, commenting on the target audience, said, "Radio. . . enables us to reach that *unknown* decision maker who is not listed in the directories but does listen to radio."

The ADP commercials have consistently been built around the same dramatic device—an ADP spokesman talking with a satisfied ADP user. They are soundly written, professional commercials but they don't win awards for outstanding creativity. What makes them so successful is that they *sound the same* year after year. Though each year's announcements are current in content and newly produced, the familiar format lets each new commercial build on the ones that ran previously. Even though a listener does not hear an ADP commercial from one fall to the next spring, ADP's radio works like a snowball rolling down a hill. It picks up weight from what has gone before.

Automatic Data Processing is an outstanding radio success story for two reasons: the company advertises consistently on the medium, and each year's advertising builds on the foundation of previous years' advertising.

Reacting to Mother Nature and Other Forces

When Mother Nature flexes her muscles, just about everyone snaps on the radio and tunes into the station that reports what's going on. The versatility that radio exhibits when emergencies—or, for that matter, fast-breaking news stories—arise enhances its value as an advertising medium. Radio has totally replaced the newspaper extra ("Read all about it!") as the carrier of extraordinary public information. Certain formats, notably All-News, News/Talk and, to some degree, stations with strong personalities, attract listeners from all over the dial at times of crisis.

On April 14, 1983, a sudden spring blizzard hit the Minneapolis-St. Paul, Minnesota area. More than 400 schools and many businesses called one radio station, WCCO, to report closures because WCCO is *the* emergency clearing house for an area with a radius of 100–150 miles. It is an accepted fact in this storm-prone part of the country that if life is disrupted by a natural calamity, you find out what's going on by listening to WCCO.

Some radio stations will even accept stand-by schedules from advertisers to run, for example, during heavy rain- or snowstorms or when the temperature drops below a certain level.

It would be almost impossible to have a nonweather emergency trigger a commercial schedule. (The reverse does happen, however. Almost every airline specifies that its announcements be cancelled for a designated period of time after a major air crash.) The benefit to the advertiser of emergency coverage and the subsequent swelling of radio stations' audiences is inadvertent but nonetheless valuable. In covering a major disaster, however, announcements are frequently dropped in order to provide more time for the coverage of hard news.

When a catastrophe occurs, radio is invariably the first source of the news. A listener from Carmel, California, wrote to KCBS in San Francisco:

> At the time of the recent [1983] earthquake which was felt quite strongly here in Carmel Valley, I immediately tuned into KCBS Radio. Within 120 seconds, your news reporter commented on the earthquake and stated there would be a continued follow-up to determine the extent of the quake. We wish to commend you on your excellent coverage of the quake and of other important news events.

The space shuttle *Challenger* exploded and plunged into the sea on Tuesday morning, January 28, 1986. KNX, Los Angeles, had prearranged with Scarborough Research to execute a special audience study three days after the next major catastrophe and accordingly the survey was conducted. It showed that the All-News station's audience increased in size by six times and that 18 percent of all radio listeners in Los Angeles had tuned to the station that morning. The other All-News station, KFWB, had a 12 percent share. A combined radio audience of 30 percent was following news of the disaster on two radio stations.

Station and program managers believe—and the ratings services bear them out—that regardless of the reason why new listeners tuned into a station, some of them will stay with that station after the original experience. There is, therefore, an increased continuing audience for advertisers as a result of a radio station's emergency coverage.

"This Bud's for You"

Per capita beer consumption has been declining for years but you wouldn't know it looking at Anheuser-Busch. The St. Louis-based brewery sold twice as much beer in 1987 as it sold in 1977, more than its two largest rivals combined.

Anheuser-Busch follows a strategy called "total marketing," which means that it pours money into everything—all media, all kinds of advertising, point-of-purchase, sporting events, rock music concerts, and more. This strategy, however, is based almost entirely on target marketing. Advertising for its various beer brands—Budweiser, Bud Light, and Michelob are the most important—has been specifically aimed at blacks, whites, Hispanics, women, blue-collar workers, computer fanatics, auto racing fans, skiers, waitresses, bartenders, servicemen and -women, immigrants, Texans, Californians, New Yorkers, and baseball umpires, among other varied market segments.

With radio, the company's practice is to design commercials for Country, Urban Contemporary/Black, Album-Oriented Rock (AOR), and Contemporary Hit Radio. Sometimes, if they consider a musical spot with a Lou Rawls or B. B. King to have a lot of crossover value, they may run it in three or four formats.

Most of Anheuser-Busch's efforts go into Los Angeles, New York, Boston, and thirty-three other markets where 75 percent of all beer is consumed. Seventy percent of the company's estimated $450 million advertising budget goes into sports programming. Anheuser-Busch owns the St. Louis Cardinals baseball team and in 1987 had exclusive advertising rights with 21 of 24 major league baseball teams, 21 of 28 National Football League franchises, 300 college sports teams, and most professional basketball, hockey, and soccer teams. Though many of these rights include television, the company is by far the world's largest sponsor of radio sports.

Anheuser-Busch's top advertising strategist is Mike Roarty, its marketing vice president, who has been forthright in justifying his company's heavy investment in radio. In an address for the Radio Advertising Bureau, he set out these reasons:

- Radio is allied more directly than any other medium with the diverse life-styles of virtually all of Anheuser-Busch's target consumer populations.

- Unlike TV with its reruns, radio doesn't go on vacation, and summertime is the peak selling season for the beer business.

- Radio reinforces the momentum and continuity of other advertising.

- Radio provides a decided edge for reaching special audience segments like young adults, blacks, women, Hispanics, as well as more mature customers—all being consumers the company has to influence to meet its sales objectives.

- Thirty percent of beer drinkers account for 70 percent of all beer sales. Radio is the prime medium for reaching Anheuser-Busch's prime target, that most sought-after consumer, the 21–49-year-old male heavy beer drinker.

- Radio is the most flexible of all of the mass media, allowing for everything from special programming on Black format radio stations to live broadcasts of country-western concerts.

Let's Hear It for Parsimonious Phil

An entire class of advertisers use radio because it is all their budget will allow. Unlike an Anheuser-Busch, whose radio advertising is complemented by massive efforts in other media, these radio efforts represent total win-lose situations. This is pressure-cooker advertising.

Purex laundry products compete with other household products whose manufacturers spend more money supporting one brand than Purex spends on its entire product line. The advertising dollars used to promote Purex's eleven nationally distributed products represent a mere 1 percent of expenditures in a category that includes such big league marketers as Procter & Gamble, Colgate-Palmolive, and Lever Brothers. For example, P&G spends $50 million annually on Tide alone.

Because all eleven products carry the Purex brand name, the agency, Ramey Communications of Los Angeles, recommended an umbrella advertising strategy. The plan was to sell right across the entire line. Though television was not affordable, Purex needed the immediacy and impact of broadcast. Ramey decided to use wired and unwired network radio to target 25- to 54-year-old women.

The agency had to get its campaign approved twice. Just when the commercials were being produced, Purex was sold to Armour-Dial, a giant package goods company whose use and faith in radio was virtually nonexistent. With some skepticism, however, Armour-Dial went along with the plan.

Purex had the reputation of selling parity products. Its bleach, for example, is considered by many housewives to be "about as good as Clorox," the market leader, but less expensive. Accordingly, the advertising campaign was based on a value claim.

That value claim was personified by a character, called Phil. Phil was honest, down-to-earth, and earnest—an all-American entrepreneur with a midwestern accent whose creed was fair price for fair value and whose mission was to put Purex "back on its feet." In each commercial, there was Phil on his own in an overpowering environment, such as a forest of giant redwoods. Phil personified Purex and the environment personified the monster-sized competition.

Every effort was made to have Phil sound like a real person and not an actor. To encourage this perception, the agency decided to drop a rhetorical request in the commercials. No mailing address was given because there was no real intent to induce listener response. Phil just said let me hear from you.*

PHIL: Hi, I'm Phil and I'm out here alone, in the fresh air among the giant redwoods with the whole family of Purex cleaning products. You should see these redwoods. They're big. Well, actually, that's why I'm here. To make a point. You see, at Purex we sometimes feel like we're surrounded by giants...all those big companies that make cleaning products and then

---

*Purex commercial printed by permission of Armour-Dial Corporation.

charge big prices for them. And here stands Purex. All alone. Oh, sure, we make quality cleaning products, too, but we charge a lot less than those big guys.

SFX: *(chipmunk)*

PHIL: Even that old chipmunk knows what I'm talking about. But you know what gives me heart? Knowing there are millions of you using Purex. 'Cause a lot of you out there know an honest value when you see one. And that's nice. So while we're going to go right on making quality cleaning products for less, it's tough standing up next to the giants. So, could you do me a favor? Maybe send me a card, or a Purex boxtop, and say, "Dear Phil...We hear you." Oh, just one thing, I can't promise we'll send anything back. It just helps knowing you're out there.

ANNCR.: Purex. America's first choice in quality.

Thousands of listeners sent cards that eventually ended up, somewhat to their consternation, at Armour-Dial's offices in Phoenix. Phil was perceived as a real person. He was invited to dinners all over the country. Women wrote him asking for dates. Radio stations tried to set up interviews. A carpenter built and sent him a case specially constructed to hold samples of all eleven Purex products.

Follow-up research showed that the four-month campaign which cost around $3 million built up enormous brand awareness and good will for Purex. Fifty percent of the target market heard Phil's call. And though Phil, unlike David, did not slay his Goliath, he demonstrated that he had chosen the right slingshot.

Get 'Em While They're Hot

Top-of-mind awareness is crucial in the fast food business. McDonald's research shows that 40 percent of all its customers make the decision to visit a McDonald's within *two minutes* before they arrive at the restaurant. Almost 80 percent of all customers decide on eating at McDonald's within two hours.

Of all fast food customers, 85 percent travel to the establishment by car and 81 percent listen to the radio en route. It's logical that McDonald's is a heavy and enthusiastic radio advertiser because they do get 'em while they're hot. (See Table 13–3.)

That's not the chain's only rationale for using radio. When McDonald's introduces a new product, it considers the key to trial to be the frequency of its advertising message. The "magic number" used at the Golden Arches for stimulating trial is three advertising impressions a week. When the fast food chain began offering breakfast dishes about a decade ago, it found that al-

Table 13–3.   **Car Usage and Radio Listening**

	Shopping		Eating Out	
	Food	Department Store/Retail	Fast Food	Regular Restaurant
Percentage Using Car	91	91	85	88
Average Time Spent in Car (minutes)	27	33	25	34
Percentage of Shoppers Listening to Radio All or Part of Time	85	86	81	82

Source: *Media Targeting for the 90's* produced by R. H. Bruskin Associates for the Radio Advertising Bureau. Used by permission.

though its television was viewed by 95 percent of all 18- to 49-year-old adults, it could only reach 60 percent of the target group the necessary three times a week.

McDonald's opted to add a healthy amount of radio to raise the advertising frequency against the hard-to-reach light viewing television quintiles. For a radio expenditure amounting to 18 percent of the original television outlay, McDonald's was able to achieve acceptable frequency for the breakfast message with 84 percent of the target demographic. Spending more television dollars to add 24 percent more reach would have been prohibitive.

Keep the Cash Register Humming

A lot of cooks get involved in stirring up the advertising broth in major department stores. Each merchandise manager and buyer has something to say about how his or her department's funds should be spent. Because co-op funds that are extremely important to retailers have to be used to support specific items, the situation is doubly complicated. The advertising director who has to be participant, judge, and referee sometimes resembles a circus juggler trying to keep a variety of objects flying through the air.

In the early 1980s, the Broadway Department Stores, a multistore retailing giant in Southern California, was becoming a heavy television advertiser but making irregular and patternless use of radio. At the end of 1981, Jan Wetzel, then vice president of marketing, decided to run a definitive test to prove to merchandisers and buyers that radio could become a potent promotional tool. His counselor was Harry Spitzer, then sales director of the Southern California Broadcasters Association and today an independent retail radio consultant.

Spitzer insisted that radio be the single variable in the structure of the test. Accordingly an annual Columbus Day promotion that had run successfully in prior years was unchanged except for the addition of the radio advertising. The target demographic segment was 25- to 54-year-old women with household incomes of $25,000 and up.

The sale event ran over five days, from the preceding Thursday through Monday, Columbus Day. Thursday was a courtesy day for Broadway's regular customers, promoted by a special mailing. On the Friday, the first day of the public sale, a sixteen-page special section in the *Los Angeles Times* shouted "Sale Starts Today!"

The radio campaign that Wetzel and Spitzer constructed was designed to reach 60 percent of the target group three times. It utilized seventeen Los Angeles-area radio stations and cost $90,000. (The cost would probably be double in 1988. This represented a serious expenditure.) Broadway commercials, announcing the Friday sale, began on Tuesday, "heavied-up" on Wednesday, Thursday, and Friday and then, contrary to established practice, continued through Saturday and Sunday.

In the past, retailers, including the Broadway, who used radio to promote sales ceased radio advertising when the sale began. In this instance the first sale day was Friday, but Spitzer urged that the commercials continue right through Sunday evening. This innovation made all the difference. The increased volume over the preceding year for the entire Columbus Day promotion was $900,000. Previously, volume dropped off sharply on the last days, but this year all the sales gains were made during the last two days of the sale. Listeners, hearing the Broadway's commercials on their radios at the last minute, reacted to the message and kept the cash registers humming.

The Broadway has become and remains the largest retail user of radio in its geographical area.

One on One

Almost every radio station in America has a local, narrowly targeted success story. It's a far cry from McDonald's and AT&T, with their multimillion dollar budgets, to Jim Lebenthal, a Manhattan bond broker, who spends a couple of hundred thousand dollars a year on radio. Lebenthal, who has been writing and doing his own commercials for tax-free municipal bonds for close to twenty years, is the quintessential entrepreneurial businessman.

In the context of the total radio audience, Lebenthal's audience is minute. He can be heard on New York's All-News, News/Talk and Classical radio stations talking to a relatively small group of prospects. "I buy where my belly tells me the well-to-do, upscale listener is listening," Lebenthal explained. His typical customer is over fifty, earns more than $50,000 a year, and has most heavy expenses behind him. "I sell a most esoteric product. One could say we don't belong on radio...on mass media. We should be making housecalls." His continued success indicates, however, that Jim Lebenthal knows what he's doing.

An advertiser like Lebenthal is frequently the only radio advertiser in his category. Being the only game in town is a wonderful position. Some advertising is more successful in selling the category than it is the advertiser. Commercials may do as much good for the competition as they do the company that's footing the bill. But when Lebenthal & Co. alone is advertising a municipal bond issue, the call is unlikely to go to another bond broker.

The Commercial That Never Was

All radio successes don't follow the same pathway.

The following appeared in the April 1981 issue of *Travel & Tourism Executive Newsletter:*

> "Someday Never Comes"...the catchy jingle used by Boeing to get people aloft, hopefully on a Boeing commercial aircraft. We've heard and seen it on TV, spot radio and in magazines. It's a winner!...We vote this campaign tops in all categories— industrial relations with the airlines, believability of consumer message, and the class [of] the acknowledged leader in the airplane biz.

A nice testimonial—but not quite accurate.

"Someday Never Comes" *never ran on television!* The entire broadcast portion of the campaign was on radio. The only pictures the editors of the newsletter saw were in their minds. The radio commercials, produced by Cole & Weber, Seattle, were superlatively visual and the errant editors could be forgiven for feeling that the images were so real they *must* have been on a TV screen.

The Cincinnati Hoax

In 1985, all the Cincinnati radio stations banded together to perpetrate a hoax on the local citizenry. They carried advertising announcing the establishment of "Plummet Mall," the world's first vertical underground shopping center—a shopping center that did not exist—as a demonstration of the efficacy of radio advertising. During the month-long test, a different announcement ran each week, and to duplicate a realistic buy, a local advertising agency set up the station schedules. Each participating station ran between fourteen and thirty Plummet Mall commercials a week.

After four weeks of advertising, Burke Marketing Research noted that 60.5 percent of the people in Cincinnati had some awareness of the imaginary mall and 41 percent were able to volunteer information without prompting. "The results are extraordinary awareness figures no matter what the qualifications," Jim Russell, Burke vice president, stated. "A 41-percent unaided number in just four weeks is, to my knowledge, unprecedented and was achieved with a relatively modest budget. Most product managers are very happy with 10–15 percent figures which are gained only after significant television advertising, supplemented with couponing, sampling, et cetera."

Even before Burke began measuring, the Cincinnati Chamber of Commerce received a large number of telephone inquiries as to when Plummet Mall would open. One woman complained that her basement was flooding because of the mall's construction and she wanted to send a $5,000 bill for repairs to those responsible. A waste disposal company wanted to bid for the right to handle the shopping center's refuse.

Too bad the place did not exist. The advertising certainly worked.

Greatness Kills!

The late Bill Bernbach, the creative genius whose body of work is unmatched in advertising annals, spoke frequently about the need for a good product to advertise. It's an industry truism that effective advertising will induce trial but that a bad product cannot be advertised into success.

Bernbach also made the point that outstanding advertising will be the quickest to kill off a poor-quality brand. A frequently cited example is a memorable radio campaign for Piel's Beer in which the veteran radio comedy team of Bob Elliot and Ray Goulding portrayed the fictitious Bert and Harry Piel. Bob and Ray's riotous spots were so compelling that thousands of beer drinkers switched to Piel's. In short order, they recognized they didn't like the way it tasted and they went back to other brands. Piel's derived no great benefit from a prize-winning campaign.

A Multimedia Evaluation

In the mid-1980s, a combination of factors spurred tourism to the South Pacific. A rash of terrorist activities in Europe inhibited normal tourism to that part of the world. Many American travelers had become jaded with Hawaii after multiple visits. The Australian Tourist Commission picked the perfect time to break with outstanding advertising.

Australia's memorable television and radio campaign began in 1984. Their commercials featured an entertainer named Paul Hogan as the spokesperson for Australia. Hogan is an *ocker*. An ocker is the down-under equivalent of a redneck, a working stiff, common and earthy.

MOJO, the Australian agency that conceived and produced the advertising, faced a considerable amount of criticism when it was announced that Hogan would be featured in the commercials. The better elements in Australian society didn't appreciate that the language of Hogan's nightclub performances leaned heavily to the blue side and that his accent was definitely working class.

People have been more wrong—but not much. If there ever was an ideal bit of casting, having Paul Hogan speak for Australia ("G-day, mate.") was it. The advertising was successful from the start and its timing was impeccable. Australia offered an alternative to the affluent travelers who were scared away from Europe by bombings and other terrorist atrocities. In 1986, *Forbes* reported that Australia was the number one foreign holiday destination on American "wish lists," up from forty-ninth in 1983, and that 1985 visa applications showed a 25 percent increase over the previous year.

The television and radio advertising initially ran only in large West Coast cities while a limited amount of magazine advertising provided a national umbrella. A second broadcast flight then ran in four West Coast and four eastern markets. Television and radio were flighted so that they never ran at the same time. The advertising schedules in the United States were planned and executed by NW Ayer's Los Angeles office under the direction of a veteran international advertising man, Bart Stoner.

The commercials and ads urged the public to call an 800 number for a free brochure about Australia. After the first flight, the Tourist Commission had to go back to the Australian parliament for an additional budget so that more brochures could be printed. Just a few weeks of advertising had developed more responses than had been expected over the entire first year.

After the second flight, Stoner commissioned a segmentation study to determine which of the three media most effectively reached the target audience defined as 35–64-year-old adults who had attended college and had household incomes of over $50,000. More than 100,000 responses were analyzed, using ACORN (A Comparison of Residential Neighborhoods) norms.

The overall cost per response for radio was 15 percent lower than that for television. A more crucial measurement, the cost per target market response—those people most likely to take a trip to Australia—showed radio to be 36 percent lower than television. (The national magazine schedule cost per response was lower but the two broadcast media outpulled print by five to one.)

Everyone involved with Australia's tourism marketing is rightly convinced that its success was built on the use of multiple media, outstanding commercials featuring Paul Hogan, and a shrewdly executed plan. They are also convinced that the radio effort was integral to the campaign. Radio complemented the broad-reach television and magazine advertising by zeroing in on those people who were most likely to take the desired action.

Selling Subscriptions

The *Wall Street Journal* reader, according to Simmons, is well educated, well compensated, and in a professional/managerial occupation. This same profile also fits the listeners to certain radio formats, therefore these listeners should be prospective *Wall Street Journal* subscribers.

The *Wall Street Journal*, through the Lawrence Butner Agency of New York, has used direct response advertising for new subscribers on radio consistently since 1976. Direct response advertisers evaluate the success of their advertising on hard numbers. In the case of the *Wall Street Journal,* how many subscriptions for how many advertising dollars? The relatively few stations that Butner uses are the ones that produce the most subscription orders.

The success of the *Wall Street Journal's* direct response advertising spawned an equally successful image radio campaign. Beginning in 1982, parallel network radio advertising, first placed by BBDO, New York, and later by Fallon McElligott, Minneapolis, has extolled the quality of the newspaper. From 1982 to 1985, the *Wall Street Journal* took special advantage of radio's unique production flexibility. Commercials incorporating headlines from the current day's edition were written and recorded late the evening before and carried by the radio networks the morning of publication. It was a dramatic concept.

Even today the image advertising solicits subscriptions and includes an 800 number for the listener to call. Although that is not the main thrust of the Fallon McElligott commercials, it is a reminder of what put the *Journal* on radio initially.

The Radio Advertising Bureau maintains a voluminous file of radio case histories, including both national and local advertisers in a large number of business categories. (See Appendix.)

14

Effective Direct Response Techniques

The Australian Tourist Commission and the *Wall Street Journal* are not the only advertisers to recognize that radio is an effective direct response advertising medium. Correctly used, radio is a potent direct response medium.

What Is Direct Response, Anyway?

Direct advertising is a hot category. Over the last several years, many large advertising agencies have acquired direct advertising subsidiaries. In most cases, the acquired organizations had originally been *direct mail* agencies.

There is a big difference between *direct response* and *direct mail*. One form of direct advertising involves the use of direct mail to elicit response. The category includes any advertising whose purpose is to generate response. In the direct mail business, technique is highly formularized and, in essence, everyone does it like everyone else. That accounts for the striking similarities in the vast quantity of mail solicitations sent out on behalf of charities, publications, political candidates, and other worthy causes.

Although direct advertising specialists whose emphasis has been on direct mail and coupon advertising in print media may suggest that they have expertise in developing response in all media, they rarely have experience with broadcast of any type. Many feel that radio can be used only to instruct the listener to seek out ads in newspapers and magazines. This concept is totally off the mark. Let the advertiser beware.

Radio is a logical direct response medium because radio stations design their programming to be selective and to appeal to listeners with similar interests. A specific radio format, with listeners who share demographic and psychographic characteristics, is akin to an aural mailing list. But the dynamics of eliciting response on the radio differ substantially from the dynamics of direct mail.

The Direct Response Commercial

Radio works for direct response when the radio commercial is designed to elicit phone calls. It won't work if a direct response appeal is simply appended to a conventional commercial. Forget about adding a tag that says, "and, by the way, if you would like more information, call this 800 number." The entire thrust of the announcement must be geared to developing response. If the objective of a commercial is to draw requests for a brochure, the commercial should talk about the brochure. If the commercial is selling a subscription, this should be clear throughout the entire sixty seconds. Subtlety is not a virtue in direct response commercials.

Direct response commercials must be fine-tuned. This is pragmatic advertising at its ultimate. Sometimes just changing a few lines can make a dramatic difference in the response rate. Saddling an unproven response spot with an excessive amount of production cost can be a big mistake. Certainly at the outset, simplicity is desirable.

Direct response radio commercials work at once or they don't work at all. Effective messages immediately have a high response rate and then, over time, their impact tends to diminish. It is imprudent to stay with a low-pulling commercial in the hope that response will build. When hitherto effective spots bring an inadequate return, taking a hiatus may help. Getting off the air, or off a particular station, for a few weeks allows the audience to freshen.

Too many copywriters follow a vestigial print practice when constructing radio commercials. They try to hide unpleasant information by burying it at the end of a commercial as they would with an asterisk and six-point type in a print ad. Neil Elliott, an advertising man who has served broadcast direct response advertisers with great success over a long career, put it this way:

> What these print copywriters do not grasp is something every listener and certainly every competent writer of radio copy knows: the point of greatest emphasis in a radio commercial is at the end.
>
> The worst examples are in bank and savings and loan copy. For fifty seconds, we hear persuasive arguments why we should put our money in a particular kind of account. Then—during the precious remaining seconds that should be used for impassioned exhortation to do it before another sun sets—we hear a tag that

is usually a warning of mysterious penalties we will suffer if we dare to put any money into such an account. The place for this required disclosure is early in the commercial where it can artfully be buried by a writer of any skill at all.

The unhidden disclaimer can be deadly in radio direct response because the end of a commercial will contain the action inducement message. That is what the listener should remember, not some extraneous legality. Even the phrase "an equal opportunity employer" in a direct response recruitment commercial is better off in the body of the spot.

The impact of a response radio commercial is in direct proportion to the immediacy of the message. You can get by with less advertising weight if you include a forced response mechanism. A commercial that includes a time limit will set up an immediate yes–no situation in the listener's mind. "Seminar takes place on April 15th"; "Offer ends June 30th"; "Sale ends Friday."

Yes, I am interested—in which case I have to act quickly. Or no, I am not interested—in which case I can ignore this commercial now and forever.

Several computer companies who have staged seminars for business executives have found that ten days to two weeks of radio advertising will fill the largest hotel meeting room. Ship lines advertising "Cruise Night" promotions have come up with similar findings.

The Oral Coupon

Will they really call? Don't let anybody tell you they won't.

Company presidents, people interested in career improvement, consumers who want information about products and services, customers who want to buy things, homemakers, motorists going sixty miles per hour on the freeway all will respond to a telephone number in a radio commercial. Consider the following:

- Tens of thousands of radio listeners called to ask for a brochure about Australia after hearing Paul Hogan suggest they do so.
- Chicago's WBBM/Newsradio posed an on-air question relating to city government and received 30,000 phone calls in one day!
- In a two-week, one-station, one-market test, the state of Alaska received close to 6,000 phone requests for its travel brochure.
- A computer company ran commercials on two stations in each of five markets asking business executives to sign up for a seminar on data processing. More than 1,500 called in and attended the meetings.
- A metropolitan New York realtor wrote the general manager of WCBS-AM that the station had pulled "thousands of responses to our 800-USA-SOLD telephone offer in only four weeks."
- The senior deputy commissioner of commerce of the state of New York concluded that radio had been highly effective in targeting business people. "In terms of response," said Natel Matschulat, "it has

been terrific. We found on a cost per thousand basis, radio gave us 30 percent more responses than our print advertising.

- A *Business Week* story about the introduction of an IBM small business computer in the late 1970s reported that IBM used radio and other consumer media to obtain responses. "Of the 5,500 inquiries generated," said the magazine, "3,220 came from radio."
- The first announcement featuring a special offer by an investment newsletter that ran on Michael Jackson's program on Talk Radio KABC, Los Angeles, drew more than 500 phone calls.

Sometimes there need not be many callers. Several years ago a division of Computer Sciences Corporation was organizing a seminar for executives involved with accounting procedures covered by the Federal Accounting Standards Board Regulation 13. FASB 13 concerns major real estate leasebacks, a matter of interest to financial officers of the largest corporations and their accountants.

With great skepticism, Computer Sciences ran a one-week schedule on KNX/Newsradio in Los Angeles. The live commercial invited people who wanted to delve into the intricacies of FASB 13 to respond by telephone. If fifteen responses were recorded, the advertising would be considered successful. Forty-five calls were received.

How does it happen? The listener at home has no particular difficulty, but how can a business executive driving at high speed on an interstate highway record a telephone number he or she has just heard on the radio? It is a function of recognition. The first time a commercial is heard the listener is probably unaware that there will be a telephone number to be called. If, however, the commercial made the right impression, the next time it is heard, recognition will be almost instantaneous. Now there is close to a minute to reach for a pad and pencil in the glove compartment or handbag or an envelope in a coat pocket.

The proof is empirical. They do call.

Some Do's and Don'ts

Forget about drawing response by mail. The telephone is the only way to go. Repeat the phone number three times. The specialists in radio response advertising swear this is the magic number. Do not let *one single word* follow the final reading of the telephone number. The last sounds of a commercial will hang in the brain for many seconds. The phone number will be remembered and recalled if listeners know they do not have to be bothered listening to anything else. Copywriters who insist on ending a direct response commercial with a quip should be trussed up with used typewriter ribbons and forced to listen to twenty-four hours of real funny stuff, like nonstop Howard Cosell tapes.

Figure 14-1.   Sample Computerized Telephone Response Reports

```
5007                      8006 | 5007                      8008 | 5007                      800A
CLIENT COMPANY     800-632-2122| CLIENT COMPANY     800-632-2122| CLIENT COMPANY     800-632-2122
  0  INFO BROCHURE 4061 09 10  3:19P|  0  INFO BROCHURE 4001 09 10  3:21P|  0  INFO BROCHURE 9000 09 10  3:26P
NAME: MAXINE RODGERS        | NAME: SAMANTHA DOERR        | NAME: ROBINSON GEOFFREY
ADDR: 140 VALLEY DR         | ADDR: 1954 GEARY ST         | ADDR: 19489 BIG CREEK RD
CITY: BRISBANE              | CITY: SAN FRANCISCO         | CITY: APTOS
STATE: CA  ZIP: 94005       | STATE: CA  ZIP: 94116       | STATE: CA  ZIP: 94125
TEL#: (415) 468 5100        | TEL#: (415) 751 3536        | TEL#: (408) 988 6125
SOURCE: YYY                 | SOURCE: ZZZ                 | SOURCE: XXX
3                           | 3                           | 3

5007                      800C | 5007                      000E | 5007                      8010
CLIENT COMPANY     800-632-2122| CLIENT COMPANY     800-632-2122| CLIENT COMPANY     800-632-2122
  0  INFO BROCHURE 5000 09 10  4:35P|  0  INFO BROCHURE 4061 09 10  4:55P|  0  INFO BROCHURE 5555 09 10  5:00P
NAME: DONNA CHILDERS        | NAME: JOSEPH WEINSTEIN      | NAME: JACK SMYTHE
ADDR: 24 SYCAMORE LANE      | ADDR: 1800 SUN VALLEY MALL RD| ADDR: 1267 RIVERA ST. SUITE 2505
CITY: SANTA CLARA           | CITY: RICHMOND              | CITY: ALAMEDA
STATE: CA  ZIP: 95025       | STATE: CA  ZIP: 94390       | STATE: CA  ZIP: 95090
TEL#: (408) 233 5500 X2190  | TEL#: (415) 354 6708        | TEL#: (415) 655 5454
SOURCE: YYY                 | SOURCE: ZZZ                 | SOURCE: YYY
3                           | 3                           | 3

5007                      0012 | 5007                      0014 | 5007                      C016
CLIENT COMPANY     800-632-2122| CLIENT COMPANY     800-632-2122| CLIENT COMPANY     800-632-2122
  0  INFO BROCHURE 9009 09 10  5:03P|  0  INFO BROCHURE 9009 09 10  5:37P|  0  INFO BROCHURE 4061 09 11  1:35P
NAME: MRS EDWIN MARLEY      | NAME: REBECCA D'AMICO       | NAME: PATRICK FITZGERALD
ADDR: 947-A OLD COUNTY RD   | ADDR: 1890 PACIFIC AVE      | ADDR: 2402 SOUTH MAIN ST
CITY: SANTA ROSA            | CITY: FOSTER CITY           | CITY: SAN MATEO
STATE: CA  ZIP: 94695       | STATE: CA  ZIP: 94165       | STATE: CA  ZIP: 94039
TEL#: (707) 742 1987        | TEL#: (415) 661 2000 X340   | TEL#: (415) 344 8989
SOURCE: YYY                 | SOURCE: YYY                 | SOURCE: XXX
3                           | 3                           | 3

5007                      0018 | 5007                      801A | 5007                      801C
CLIENT COMPANY     800-632-2122| CLIENT COMPANY     800-632-2122| CLIENT COMPANY     800-632-2122
  0  INFO BROCHURE 4444 09 11  1:37P|  0  INFO BROCHURE 5555 09 11  1:47P|  0  INFO BROCHURE 1000 09 11  1:54P
NAME: AMY LOWELL / CAMBRIDGE INSTITUTE| NAME: DON YEAGER     | NAME: CHARLES LEE
ADDR: 45090 HEATHER PARK BLVD| ADDR: 4466 8TH AVE          | ADDR: 1736 LINCOLN AVE
CITY: SAN JOSE              | CITY: MILPITAS              | CITY: SAN FRANCISCO
STATE: CA  ZIP: 95889       | STATE: CA  ZIP: 95243       | STATE: CA  ZIP: 94120
TEL#: (408) 478 3000 X3964  | TEL#: (408) 687 4500        | TEL#: (415) 668 1432
SOURCE: YYY                 | SOURCE: ZZZ                 | SOURCE: YYY
3                           | 3                           | 3

5007                      001E | 5007                      8020 | 5007                      8022
CLIENT COMPANY     800-632-2122| CLIENT COMPANY     800-632-2122| CLIENT COMPANY     800-632-2122
  0  INFO BROCHURE 2000 09 11  2:11P|  0  INFO BROCHURE 4000 09 11  2:14P|  0  INFO BROCHURE 4010 09 11  2:20P
NAME: ANDREW MAC DONALD     | NAME: J. EDUARDO VASQUEZ    | NAME: ROBERT VEJNONSKA
ADDR: 211 SUMNER PLACE      | ADDR: 1011 DOLORES ST       | ADDR: 757 SUTTER ST
CITY: SACRAMENTO            | CITY: SAN FRANCISCO         | CITY: SAN FRANCISCO
STATE: CA  ZIP: 93456       | STATE: CA  ZIP: 94110       | STATE: CA  ZIP: 94102
TEL#: (916) 898 5409        | TEL#: (415) 824 0836        | TEL#: (415) 781 5769
SOURCE: XXX                 | SOURCE: ZZZ                 | SOURCE: ZZZ
3                           | 3                           | 3
```

Prototype report provided by Proxy/Voicebank, Brisbane, California.

If it possibly can be avoided, advertisers who are looking for leads or fulfilling requests for literature should not handle telephone calls with their own personnel. When they do, there is an overwhelming tendency to qualify respondents. A dialogue between caller and answerer inevitably will occur. Such a dialogue ties up lines when others are trying to get through. Radio listeners will try a couple of times but too many busy signals will discourage them. Also most businesses can only accept calls during business hours and this will put a damper on response.

Instead use a professional broadcast telephone answering service (or where callers are ordering merchandise or making reservations, a company's own bank of trained operators). Such services exist in most large cities and the national companies who sell 800-number services can function almost anywhere. Their cost is moderate. They will record time of call, names, addresses, phone numbers, the radio station on which the commercial was heard, as well as any other required information and forward this data on computerized reports. Good records are the mother's milk of the direct response business and this is how to obtain them. (See Figure 14-1, for example.)

Until recently, it was preferable to use a local number rather than an 800 number. Despite being "toll free," calling an 800 number was perceived as a long distance call and its use definitely cut response. With the increased use of all types of telemarketing in the last few years, 800 numbers have proliferated and the problem has virtually disappeared.

In many large metropolitan areas, there are multiple area codes. To take calls with local numbers in the metropolitan area covered by Los Angeles radio stations, for example, the commercial would have to include three different telephone numbers. This would be time consuming and confusing.

AT&T now sells a tracking and switching system that assigns each radio station in a market its individual 800 number. With this level of sophisticated equipment, the direct response advertiser can ascertain how many and what kind of respondents each radio station is producing.

Eliciting Sales on Radio

Making a sale is the ultimate direct response. Great quantities of merchandise can be sold through radio advertising if the advertiser knows precisely what to do.

In 1984, an enterprising entrepreneur named Jim MacAlister started a direct sales company with a single product. It was "Verbal Advantage," a vocabulary-improvement audio cassette that he sold for $99.95, and it was, and is, sold only on radio.

Today MacAlister's company, the hugely successful National Dynamics, using radio exclusively, markets nineteen different taped educational programs. Calls are answered by a bank of operators who receive hundreds of hours of training under close supervision. Eighty-six percent of the company's sales are prepaid and charged to listener's credit cards. Satisfaction is guaranteed. Not only are sales consummated over the 800-number telephone lines but MacAlister develops new products through the evaluation of his respondents' demography.

Commercials are live and copy changes are made every week. National Dynamics runs in selected time periods during daytime and evening hours and responses are carefully tracked daily. MacAlister tests various stations, jumping around from market to market, but his advertising is consistent in about eight major markets.

National Dynamics' success can be attributed to these factors:

- Good products
- Concentration on one selling technique and one medium
- Proven commercials
- Highly trained telephone operator/salespeople
- Assiduous and detailed response record keeping

Radio for Recruitment

Recruitment advertising is a form of direct response advertising that meets two important objectives. It serves a specific need and it presents a corporate message.

Recruitment advertising in the classified section of the newspaper is seen only by those people actively seeking jobs. Recruitment advertising on radio is heard not only by prospective employees to whom the message is specifically addressed but also by the company's present employees, stockholders, competitors, and neighbors, plus the government, business, and financial communities. Thus recruitment advertising on radio is *corporate advertising*. Any recruitment commercial that does not, by content and production value, put the advertiser's best face forward could be damaging corporately, whether it achieves its recruitment objective or not.

In specific terms, using radio for recruitment allows the advertiser to talk to prospective employees who are presently working. Most gainfully and happily employed persons do not read help wanted ads in the newspaper, but, like everyone else, they listen to the radio. A well-crafted recruitment commercial can plant the idea that here are advancement opportunities for individuals willing to switch employers.

During a period when airplane production was booming at Boeing, the Seattle-based airplane manufacturer successfully ran radio recruitment advertising in St. Louis (home of McDonnell-Douglas), Los Angeles (the base for McDonnell-Douglas, Hughes Aircraft, Northrup, and Lockheed), and other cities where aircraft engineers and construction specialists were to be found. They talked to and hired individuals who could have been reached in no other way.

Loral Electronics Systems used radio to recruit engineers and computer scientists in the New York area. In the first two weeks of advertising, the company received 250 telephone inquiries and the average number of resumes it received climbed from 20 to more than 200 per week.

Nurses, accountants, bookkeepers, temporary employees, assembly line workers, and salespeople have been recruited through radio advertising. The medium has been effective when only a few jobs are open. A computer company sought two college graduates with some business experience to enter a marketing representative program. Three large ads in the classified section of a big city newspaper drew virtually no response. A one-week schedule that cost less than one of the classified ads ran on an All-News radio station. One hundred and nineteen individuals responded.

Even though a powerful radio station's coverage will far exceed the circulation area of even the largest newspapers, some recruitment advertising agencies, classified advertising specialists, persist in viewing radio as a "referral medium." They contend that all radio should be asked to do is send an interested individual to the newspaper.

Hughes Aircraft, Boeing, and TRW, among others, who have successfully used radio for recruitment, regularly run radio commercials that do not mention their newspaper ads. Although there is no harm in mentioning that the advertiser is also running ads in the classified section of the newspaper, the radio advertising must stand on its own feet. If radio commercials are designed only to force better readership of a newspaper ad, the recruitment advertiser prevents those people who cannot or will not look at a newspaper from responding. Those prospects that are forced to the newspaper will also get a healthy look at competitive offerings.

When the Sun Goes Down

During a late night interview show on KMOX, St. Louis, a booklet on government spending was offered. The 50,000-watt clear channel radio station received 963 responses from twenty-two states.

A direct response commercial advertiser on the same station ran announcements between 11:00 P.M. and 5:00 A.M. One night's log showed the time the commercial ran and the response, as follows: 11:40 P.M., 54 calls; 1:55 A.M., 45 calls; 4:40 A.M., 138 calls.

Big booming AM radio stations send their signals over incredible distances when the sun goes down. (See Chapter 3.) No matter what time of night it is, large numbers of people are listening to the radio. These late night listeners are especially susceptible to direct response advertising. Only small advertising budgets are needed because most stations practically give away overnight commercial time.

Hooray for Synergy

Does radio advertising have a positive effect on the response to print advertising? Yes, it does. Not only will radio advertising increase both awareness and readership of magazine and newspaper ads, it will also affect the coupon response of the print ads. It will have the same salutary effect on direct mail advertising. This does not require any mention of print advertising in the radio commercials. It is a result of the synergy of the various media.

Because direct response advertisers are chary about releasing their numbers, it is difficult to document these conclusions quantitatively. Most of the best creative work in advertising resists copy testing. The proof is in the running. The positive synergy of using radio in conjunction with direct response print can be proven the same way. Use print alone in one matched market and add radio in the second. The results may then be compared.

15

Barter
The Two-Edged
Sword

In broadcasting, the word *barter* can have two sharply different meanings. When broadcast programmers refer to barter, they mean *barter syndication*. In a barter syndication, a syndicator provides a radio or television station with a program in return for a certain increment of commercial time, usually from 20 percent to 30 percent, which the barter syndicator then sells. The remainder of the commercial time is sold locally for hard dollars by the station.

When an advertiser refers to barter, he means a trade of products or services in return for air time. A number of media companies specialize in bartering broadcast time.

In the mid-1980s, there was a rash of activity on the part of advertisers who wanted to trade a product or service for radio time. Movies, theaters, and rock concerts liked to swap tickets for advertising. Hotel and cruise lines, with their perishable inventories, had been long-time barter advertisers. After deregulation, airlines moved strongly in that direction.

In the swiftly changing hi-tech arena, manufacturers of computers, telecommunications equipment, and the like frequently found themselves with hefty amounts of obsolete products and began offering them in trade for broadcast time, as did companies in other industries who had close-outs for whatever reason. Producers with excess manufacturing capacity and high fixed costs found it more profitable to trade goods at cost than to shut down huge assembly lines. Similarly, businesses whose excess production came in at low incremental cost found that barter was a practical way to open new distribution and fund advertising.

Radio barter, like other games, has its own set of rules. Major radio stations operate with grid rate cards that allow the stations to charge varying rates for identical announcements. The question logically arises as to the price of the time being bartered. If an announcement that could be bought for $100 cash was bartered for $200, the company bartering products or services would not be getting much of a deal. Invariably, however, the value of the products or services is *also* being inflated. Practically all barter is based on the retail list price of goods or services, an amount that the manufacturer could never recover from his conventional customers.

Another concern in barter is commercial clearance. The best administered radio stations are oversold from time to time. In this situation, whose announcement is likely to be shunted aside, the advertiser who bought for dollars or the advertiser who has traded for time? The bartered spot inevitably will be dropped. To prevent this from occurring, the most sophisticated barter specialists no longer seek 100 percent trade. Instead they offer radio stations and radio networks deals calling for part trade, part cash. Now, if a station drops a spot, it is losing hard money.

The addition of cash to trade also enlarges the marketplace for barter. Many stations will not accept pure barter arrangements but are amenable to combinations of products or services and money.

In the hotel, cruise line, or airline business, the case is repeatedly made that unoccupied hotel rooms, empty staterooms, or surplus airplane seats have no value. No matter at what price they are traded, in theory the advertiser will be ahead of the game if he trades them for broadcast time.

The same point, in theory, can be made about broadcast time. If commercial time on a given day is unsold, it is worthless when that day has ended. In practical terms, this is not the case. The grid rate card allows the radio station to drop prices at will and for most major stations, selling all available time inventory is a pricing consideration. On the other hand, the hotel that is running at an average 85 percent capacity cannot simply reduce prices on the unsold 15 percent and fill those rooms.

Most barter commitments extend for considerable time periods. A year is customary. In the case of perishable travel-related services, the provider of the service cannot normally isolate those times when the barter is applicable. A hotel, subject to availability, must provide the bartered rooms during peak seasons when it could easily fill them with paying customers.

Though some barter radio contracts extend over substantial stretches of time, the buyer usually negotiates for schedules that run in a set period in order to meet the desired advertising objectives. This does allow the station to accept or reject barter depending on seasonable demand. Most good radio stations are not particularly interested in trading time in the fourth calendar quarter.

Many important radio stations in large metropolitan markets have restrictive barter policies though there are only a handful that totally reject all trades. Although some broadcasters will stockpile products and services for which they have traded and broker them for cash at discounted prices, CBS Radio stations, for example, will not barter time for products or services they cannot themselves use. Radio stations, like all businesses, have needs and will often seek barter to fill them. They require automobiles for news reporters; carpeting, furniture, and other hard goods; a certain amount of airline and hotel credits for business travel; outside meeting facilities; prizes for audience promotions and sales incentive programs, and so forth. Internal Revenue Service regulations require broadcasters to consider barter compensation as income.

If an advertiser barters computers or telephones or any other product that has fixed cost of manufacture, trading can be hazardous. Unlike the empty hotel room that is worthless once the evening passes, the value of a hard product should never be less than its intrinsic cost. Often the *real value* of the traded air time is less than the *real value* of the traded product despite the fact that the prices for air time and the product have been inflated.

Conceptually barter is wonderful. The reality depends on who is executing. Skilled experts do an excellent job for their clients. Bunglers, and there are scores in this delicate business, do not.

Some barter companies take a principal's position themselves and work with a bank of products and services. For them, three- or four-sided trades are common. The barter company provides hotel space to an outdoor advertising company which needs it for its sales representatives, outdoor boards to a broadcast company to promote its stations, and broadcast time to the hotel company for advertising its properties. In this type of transaction, the barter company could negotiate independently with its three clients who would never have to deal with each other.

By 1987, enthusiasm for barter had waned. Some hi-tech companies which exchanged their products for broadcast time were distressed about what they received for their merchandise. The airlines, who had been consolidating at an unprecedented pace and had a shrinking number of empty seats, recognized that broadcast time was too important an advertising component to be frivolously whirled about in the winds of barter. Though some airlines still seek trading partners, they generally put advertising considerations first.

Barter Rules to Remember

The key principle is: Never barter for that which you would not purchase for cash. If an advertiser must barter, he should make an attempt, independent of the transaction, to learn what he would have to pay in cash for similar announcements. The unsophisticated trader too often ends up with schedules based on *what he can get* rather than *what he should have* to make his advertising effective. If he barters a product or service that the stations or networks want, he can strike a more advantageous trade. In all barter situations, an advertiser will do better if he offers a combination of cash and barter rather than 100 percent barter.

16

Using Co-op Advertising Dollars

Advertising allowances and cooperative advertising allowances provided by manufacturers to their wholesale and retail outlets amount to big money. The national estimate was $8 to $10 billion in 1987. These vendor funds, universally called co-op, are not the same, though both types of allowances may be administered similarly.

An advertising allowance is a percentage of a purchase order. If a dealer places an order for $100,000 with a company that offers a 3 percent advertising allowance, under established guidelines the dealer may expend $3,000 to promote the company's product. Advertising allowances are standard in the electronics and computer industries, among others.

A cooperative advertising allowance is usually a matching arrangement. To promote a company's product, a dealer may spend up to a certain amount based on his purchase volume. What the dealer spends will then be matched by the manufacturer. It is truly a cooperative effort. Real co-op is common in apparel and package goods.

Traditionally newspapers have been the beneficiaries of most vendor funds, but over the past twenty years, radio, television, and cable have made healthy inroads. In 1962, only 500 companies authorized the use of radio for co-op advertising. Today the total number is in excess of 5,000, of which more than 1,000 offer 100 percent advertising allowances.

In 1987, radio co-op alone amounted to approximately $800 million. Radio stations all over the country are aggressively soliciting this kind of business, many employing co-op specialists who work directly with retailers and dealers, showing them how to use manufacturer-provided funds on radio to the maximum advantage. The Radio Advertising Bureau, which devotes considerable effort to this area of the business, estimates that 15 percent of all local radio revenue comes from co-op.

There is a substantial body of business literature on cooperative advertising, mostly written from the vantage point of the advertiser. Radio rarely receives more than token attention. Despite the inroads made by all broadcast media, co-op is *perceived* to be the province of newspapers. For radio stations, as sellers, the authoritative text is *Making Money with Co-op,* written by Miles David in 1986 and published by the Radio Advertising Bureau.

For a dealer or retailer, the co-op dollars received from its vendors may finance a substantial percentage of total advertising. Under most present plans, there is considerable leeway as to how this advertising is run. Larger outlets, like department stores and mass merchandisers, have well-staffed internal advertising departments who can incorporate co-op messages into their overall advertising. Smaller stores may take material prepared by the manufacturer and merely add a signature line to a newspaper add or a tag to a radio commercial.

For a national advertiser who has a co-op or advertising allowance plan, the advertising it funds for dealers and retailers can be effective, ineffective, or even destructive depending on how well it is conceived and executed. Most retailers, large and small, are most skilled, or at least have the most experience, in preparing newspaper advertising, and here the manufacturers need to exercise the least control over their co-op partners. But with radio, as with all broadcast, retailers are likely to be relatively inexperienced. In these instances, control of co-op should be a major vendor consideration.

The Invisible Wall

In many firms, an invisible wall divides a company's own advertising from the dealer advertising financed by co-op or advertising allowance funds. The two advertising budgets are almost always separate; frequently the co-op funds are administered not by specialists in the advertising department, but by the sales department.

This barrier inhibits the company's ability to control the allowances being doled out. The co-op plan details what will and will not be sanctioned. The dealer selects and places the co-op advertising. The company's advertising department usually prepares some newspaper mats and an occasional radio commercial that it gives to its customers. Sometimes a co-op version of a television commercial will be part of the dealer kit. Beyond that, most companies exert little influence.

Control of how the dealer expends these funds, however, is no small matter. There are a considerable number of manufacturers who exceed $1 billion in sales annually. At this level, a 3–4 percent advertising allowance, which is not uncommon, amounts to $30–$40 million. One method of controlling these expenditures is to put some of a company's own advertising money into a market in a way that makes it economic, prudent, and effective for the dealer, retailer, or distributor to join the company's advertising effort.

The 30–30 Plan

The 30–30 approach works particularly well on spot radio where a thirty-second commercial normally costs 80 percent of a sixty-second commercial. The company can buy a sixty-second spot, use thirty seconds for its own message and then "sell off" the other thirty seconds to its dealer. The dealer pays less for his thirty seconds than he would if he had purchased it himself. If the sixty seconds cost $100, company and dealer each end up paying $50. Had the dealer purchased a thirty-second announcement on his own, he would have paid $80.

The dealer then compensates the manufacturer for his portion of the time with his advertising allowance. Because his thirty seconds are contiguous with the vendor's thirty seconds and because the dealer's broadcast time is bought by the vendor and sold back to him, the dealer gives up some advertising independence in return for a monetary saving.

Under the provisions of the Robinson–Patman act, this type of program must be offered to all dealers in a designated market in accordance with the amount of business each does with the manufacturer but the manufacturer may choose as few or as many markets as he wishes.

With a 30–30 plan, the manufacturer controls the use of the co-op funds, selects the stations, and buys the radio time. He also benefits from the cumulative effect of having all the participating dealers using radio advertising in the same way, that is, appending their individual thirty-second announcements to the manufacturer's consistent thirty-second message.

In addition to obtaining $80 worth of radio time for each $50 of his vendor funds, the dealer is able to utilize the media buying expertise of the manufacturer and his advertising agency. Because of radio's flexibility, his thirty-second portion of the total announcement may easily be tailored to whatever best suits his interest within the manufacturer's established ground rules. He is not merely limited to a name and address tagline.

These 30–30 plans have long been used by package goods companies to spur promotional sales efforts. In some cases, the manufacturer pays for all the radio time but rewards customers with thirty-second increments in return for purchasing varying quantities of merchandise.

Don't Sell Co-op Short

Both the provider and the recipient of co-op funds should carefully scrutinize radio advertising opportunities. Significantly, radio reaches more consumers immediately before they buy than any competitive media, covering more than 50 percent of all adults within one hour of the day's largest purchase, compared to television's 16 percent and newspapers' 9 percent. Whether announcements are placed and run by the retailer or whether less conventional approaches, like the 30-30 plan, are utilized, the medium offers some powerful benefits to co-op advertisers.

Vendor Support Programs

Relatively new entrants in the dealer/supplier advertising mix are the vendor support programs that go under a variety of names—vendor promotion programs, vendor discretionary funds, vendor fund development, and others. These are undertakings instituted, not by the manufacturer or distributor, but by the retailers and they usually support major storewide or chainwide merchandising events. They are funded, however, by the participation of key suppliers *chosen by the retailer* and the money expended is almost always over and above any co-op advertising allowance.

Vendor support programs are designed to generate a very high level of awareness of the advertised event and almost always involve multimedia participation. Radio stations have been recipients of substantial vendor support business and many stations are now aggressively cooperating with large retailers to organize them.

Here's how a vendor support program works:

A high-volume retailer or chain or dealer association prepares a plan for a specific promotional campaign in a specific market, usually in the context of a special event, and presents it to a vendor or a group of vendors to underwrite.

The vendor is thus provided with an opportunity to enhance a significant relationship, and, at the same time, to sell additional merchandise for the retail promotion. The required funds are almost always derived from special vendor budgets set up under a variety of names such as key city funds, strategic market funds, new market funds, special opportunity funds, and the like. It is estimated that the pool of vendor dollars is in the billions per year.

Vendor programs neither affect nor detract from co-op or advertising allowance plans. The money is unencumbered and its use is not predetermined. The amount a vendor will apply to a promotion is normally based on *projected* sales while co-op money accrues from *actual* purchases.

Several advertising agencies now specialize in establishing vendor-supported promotions, particularly those representing dealer associations where coordination between a group of independent retailers or franchisees is essential.

Some radio stations, recognizing that like all local media they have a strong stake in vendor support programs, have also taken the lead in organizing informal dealer groups in order to tap vendor money. The Radio Advertising Bureau has published an excellent brochure, *Introducing Radio Vendorization,* which, though prepared with radio stations in mind, serves as a step-by-step guide for establishing complicated vendor support programs.

17

A
Smattering of
Intelligence

It is impossible to neatly categorize every facet of radio advertising. A business is being examined, not a pure science, and there are the inevitable loose ends.

When Yogi Berra was a rookie catcher with the New York Yankees, his mentor was the Yankee veteran, Bill Dickey. Asked how the relationship was progressing, Yogi declared, "Bill is learning me his experience."

Let me cover a few loose ends by learning you some of mine.

Radio and Suburbia

In 1980, according to the U.S. Census, 60 percent of metropolitan populations lived outside of the central cities. If a *Los Angeles Times* study on attitudes toward Los Angeles by residents of suburban Orange County is typical of the whole country, most suburbanites disassociate themselves emotionally from the city. In a practical extension of this attitude, very few indicated they would go to the central city to make a major purchase.

Metropolitan newspapers have been severely affected. From 1980 to 1986, the majority of big city newspapers showed little if any circulation growth. According to data assembled by *Media and Marketing Decisions,* the *Los Angeles Time's* circulation rose 1 percent in the six-year period. The *Chicago Tribune* showed a 3 percent circulation loss. Suburban newspapers, however, have been prospering, and newspaper advertisers, particularly retailers, have recognized the need to place ads in community papers.

Though loyal to local newspapers, suburban residents aren't enamored with local radio stations. They listen principally to the major city stations. In one recent Southern California Arbitron survey, the highest rated Orange County station was in eighteenth position *in Orange County.* Seventeen Los Angeles stations had larger listening audiences in this suburban area.

Substantial numbers of the affluent are moving out of the big cities. But, unlike their big city newspaper, radio signals from the metropolitan centers follow them. Because almost all advertisers wish to communicate with both urban and suburban dwellers, radio's competitive position is enhanced.

The Age/Sex Demographic Trap

Targeting prospects by broad age/sex demographics—the norm in broadcast advertising—is fraught with danger. Consider this example: the 1987 Simmons Market Research Bureau survey discloses that 40.5 percent of *all men* 18 years of age or older in the United States are either unemployed or earning less than $10,000 annually. Another 21.3 percent earn $10,000 to $20,000. Assume a radio buy for an expensive product aimed at all adult men was made solely on the basis of gross rating points. The largest portion of the expenditure could be consumed reaching men least likely to make a purchase.

The radio advertiser who wants to talk to the 38.2 percent of men who make more than $20,000 a year should select the formats and stations these men listen to before considering raw numbers, the so-called media efficiencies. Unfortunately, such preliminary selections are not the norm.

The Perception of Value

It is an unhappy truth that radio is generally not perceived to be worth very much by the advertising community. And we live in a world of *perceived value.*

In 1983, the CBS Television Network aired the final episode of one of the most successful television shows of all times, *M*A*S*H.* The event was highly publicized and to increase its revenue opportunities, the network lengthened the total air time of the episode. Additionally, many of its local television affiliates created special lead-in shows. The *M*A*S*H* troops were breaking camp and going home.

In any city in America, the money needed to buy one local thirty-second announcement during or directly adjacent to the final episode would have bought a heavy schedule for a full month on a leading radio station. Would the one thirty-second television spot be equal, greater, or less effective as an advertising vehicle than the month's radio schedule? It's a question worth pondering.

The same media buyer who perceived the *M*A*S*H* spot to be worth many thousands of dollars would likely question the worth of the radio station—particularly if it was priced higher than the average market cost per rating point. When worth is perceived by buyers only as a numerical factor, without consideration of how a particular station is listened to, without factoring in the quality of the audience, and without evaluating the results the advertising achieves on that station, neither the advertiser nor the radio station is getting a fair shake.

The Sounds of Summer

When the warm weather arrives, it's time to remember that the radio's summertime audience stays at the same level while television audiences decline. It is also a good time to note that 20 million battery-operated radio sets are sold every year, a large number of which are played at beaches and poolside.

The Drive Time Only Fallacy

Not that anyone needs to be reminded, but 95 percent of all automobiles in the United States are equipped with radios, almost 129 million of them. That's a larger number than the combined circulation of every morning and evening newspaper in the country. There are more car radios than there are homes with television sets.

A tremendous number of people go to and from work in their automobiles, listening to the radio as they drive. That is why announcements run during the morning and afternoon drive time dayparts reach the largest audiences and are the most costly. That also is why countless numbers of advertisers honestly believe that the people they want to reach *only* listen to the radio driving to and from their jobs. In virtually every situation, regardless of how the target market is defined, they are wrong.

In the Los Angeles/Orange County area of Southern California, the largest automobile market in the country, 1,900,000 cars are on the freeways between 7:00 A.M. and 8:00 A.M. every weekday morning. But between noon and 1:00 P.M., there are more than 1,400,000 cars on those freeways. If you look at the faces in those cars, you'll surely see housewives going shopping. You will also see executives going to luncheon meetings, company presidents out to visit their friendly bankers, engineers making service calls, advertising agents visiting clients, salespeople calling on prospects, and entrepreneurs sneaking off to the golf club. These are just the people in automobiles on freeways. There are probably as many again on the surface streets.

There may be more cars on the roads in Southern California than in other sections of the country but the area is not atypical. Bumper-to-bumper traffic at midday can be seen in every major metropolis. On Saturdays and Sundays, there are actually more cars on the roads between 9:00

A.M. and 3:00 P.M. than there are on weekdays. It just doesn't look that way because weekend highway traffic tends to move equally in both directions.

Because radio pricing is based on two factors, audience *and* demand, when advertisers and their agencies insist on placing schedules during drive times only, in most cases they end up getting less advertising weight for their dollars.

Where the Listeners Are

Because there are so many cars with their ubiquitous radios in Los Angeles and the driving distances are substantial, there is a prevalent feeling that folks out west are the heaviest radio listeners. The fact is, according to Arbitron, that both men and women in New York and Chicago spend more hours each week listening to the radio than Los Angelenos, and that the Northeast has the highest level of radio listening for every Monday–Friday daypart.

On Second Guessing

In the advertising and marketing communities, media experts have one heady advantage. They understand the jargon and the numbers. Most of the people they are dealing with do not and subsequently these "expert" recommendations are infrequently questioned.

The advertising agency account manager has yet to be born who has not, one time or another, questioned the recommendations of his creative department. The adversary relationship between the creatives and the "suits" comes with the territory. *Everyone* feels capable of making a creative judgment. You like something or you do not like something. The solution fits the problem or it does not fit the problem. There is no neutrality where creativity is concerned.

Without maligning the large number of competent media people in the business, it is shocking to hear agency account managers state, as many do, that they do not question the recommendations and executions of their media departments. When a mass of numbers, a mathematical mélange, is placed before those who do not know precisely how the numbers were generated, there is a common assumption that the numbers and the conclusions flowing from them are graven in stone. Rarely are piercing questions fired back from account management to media strategists. Radio particularly suffers from this reticence.

The work of *every advertising department*—creative, production, research and media—should be subject to constant scrutiny.

The Copycat Syndrome

Radio commercials copy radio commercials. TV commercials copy TV commercials. Ads copy ads. Promotions copy promotions. The propensity in the advertising community for hopping on a successful bandwagon is too well documented. "We'll do it like they did—only better."

Leadership counts—in advertising as in politics. The irony is that followers' ads and commercials are almost always categorized as "Oh, yes, just like (fill in leader's name)."

On Filling Vacuums

There is *always* a potent advertising opportunity on radio if you can fill a vacuum. If no one in its category is using the medium, a company's commercials will jump out.

Good Sales Management

Don Beveridge, a radio industry consultant, points to four principles of effective sales management.

1. Disciplinary action must follow nonperformance.
2. Emphasis should be on results, not activities.
3. Salespeople must learn by doing.
4. Sales managers should be coaches, not players.

Too often, when sales managers make calls with salespeople, they take over and do all the talking. Beveridge says this is a critical error. Salespeople should deal with their customers' needs. Sales managers should deal with their salespeoples' needs.

The Nonexistent Demonstration Reel

Every advertising agency has a demonstration television reel. Its purpose is to convince clients and prospective clients that the agency can turn out creative and effective TV commercials. Additionally, agencies spend big bucks to make individual demos when they are trying to sell a high-budget spot.

It is the rare agency that will spend money to do a solid demo tape for radio.

This is a paradox because it is harder to present radio creative to clients than television. A radio script is unequal to a television storyboard. With radio, the blend of words, voices, music, and timing is critical. What's more, with radio there is a strong likelihood that the medium itself will have to be sold to the advertiser.

National and Local

There's an old marketing chestnut: all sales are local. Because it's a tired selling line, does that make it inaccurate? No.

It is inaccurate, however, to assume that a truly national market exists. Generating national numbers for television, radio, magazines, and Sunday supplements perpetuates the simplistic concept that advertising weight everywhere is equal. Only by evaluating the effect of advertising in individual markets can a true measurement be achieved.

A 25 household network TV rating makes it appear that every fourth home is receiving a television impression. The fact is in some markets the number of homes will be greater and in some, less. In a study of the top twelve network television programs of 1980, the combined national Arbitron rating was 24.9. The rating in the Los Angeles ADI was 18.4. In other words, the Los Angeles audience was 26 percent less than the national average.

Unequal weights give unequal results. An advertiser could easily be underpenetrating in some of his most important markets and overachieving in others. The swing with network radio ratings is markedly more severe than network television, but all *national* advertising should be subjected to market-by-market analyses.

You May Not Be in the Right Business

A few years ago, in a Gallup Organization's report on the public's perception of honesty and ethical standards, advertising executives ranked behind the clergy, physicians, police, journalists, and business executives. But congressmen ranked last.

A Discouraging Fact

Most advertisers, if asked, would have no difficulty in making a list of magazines that would be acceptable to them and a list of those magazines that would not. Similarly, they could identify television programs with which they would like to be associated.

When it comes to radio, however, most cannot make any comparable judgment about specific stations or various formats. There are too many formats and far too many radio stations for them to deal with. The result is that there is less advertiser oversight with radio than with the other leading media.

The Problem of Attrition

Advertiser attrition is a major problem faced by the radio industry. Why isn't the advertiser who was on the air last year still on the air this year? The answer rarely relates to whether or not the campaign was successful. Radio's advertising success ratio is as high, if not higher, than any other medium's.

Some say once an order has been booked, the stations no longer care. This may be true in isolated situations but no more so than in other media. Others have claimed the medium lacks glamour and that advertisers and agency people, hungering for the plaudits they receive with television and magazine campaigns, are *always* seeking to trade up.

There is no simple answer for advertiser attrition. The boredom factor is probably as significant as anything else. "We were on radio last year. What are we going to do this year?" That is the reasoning that causes advertisers to drop campaigns when they are starting to approach their highest level of effectiveness. Overfamiliarity can be deadly. The client is so sated with his advertising that he perceives it as totally worn out. The campaign is killed just when it could really be paying off.

One fact is unassailable. If radio is utilized on a hit-and-run basis, it will lack effectiveness for the advertiser who pays the bill. Neither advertiser, agency, station, nor network will be well served.

The Tyranny of Time

Let no one kid you. Television commercials were not cut back in length because thirty seconds and fifteen seconds were found to be as effective selling increments as sixty seconds. Advertisers were forced into these reduced time slots because of the escalating cost of television time.

It is far easier to fit a *sales message* into sixty seconds of radio than into thirty or fifteen seconds of TV time.

The Big Radio Agencies

The ten advertising agencies which spent the most money on radio in 1987, according to the trade magazine, *Broadcasting,* were, in order: Young & Rubicam, BBDO, Bozell Jacobs Kenyon & Eckhardt, J. Walter Thompson, Ogilvy & Mather, D'Arcy Masius Benton & Bowles, Lintas Worldwide, Foote Cone & Belding, McCann-Erickson, and Saatchi & Saatchi-DFS-Compton.

The Latest Creative Credo

The old advertising master, David Ogilvy, is credited with the line, "If you have nothing to say, sing it."

Today's creative radio star, Chuck Blore, revises this to, "If you have nothing to say, say it funny, and if you can't say it funny, then sing it."

When Times Are Bad

Historically, there are good times and bad times. Advertising is merely one marketing component for business and no one with a grain of sense will contend you can advertise yourself out of a recession. In bad times, the problem faced by an advertiser is how to succeed in spite of the economic downturn.

One solution is to consider practical alternatives to procedures that flourished in prosperity. Using radio as a television extender is one example. Another is to replace costly television and magazine advertising with radio.

During the deep recession of 1973–75, radio served those advertisers who used it extremely well. There is every probability that it will do so again during future periods of economic unpleasantness. Radio is a very cost efficient medium.

Sophie Tucker was quoted as saying, "I've been rich and I've been poor—and rich is better." Prosperous times are better than hard times, for individuals, business, and media. Radio works in both.

Advertising and Inventory Management

There are some marketers of discretionary products and services whose inventory is inflexible and perishable. Prominent examples include airlines, hotels, cruise lines, broadcast media, and motion pictures—essentially the same group of advertisers who are attracted to barter.

These products and services are more sensitive to competition and promotion and less flexible in cost than high-volume, low-unit-priced manufactured goods. Regulating the flow of business through production management, a conventional practice with package goods, is difficult.

Inventory management becomes a vital marketing issue that influences advertising priorities. Advertising in turn becomes an instrument of inventory management with these implications: a medium is required that needs only a short lead time to develop a creative communication, that can turn on a dime in order to meet immediate marketing needs, and that is highly selective and efficient in reaching precise qualitative target markets.

Radio is the natural.

A Significant Difference

In a speech before the Association of National Advertisers' Television Workshop, Gregory W. Blaine, vice president and media director, Foote Cone & Belding, said:

> Use commercial audiences, not program audiences, to evaluate where [television] advertising should be placed. Regardless of your individual research persuasion and with all due respect to Nielsen and Arbitron, there are undeniable truths about commercial and program audiences that are often ignored and lead to [advertising] waste. Commercial audience does not equal the program audience. In fact, *the commercial audience is always less than the program audience.*

He points up another reason why it is fallacious to use techniques designed to analyze and buy television, a program-driven medium, for radio, a format-driven medium. No one leaves the radio set during a commercial break. The only fall-off in radio audience between programming and commercial is in attention. Superior creative commercials can beat that rap.

Rethinking Network Radio Overlays

Many network radio advertisers who wish to place additional weight in major markets supplement their network schedules with spot radio overlays. When an overlay plan is being prepared, it is common for the network affiliates to be dropped from consideration. For example, if WBBM in Chicago is carrying eight CBS Radio Network announcements for Advertiser X, because it is already being utilized, many media buyers will not consider WBBM for the spot overlay schedule. Such a decision might be a real tactical error. Network schedules tend to be on the light side to start with. Restricting an ad campaign's overall frequency to network spots on a qualitatively correct station often results in underbuying that important station.

Consider the Competition—Or the Lack Thereof

A truism: The more crowded the category, the heavier the weight of advertising required to be heard or seen.

Each quarter, a publication called *Radio Expenditures Report* details the radio expenditures made by all market-by-market advertisers. A careful analysis of these numbers may indicate a category in which radio advertising is noticeably light.

Even in situations where objectively other media may appear to be superior to radio, filling a radio advertising void can be effective to an astounding degree. If you can dominate the medium for your product or service, the penetration of your announcements is markedly increased.

The Last Chance

There is reliable research that shows when traveling to shop, 81 percent of all adults eighteen years of age or older travel by car. Radio has always been characterized as an action-inducing medium but never is it more influential than on the drive to the shopping center.

Some Statistics That Could Induce Illness in Advertisers

A research organization called The Pretesting Company, of Englewood, New Jersey, contends that all the following statements are true:

- Nearly 70 percent of all television commercials are ignored.
- Two out of three print ads are quickly forgotten.
- Just one out of ten billboards is read.
- Only 22 percent of all radio commercials communicate their message.

Obviously poor comprehension and ineffective penetration are advertising concerns within all media. The leader, however, gets the most heat.

In a monumental 1980 study, the Education Foundation of the American Association of Advertising Agencies disclosed that "the vast majority [96.5%] of the 2,700 respondents to this investigation miscomprehended at least some portion of the sixty seconds of televised communications they viewed...approximately thirty percent of the relevant informational content within each communication was miscomprehended."

John J. O'Conner, the broadcast critic of the *New York Times* wrote, "I am getting more letters than usual from [television] viewers complaining about their inability to tolerate commercial interruptions....[Advertisers] can no longer count on the captive audience which was once confidently exploited by commercial television."

Take My Boyfriend—Don't Touch My Radio

Donnelly Marketing produces a continuing survey called "Teen Life." In 1987, it reported that among 100,000 girls and young women, aged 12–19, boys were definitely less important than radios. Among activities they enjoyed most, boys came in sixth and listening to the radio second.

Here are the top six activities and the percentage of respondents who voted for them: shopping (93%), listening to the radio (92%), hanging out with friends (91%), listening to records (90%), going to the movies (89%), boys (87%).

Remember This

It really doesn't mean much to reach a large number of *people*. What you want to reach is a large number of *prospects*.

In Support of Gut Feel

It's acceptable for creative people to follow their instincts. When media is under consideration, however, value rigidity rules supreme. Nowhere is this more prevalent than in broadcast buying. When there are numbers for a backup, gut feel is usually ignored.

A Harvard Business School professor reported that large Japanese and German companies, as well as most small U.S. high technology companies, rely much more heavily on gut feel than do the large U.S. corporations which have the largest advertising budgets. In fact, a Japanese businessman observed, "The most rational competitor is the easiest to drive out of the market; all you have to do is convince him you are not rational."

Do not denigrate instinctive media decisions.

A Real Sleeper

What percentage of American workers work at night?—16 percent or almost ten million adults. Their companion is the radio.

Early Birds

A survey done for Robert Half International found that 32 percent of American executives arise no later than 5:30 A.M. This early rising pattern is one reason why many radio stations begin their morning drive time at 5:30 A.M. and some even 5:00 A.M., even though Arbitron measures the daypart from 6:00 A.M. Business people turn on their radios when they get up.

These early rising executives have an average arrival time at the office of 7:35 A.M. and they average fifty-one minutes a day commuting to and from work. Other studies show that of the executives who commute by auto, 98 percent have their car radios on while driving to and from work.

On Evaluation of Radio Advertising

"Let's test radio" is a statement that is heard again and again at advertising agencies and departments. Radio doesn't have to be tested. For more than sixty years, radio has amply demonstrated that it works. When testing is involved, it should concern the product or service being advertised, the advertising strategy, the commercials, the formats, and stations being used and the markets. Don't worry about the medium.

To know whether any advertising worked, on radio or elsewhere, expectations must be plotted in advance. If you don't know what you want the advertising to do, you'll never know whether it worked or not.

Here are some valid expectations from radio advertising:

- Build brand awareness
- Increase name recognition
- Increase reach against present market segment
- Develop reach against additional market segments
- New market introduction
- Develop new outlets for distribution
- Provide additional frequency
- Reinforce other media
- Support in-store promotions
- Draw two or more advertisers together
- Special product/service announcements
- Quick competitive reaction

- Direct response
- Local market promotion
- Public relations
- Employee relations

Abhor the Vacuum

No medium should be considered in a vacuum. All media employed in an advertising campaign are interrelated. In the cold, real world, the fact that media are complementary is often overlooked.

Ogilvy & Mather, in a study analyzing the effect of complementary media, concluded that the combination of television and radio was more effective than television alone. Martin Himmel, the CEO of Jeffrey Martin, Inc., a company that has had tremendous success marketing a variety of relatively low-volume brands of toiletries, put it this way, "By using radio to complement television, you can get a lot more mileage out of a small budget than you might through the use of TV alone."

Considering the Competition

Although all media are complementary, they are also all competitive. Each has its strengths and weaknesses. The more aware an advertiser is of these media highs and lows, the more likely he or she is to use each medium to maximum advantage.

In a competitive sense, radio is its own worst enemy. A continuing flaw in radio selling is its overriding internal competition. Radio sales management and salespeople almost all perceive the media buyer to be the decision maker and the opponent to be another radio station or network.

Radio is severely underrepresented at the advertising strategy level. Promotional and research material rarely addresses the intermedia relationships that are basic to strategy. Graphic design of printed material is thought to be a minor consideration and consequently radio tends not to "look good." Too few radio executives recognize that prospective advertisers and their agencies compare presentations from radio to those from other media. Form as well as substance may determine how intently they are perused. And magazines, television, and newspapers all devote far more money and energy to en masse meetings with the upper strata of the advertising community than does radio.

Pure economics, margins and profits, play the largest role in how a business entity sets its competitive stance. Radio has never been a fat cat medium, nor is it likely to be in the future. Still, it is playing in the big leagues and the other players have a lot to say about the rules of the game.

Received and Perceived Media

Radio competes differently with television than it does with print media. The two electronic media are *received* media. Newspapers, magazines, direct mail, and even outdoor boards are *perceived* media.

Dr. Tony Schwartz, in *Media: The Second God,* describes the significant differences.

> Spoken language is acquired as a received medium and functions as a received medium. The difference between perceived and received is critically important. It requires skill and learning for a person to understand most perceived media. Nearly everyone understands received media.... Perceived media require time to be understood. Received media are instantaneous. As a result, people *react* to received [broadcast] media, whereas they *interact* with perceived [print] media.

In advertising terms, radio and television are *intrusive* media. But nothing is more intrusive, in the best sense of the word, than the communication between an announcer and a single radio listener.

To Show a Picture

The novelist John LeCarre says he will never again write a novel that includes the master spy, George Smiley. Having superbly portrayed Smiley in two films, Sir Alec Guinness has *become* Smiley and LeCarre is no longer free to shape the character as he wishes.

Images freeze on motion picture film and paper. For advertisers, magazines and television are literal media. The precise depiction of a product can destroy a consumer's illusion and limit advertising effectiveness. Sometimes the light is just too bright.

Corporate Interaction or the Lack Thereof

This paragraph is from a *New York Times* house ad:

> We have entered a new age...the age of corporate clutter. Page after page of every business publication is devoted to the paid corporate message. Yet, because of the sheer number of them, few retain their power and importance. For the most part, the nearly one billion dollars of corporate advertising is blended into one amorphous logo.

The next time you are on an airplane, observe a business type reading *Forbes, Fortune* or *Business Week*. A single issue may contain as many as 125 different advertisements. Note how frequently the reader turns the pages without reading a word. "There's a lot of talk today about how people use remote control devices to zap TV commercials," says Elliott Young, president of Perception Research Services, as quoted in the *Wall Street Journal,* "but advertisers forget how easy it is for readers to turn over the page of a magazine."

On Clutter

Clutter does not apply to broadcast. Hearing or seeing too many commercials is a bona fide problem but it is not clutter. Clutter is a magazine term meaning that more than one message is competing to catch the reader's eye at the same time. To combat clutter, magazines have promoted four-color, full pages, multipages, inside covers, bound-in supplements, and pop-outs, all of which have helped escalate the cost of magazine advertising.

Broadcast's "one-message-at-a-time" precludes competition for attention.

A Few Words about Newspapers

In this electronic age, the greatest weakness of the daily newspaper is that so few people read one. In 1980, total newspaper coverage was 780 per 1,000 households and trending downward.

Only three-quarters of all American households were reading any newspaper at all; the big metropolitan dailies were falling dramatically below that circulation level. According to Audit Bureau of Circulation figures, the combined penetration of the *New York Times, Daily News,* and the *Post* was 37 percent at the end of 1985. The combined penetration of the *Dallas News* and the *Times-Herald* was 53.6 percent in 1986. The combined penetration of the *Atlanta Constitution* and the *Journal* was 30.5 percent in 1987.

The *Los Angeles Times,* dominant in its market, was reaching only 24 percent of the area's households in March 1986. The *Times* and the city's other two newspapers, the *Herald Examiner* and the *Daily News,* plus twenty suburban dailies, had a combined gross reach of 66.4 percent in the Los Angeles/Orange County market. If duplicated circulation were eliminated, the reach percentage would be less. The cost of running advertising in twenty-three daily newspapers is too dreadful to consider.

Spoken Like a True Competitor

When newspaper, television, and radio salespeople struggle for local advertising dollars, the battle can become strident, but occasionally a measured note is struck.

> Unlike most other media, radio has the tremendous capacity of reaching people both in their homes and on the go. . . . By matching the known demographics of the people we are trying to reach with our radio commercials to the audience demographics of the radio stations available for our use, it is relatively simple to direct our promotion messages specifically to the people we want.

Who said that? It was Dick Collins, promotion director of the *Boston Globe,* speaking at an Eastern Regional Conference of the International Newspaper Promotion Association.

In all fairness, radio stations have been known to advertise in newspapers. And on television, too. And vice versa. In fact, Arbitron documented that more television promotional dollars in the top seventy-five ADI's are allocated to radio than to any other source. Radio gets about one-fourth of TV's promotional budget. Newspapers, *TV Guide,* and on-air promotions account for about one-fifth each.

And Our Class Won the Bible

Len Matthews, president of the Advertising Agencies Association of America, in discussing bettering the perception of advertising, said that 4A's research showed only two media, television and outdoor, contributed to the unfavorable image of advertising.

After the Super Bowl

J. Walter Thompson underwrote a research project following the 1987 Super Bowl and concluded that the thirty-six companies who paid up to $1 million for a minute of advertising time on ABC's telecast would have obtained more value for their money if they had advertised on the CBS Radio Network where an in-game minute cost only $24,000.

Ron Kaatz, the Thompson executive who oversaw the research, was quoted as saying that "in terms of absolute numbers, you'd be better off on radio. . . . The study confirmed that TV viewers are inattentive during commercial breaks, particularly during halftime. . . . Moreover, only half the male viewers and 33 percent of the female viewers were able to recall one or more commercials without prompting."

Viewing Cable Television

Neilsen's 1987 estimate of U.S. cable penetration was 49 percent but quite a chunk of major market penetration was lower.

Boston	56%	Detroit	40%
San Francisco	54	Los Angeles	39
Miami	51	Washington	36
Philadelphia	48	Minn.-St. Paul	36
Houston	42	Chicago	33
New York	42		

In terms of penetration, cable is a far stretch from radio's 99 percent; still, cable is thought by some to be directly competitive with radio. Certainly cable competes for radio budgets but has it become the "narrowcasting" rival it was projected to be?

The prevailing opinion is that cable viewers are the same people who are already a part of the highest viewing television quintiles. The added cable channels simply give them more choices to satisfy their video appetite. When they watch cable television, they do not watch conventional television and the big audience losers are the TV networks and their local affiliates. (Some cable viewing undoubtedly comes from more discerning individuals, currently in the lowest viewing television quintiles, who now have more choices of specialized programming to fit their tastes.)

Radio does not concentrate on heavy television viewers but covers all the TV viewing quintiles fairly evenly, delivering both the light and heavy viewers who are attracted to cable. There has been no indication of radio losing audience in conjunction with the growth of cable, or, for that matter, with the heavy emergence of video cassette recorders (VCRs).

Support of the Grain-of-Salt Thesis

Grains-of-salt are something to take a lot of research with. The National Academy of Sciences, after completing a study on the value of opinion surveys, gave only a qualified assent as to whether they are useful. Their concern did not relate to quantitative but to qualitative data.

Slight word changes can produce wide variations in responses. Some years ago, two questions were put to a large sample of Americans. Do you think the United States should *forbid* public speeches against democracy? Do you think the United States should *allow* public speeches against democracy?

In the first instance, 54 percent of those polled answered, yes, they were for banning such speeches. In the second, 75 percent answered, no, such speeches should not be allowed.

Marketers know from harsh experience that what people say they like and what they buy are frequently far from the same. Advertising people—advertisers, agencies, and media (radio included)—too frequently take their research unsalted.

The Perils of Recall

J. Walter Thompson did a recall study on commercials that ran during a heavily viewed television miniseries, *The Winds of War*. The survey showed that 19 percent of the respondents recalled Volkswagen commercials; 32 percent, Kodak; 32 percent, Prudential; 28 percent, American Express; and 16 percent, Mobil Oil. The catch is that not one of those companies advertised on *The Winds of War*.

Recall research is not sacrosanct. Even when an advertisement can be recalled by a reader, listener, or viewer, there can be problems. Dr. D. Morgan Neu, vice president of Starch INRA Hooper, the big print media researchers, has made the point that "many ads unsell, rather than sell." To be effective, an advertiser must have the right idea, expressed in the right way, put in the right place.

More Numbers Games

Major package goods manufacturers utilize a measurement called share of voice (SOV). If the cereal industry, for example, spends $200 million a year in advertising and Brand X spends $20 million, Brand X has a 10 percent SOV.

SOV is another purely quantitative yardstick, predicated on the assumption that each dollar spent has the same value and the effect of all advertising messages is equal—two assumptions that are obviously fallacious. When radio stations are components of SOV, the qualitative characteristics of the loyal, regular listeners receive no weight. Radio simply cannot be measured by dollars-spent alone.

Quotable Quote

Enough research will tend to support your conclusions.

Afterword

Is radio a princess in glass slippers, Cinderella in her ball gown? Or is radio just a one-dimensional stepsister? It can be either.

The advertiser will not learn how the story ends until he first knows:

How the advertising objectives were set

How the target audience was defined

How the formats, stations and networks were selected

How the schedules were bought

How the selling premise was formulated

How creatively this premise was translated into commercial form

How the results were evaluated

Radio is a *great* medium, but, Marshall MacLuhan to the contrary, the medium is not the message. The message is contained in the definitive question, *How do you use radio?*

Stay tuned.

Appendix

Essential Radio Resources

Radio Trade Associations

National Association of Broadcasters
1771 N Street N.W.
Washington, D.C. 20036
(202) 429-5300
  The broadcast industry's voice before Congress, the White House, and regulatory agencies. NAB has separate radio and television divisions. It runs conventions, management workshops, seminars, and training programs; issues publications; and conducts research.

Radio Advertising Bureau
304 Park Avenue South
New York, New York 10010
(212) 254-4800
  National organization dedicated to expanding market for radio advertising. Supported by all components of radio industry including stations, sales representatives, networks, and suppliers. Produces and distributes primary and secondary research on audience, effectiveness, and expenditures. Publishes annual *Radio Fact Book*. National sales force calls on major advertisers and agencies. Runs seminars and meetings for advertisers, agencies, and its membership.

Radio Information Center
675 Third Avenue
New York, New York 10017
(212) 818-9060

Authoritative radio station data resource with database covering all commercial and noncommercial radio stations. Provides information broken down by twenty-five criteria including AM/FM, format, location, and network affiliation.

Radio Network Association, Inc.
1440 Broadway
New York, New York 10018
(212) 382-2273

Radio network information and promotion association comprised of seven major radio organizations accounting for more than forty radio networks and syndicated programs.

Syndicated Data Sources

Media Market Guide
322 East 50th Street
New York, New York 10022
(212) 832-7170

Provides quarterly cost estimates for all media in the top 100 markets. For radio, estimates cost per rating point for Metro markets and ADIs against major age/sex demographic groups.

Radio Programming Profile
399 Conklin Street
Farmingdale, New York 11735
(516) 752-8583

Quarterly publication providing latest programming, format, personality information for radio stations in major markets. Includes voluminous details not available elsewhere.

Standard Rate & Data Service, Inc. (SRDS)
3004 Glenview Road
Wilmette, Illinois 60091
(312) 256-6067

Produces monthly publication providing detailed information about all commercial radio stations listed by city and state. Includes station addresses and telephone numbers, names and titles of key executives, sales representatives, programming and format information, technical data, and so forth. For most stations, SRDS no longer includes rates. SRDS publishes separate directories for all media.

Audience Measurement (Ratings) Services

Arbitron Ratings Company
142 W. 57th Street
New York, New York 10019
(212) 887-1300
 Measures radio listening audiences in a total of 259 markets. Report issuance varies from quarterly, for the larger markets, to annually. Provides custom market segmentation data including upper-income zip codes, county-by-county breakouts, and ClusterPlus qualitative differentiations through Arbitron Information on Demand (AID) system. Combines ADI listening data to produce annual estimate of network radio audiences.

Birch Radio, Inc. (division of Birch/Scarborough Research)
44 Sylvan Avenue
Englewood Cliffs, New Jersey 07632
(201) 585-7667
 Measures radio listening audiences in a total of 240 markets. Report issuance varies from quarterly, for the larger markets, to annual. Provides quarterly qualitative analyses for the top 100 markets covering data on income, education, occupation, and household size, as well as for selected products and services.

Statistical Research, Inc.
111 Prospect Street
Westfield, New Jersey 07090
(201) 654-4000
 Produces semiannual RADAR® national audience estimates for AM and FM radio stations in total and for selected segments of radio listeners and selected segments of the population. RADAR® also measures network radio audiences for commercials within and outside of programs.

Radio Monitoring Services

Media Monitors, Inc.
P.O. Box 55592
Indianapolis, Indiana 46205
(317) 547-1362
    Monitors by recording top ten to twenty radio stations in most major markets, generating weekly report showing advertisers, stations bought, and dayparts utilized. Weekly reports are consolidated into monthly summaries.

Radio Expenditure Reports, Inc.
740 West Boston Post Road
Mamaroneck, New York 10543
(914) 381-6277
    Authoritative source for national and regional spot radio expenditures, broken down monthly by major markets and quarterly by category. Covers all spot radio advertisers on approximately 5,000 radio stations.

Qualitative Research Services

R. H. Bruskin Associates
303 George Street
New Brunswick, New Jersey 08903
(201) 249-1800
    Produces special radio listening surveys. Used by the Radio Advertising Bureau to conduct a number of major multimedia studies and by all major radio networks to produce audience measurement studies for specific programming.

International Demographics, Inc.
3000 Richmond Avenue
Houston, Texas 77098
(713) 522-1016
    Produces *The Media Audit,* a biannual multimedia qualitative audience survey in twenty-one markets stretched across the southern tier of the country. Cross-tabulates media data, including local radio, against a large number of demographic and usage criteria.

Mediamark Research, Inc. (MRI)
341 Madison Avenue
New York, New York 10017
(212) 599-0444

Annual twenty-seven-volume national study covers media audiences and consumer data for products, brands, services. Analyzes usage and user demographics cross-tabulated for all media. Database is produced semiannually. Special cross tabs available incorporating ACORN and VISION. Also provides local market studies in a number of major markets.

A. C. Nielsen Company
Nielsen Plaza
Northbrook, Illinois 60062
(312) 498-6300

Though nominally a television industry researcher, produces specially commissioned radio listening recall studies.

Scarborough Research (division of Birch/Scarborough Research)
44 Sylvan Avenue
Englewood Cliffs, New Jersey 07632
(201) 585-7667

Produces local multimedia qualitative audience surveys, including radio, in eleven major markets. (Have announced that their *Multi-Media Consumer Profiles* will be produced in the top twenty-five markets beginning in fall 1988.) Data shows audiences of individual stations broken down by listener income, education, occupation, and other demographic categories, cross-tabulated against a substantial number of products, services, and retail store usage. By spring 1989 *Profiles* will be produced in the top fifty markets.

Simmons Market Research Bureau, Inc.
380 Madison Avenue
New York, New York 10017
(212) 916-8900

Annual forty-three-volume *Study of Media and Markets* provides national audience data for all media, including radio, by format, daypart, and major networks, cross-tabulated against users of a wide variety of products and services. Special cross tabs available incorporating VALS, PRIZM, and ClusterPlus. Simmons also produces syndicated studies on college and teenage markets.

Radio Creative Services

Bert, Barz & Kirby
1956 North Cahuenga Blvd.
Los Angeles, California 90068
(213) 462-7261

Stan Freberg Productions
911 North Beverly Drive
Beverly Hills, California 90210
(213) 273-7730

Chuck Blore & Don Richmond
1606 North Argyle
Los Angeles, California 90028
(213) 462-0944

Joy Radio
60 West 57th Street
New York, New York 10019
(212) 957-1058

Bob & Ray
420 Lexington Avenue
New York, New York 10017
(212) 867-9014

Dick Orkin's Radio Ranch
1140 North LaBrea Avenue
Los Angeles, California 90038
(213) 462-4966

Life-Style and Geodemographic Profiles

ACORN —First geodemographic clustering system using the block group level of census geography. Evaluates forty-four market segments from a base of more than 250,000 census block groups. Developed by CACI International, a British company. Available in the United States, Canada, and Europe.

ClusterPlus —A geodemographic market segmentation developed by Donnelley Marketing Information Service in conjunction with Simmons. Integrates Donnelley's 75-million-household database with Simmons product, service, and media data within forty-seven life-style clusters. Is also linked with Arbitron local radio audience data.

PRIZM —A geodemographic market segmentation developed by the Claritas Corporation. Uses census demographic data to classify all U.S. neighborhoods and communities into forty homogeneous population clusters. Based on analysis of 35,000 zip codes and neighborhoods.

VALS —A life-style segmentation system developed by SRI. Classifies U.S. population in categories in accordance with their life-styles and attitudes.

VISION —A neighborhood-based lifestyle segmentation system evaluating demographic and socioeconomic characteristics of forty-eight market segments in over 250,000 census block groups. Produced by National Decisions Systems. A marketing-oriented system that emphasizes affluent segments.

Index

About the Author

Bob Schulberg is the Western Marketing Director for CBS Radio Representatives, the national sales arm of CBS-owned and -represented radio stations, and is a recognized authority on radio advertising. He has been with CBS since 1975.

Headquartered in Los Angeles, he is responsible for the development of new business categories for major radio stations in thirty metropolitan markets. His special fields of interest are wine, travel, computers, telecommunications, finance, and corporate advertising.

Since 1978, Bob Schulberg has written *Tuned In,* a monthly radio newsletter that is read by 2,500 advertiser and agency executives. He is also a regularly published travel writer whose articles appear in the *Los Angeles Times* and other newspapers and magazines.

Unlike most executives in the broadcast community, Bob Schulberg came up the advertising and marketing route and not through broadcasting. He was a vice president and management supervisor at Ogilvy & Mather (formerly Carson/Roberts) in Los Angeles where the accounts he supervised included American Express, Universal Studios Tours, P & O Lines, Jantzen, Munsingwear, Baskin-Robbins, and a division of Mattel.

Prior to joining Carson/Roberts in 1965, he was the Los Angeles manager of Guild Bascom & Bonfigli, then the largest advertising agency in the western United States. At GB&B, he supervised the advertising that introduced Suzuki motorcycles to the United States.

Before starting in the advertising agency business in 1958, Bob Schulberg was a marketing executive and a newspaper reporter. He served in World War II as an intelligence officer with the 13th Airborne Division and a public relations officer with the First Airborne Army and 82d Airborne Division in Europe.

A graduate of Union College in Schenectady, New York, he is a native of Mount Vernon, New York. He is married and has two grown children.